Jan. 2017

Mom
Thought you might
enjoy this.
Love,
Cayla

PATRON SAINTS

Saints for Every Member of Your Family,
Every Profession, Every Ailment,
Every Emergency, and Even
Every Amusement

Thomas J. Craughwell

OUR SUNDAY VISITOR PUBLISHING DIVISION
OUR SUNDAY VISITOR, INC.
HUNTINGTON, INDIANA 46750

Nihil Obstat
Msgr. Michael Heintz, Ph.D.
Censor Librorum

Imprimatur
✠ Kevin C. Rhoades
Bishop of Fort Wayne-South Bend
August 8, 2011

The *Nihil Obstat* and *Imprimatur* are official declarations that a book is free from doctrinal or moral error. It is not implied that those who have granted the *Nihil Obstat* and *Imprimatur* agree with the contents, opinions, or statements expressed.

ISBN: 978-1-59276-782-3 (Inventory No. T1086)
LCCN: 2011934883

Cover design: Rebecca J. Heaston
Cover art: Detail from Fiesole San Domenico Altarpiece. *The Forerunners of Christ with Saints and Martyrs*: Inner Right Predella Panel, about 1423-1424, by Fra Angelico (1387-1455). © National Gallery, London / Art Resource, NY.
Interior design: Dianne Nelson

PRINTED IN THE UNITED STATES OF AMERICA

TABLE OF CONTENTS

INTRODUCTION

It's difficult to imagine Catholic devotional life without patron saints. There appear to be saints for everything: lost causes and lost objects, headaches and stomachaches, irritating in-laws and disappointing children, successful test-taking and successful real estate transactions. And new patron saints crop up all the time. In the 1950s Pope Pius XII gave us a patron saint for television. In the 1990s Catholics working in the Web industry adopted a patron for the Internet. Any day now we should get a patron saint for cell phones (my money is on St. Gabriel the Archangel — he's already the patron saint of the telephone). So it may come as a surprise to learn that in the early Church there were patron saints, but they weren't so specific.

What the early Christians called a "patron saint" we would call a "favorite saint," meaning a saint to whom we have a special devotion, to whom we turn in times of trouble, and to whom we give thanks in those times when heaven's blessings are showered down upon us. A classic example of how our ancestors in the faith regarded "their" saints has come down to us. St. Paulinus of Nola (c. 354-431), a Roman priest and poet, a friend of St. Augustine, St. Jerome, and St. Martin of Tours, had a spiritual friendship with a holy martyr who was intensely popular in Italy many centuries ago, but who is all but forgotten today — St. Felix of Nola (died 287). Paulinus declared that St. Felix was his "eternal patron," his heavenly protector. As a token of his gratitude for all the prayers St. Felix had answered, Paulinus built a shrine over the martyr's tomb and wrote poems in his honor.

Paulinus used the word "patron" in the old Roman sense. In ancient Rome, it was considered praiseworthy for wealthy, powerful, well-connected members of Rome's upper class, known as patrons, to assist less fortunate individuals, known as clients. Once a week, in some cases every day, clients gathered first thing in the morning at the patron's house to offer good wishes and perhaps a small token of appreciation, such as a poem. During these morning calls the clients were free to present requests: a doctor for a sick member of the family, funds for a wedding or a funeral, help in finding a job or obtaining a post in the government. The patron fulfilled these requests insofar as he or she was able. (Roman women of the upper class could also be patrons.)

The patron-client system was such a familiar part of Roman life that it is only natural that Christians would apply it to the saints. The saints are in glory, they gaze upon the face of Almighty God, they can present their prayers directly to the Father and call upon the other saints in heaven to join with them. Just like a Roman patron on earth, a saint in heaven procures favors for his or her clients — by which I mean us.

We do not know when Catholics came to regard certain saints as having certain "specialties," but by the year 1100 the idea was gaining popularity across Western Europe. Every ailment had its own saint; every profession wanted one; and those in every condition of life as well as every town, province, and country adopted one. In fact, as you will see as you page through this book, patients, professions, and geographical locations were rarely satisfied with just one saint. After the Blessed Virgin Mary, St. Nicholas of Myra and St. George were the two most popular saints of the Middle Ages. Everyone from lepers to saddlemakers took St. George as a patron. St. Nicholas' patronage list is even longer and includes pawnbrokers, brides, brewers, longshoremen, children, and even thieves.

The reason is simple: Catholics looked at the saints, and seeing some part of a saint's life that reflected their own, took that saint as a particular patron. Doctors took Sts. Cosmas and Damian as their patrons because Cosmas and Damian were doctors. People with toothaches prayed to St. Apollonia because in the course of her martyrdom a pagan mob knocked out all her teeth. Citizens of Catania in Sicily trusted in St. Agatha to look after their interests because she had been born, lived, and died in their town.

Sometimes the principle works in reverse. St. Meinrad unknowingly welcomed into his cabin cutthroats who accepted his hospitality, then murdered him. Nonetheless, St. Meinrad is the patron of hospitality. St. Sebastian was martyred by being shot through with arrows; he is the patron saint of archers — not because he was an archer himself, but because he was the archers' target.

Readers of this book will find that it is not unusual for there to be more than one patron for a particular cause. Students, for example, can call upon St. Brigid, St. Nicholas of Myra, St. Cassian of Imola, St. Benedict, and St. Albert the Great (who specializes in students of science and math). If you are afraid of the water, pray to St. Radegunde, St. Adjutor, St. Florian, and St. Hyacinth to keep you from drowning. And if you have a family member in the military, the patrons of soldiers are St. Michael the Archangel, St. George, St. Ignatius Loyola, St. Joan of Arc, St. Foy, and St. Theodore Stratelates. In addition, a saint can be patron of many things. St. Joseph, for example, is patron of the Universal Church, a holy death, families, virgins, realtors and successful real estate transactions, and workers (especially carpenters), as well as a host of nations, including Mexico, Canada, and Korea.

Patron saints are arranged in this book by broad themes, and then in each chapter alphabetically by topic. Each entry focuses on the reasons why the saint is patron of a certain type of person, place, or thing. Some entries are brief, but in the case of especially important or significant saints, the entry offers a more detailed capsule biography. (Note: Those saints and feast days not found in the General Roman Calendar are from other traditional or regional calendars.)

It is my hope that in this book you will develop a greater appreciation for your favorite saints, learn about saints who were unfamiliar or entirely unknown to you, and grow in your devotion to these particular friends of God, who are also our friends.

CHAPTER 1

Patron Saints
for the Family

ADOPTED CHILDREN

ST. THOMAS MORE (1478-1535). Thomas More is best remembered as the unwavering Catholic statesman who preferred to give up his life rather than give up his faith. Less well-known is More the devoted husband and father. From his first marriage More had three daughters and a son, but he also added two orphaned children to his household: Margaret Giggs, whom he formally adopted, and Anne Cresacre, who became More's ward. He loved all six children dearly, and taught all of them Latin, Greek, philosophy, and mathematics — giving them an education that at the time was rare for boys and virtually unheard of for girls.

Feast day: June 22.

ST. WILLIAM OF ROCHESTER (DIED 1201). William was a baker who lived in Perth, Scotland. One morning while on his way to Mass he discovered a baby boy abandoned at the church door. William picked up the child, had him baptized with the name David, and adopted him as his son. When David was in his teens William informed him that they would make a pilgrimage to the Holy Land; David did not want to make such a long and dangerous journey, but he kept that secret from his father. They had gotten no farther than Rochester in England when David turned on William: he struck his father in the back of the head, then slit his throat. He ran off with all the money William had saved for the journey to Jerusalem and was never seen again.

The monks of Rochester Cathedral buried William inside their church. Fifty-five years later Pope Alexander IV declared William a saint.

Feast day: May 23.

BABIES

HOLY INNOCENTS (FIRST CENTURY). The Holy Innocents are invoked to protect the life and health of all infants. We find the story of the Holy Innocents in Matthew 2:16-18: they were the baby boys of Bethlehem, none of them over two years of age, whom King Herod ordered his troops to murder, hoping that the newborn King of the Jews — the Christ Child — would be among them. Of course, God frustrated Herod's scheme.

Feast day: December 28.

ST. NICHOLAS OF TOLENTINO (1245-1305). St. Nicholas of Tolentino was one of the great wonder-working saints of the Middle Ages. So many miracles are attributed to him that it has become impossible to separate fact from legend. For example, St. Nicholas is venerated as the patron of babies because it is said that during his life he raised from the dead more than one hundred children.

Feast day: September 10.

ST. RAYMOND NONNATUS (1204-1240). "Nonnatus" is St. Raymond's nickname — it is Latin for "not born." Raymond was delivered safely by cesarean section, so he is not only the patron of babies, but especially of C-section babies.

Feast day: August 31.

St. Brigid of Kildare (c. 450-525). In the early Middle Ages the Irish told the most extravagant stories about their saints. St. Brigid, as one of the most beloved saints in Ireland, was the subject of countless legends, two of which led to her being venerated as the patron of babies. One tells how when Brigid was still a baby, her nurse developed a terrible thirst — so little Brigid changed water into the finest ale. Years later, when she was abbess of Kildare, an unmarried woman accused one of the disciples of St. Patrick of fathering her child. St. Brigid stepped forward, made the sign of the cross on the infant's forehead, and immediately the baby declared the name of his real father.

Feast day: February 1.

BRIDES

St. Dorothy (died 311). During the last gasp of Emperor Diocletian's persecution of the Church, Dorothy, a young woman of Cappadocia (now in modern-day Turkey) was arrested. The magistrate offered to spare her life if she married a pagan, but Dorothy replied that she had consecrated her virginity to Jesus Christ. Reluctantly, the magistrate condemned her to death. As Dorothy was being led out of the court a pagan lawyer named Theophilus mocked her. "Bride of Christ!" he cried, "Send me some fruit and flowers from your bridegroom's garden!" Suddenly a small child appeared beside Dorothy with a basket brimming with rare flowers and fruit. "Take these to Theophilus," she said to the child. "Tell him I will meet him in the garden." The moment after the executioner cut off Dorothy's head, Theophilus made a public declaration that he was a Christian, too; he was beheaded on the spot. Dorothy, who took Jesus Christ as her spiritual spouse, is the patron saint of brides.

Feast day: February 6.

Bridegrooms

St. Louis IX of France (1214-1270). During the Middle Ages royal marriages consolidated power, or territory, or forged a political alliance. The royal couple was not expected to be in love, and no one was surprised if the king did not remain faithful to his wife. But Louis IX, king of France, genuinely loved his wife, Margaret. During their forty-two years of married life the royal couple had eleven children, and Louis was never unfaithful. Because of his fidelity to his marriage vows, St. Louis is venerated as the patron saint of bridegrooms.

Feast day: August 25.

Childless Couples

St. Elizabeth (first century). Elizabeth was an elderly cousin of the Blessed Virgin Mary. She and her husband, Zechariah, had tried for many years to have children, but Elizabeth never became pregnant. One day, when Zechariah was in the Temple burning incense (he was a Jewish priest), an angel appeared and told him that Elizabeth would bear a son. The infant was St. John the Baptist. The full story can be found in Luke 1:5-80.

Feast day: November 5.

Children

St. Nicholas of Myra (died c. 350). For seventeen hundred years Christians of the East and West have venerated St. Nicholas, the bishop of Myra (in what is now Turkey), as one of the great wonder-working saints. Devotion to him over the centuries has been so deeply rooted that he has become the patron of countless causes and occupations.

We possess very few details of Nicholas' life so, as is often the case with popular saints, legend has stepped in to fill the void. It is said that one night as Nicholas was traveling through his diocese, he stopped at an inn. The innkeeper, delighted to have a bishop as a guest, promised Nicholas a comfortable room and a fine meal of freshly butchered meat. Without saying a word, Nicholas pushed the innkeeper aside and entered his kitchen. There he found a large wooden tub filled to the brim with fresh meat — just as the innkeeper had said. Raising his right hand, Nicholas made the sign of the cross over the tub and immediately the meat vanished and three young boys stood in the tub in its place. The innkeeper had murdered the boys, then carved them up to serve his guests. Because of the miracle Nicholas performed at the inn, he is venerated as the patron saint of children.

There is no denying that this is a gruesome story, which explains why it is rarely repeated today. But our ancestors, who were less squeamish than we, were familiar with it: if you visit the medieval wing of almost any art museum you will probably find a painting or statue of St. Nicholas in his bishop's robes blessing the three little boys in the tub. In honor of the patron saint of children, it is a tradition among Catholics of Central Europe, the Netherlands, and Belgium to give children chocolate or small gifts on St. Nicholas Day.

Feast day: December 6.

St. Dominic Savio (1842-1857). Dominic Savio's family were peasants in the northern Italian province of Piedmont, yet they scraped together the funds to send him to St. John Bosco's school in Turin. Don Bosco's establishment was part academy, part trade school, part orphanage, and part reformatory. Initially, Dominic did not fit in. He was excessively pious and especially drawn to inventing penances for himself. Don Bosco, who was devout but extremely practical, brought Dominic down to earth and insisted that he give up his self-imposed penances, saying that if he wanted to do penance he should endure irritating people patiently. Dominic flourished under Don Bosco's spiritual direction, and his reputation with his fellow students soared after he defused a violent fight on the playground. At age fifteen he developed a lung infection and died. Don Bosco wrote his biography. St. Dominic Savio is the only non-martyred youth to be canonized by the Catholic Church.

Feast day: March 9.

St. Agnes (died c. 304). St. Agnes came from a family of Roman Christians. She was twelve or thirteen when she was arrested during Emperor Diocletian's persecution of the Church. To humiliate her, she was exposed naked in the arena that stood on the site of Rome's Piazza Navona, then executed by being stabbed in the throat with a dagger. Because she gave her life for Christ at such a young age, she is venerated as the patron saint of children, especially young girls.

Feast day: January 21.

St. Pancras (died c. 304). St. Pancras was an orphan who lived with his uncle in Rome. At age fourteen he was arrested and executed for refusing to sacrifice to the emperor and the pagan gods. Like his contemporary, St. Agnes, Pancras' youthful courage and fidelity inspired Christians, and he became venerated as one of the patron saints of children.

Feast day: May 12.

Holy Infant of Prague. Catholics pray before this much-venerated statue for a variety of causes: prosperity, peace in the family, the success of the foreign missions, an increase of vocations. But since the statue represents the Christ Child it is only natural that Jesus — under the title "Infant of Prague" — is venerated as the special protector of children.

The statue was carved in Spain in the sixteenth century and came to Prague in what is now the Czech Republic in 1587 as part of the marriage trousseau of a Spanish noblewoman, Polyxena Manrique de Lara. At the lady's death the statue passed to the Carmelite Church of Our Lady of Victory in Prague. In 1631 the city was occupied by an army of Swedish Lutherans, who wrought terrible destruction on the city's churches. After the Swedes moved on, a priest discovered the statue, its hands broken off, in the ransacked Carmelite church. As he picked it up he heard a child's voice say, "Give me my hands, and I will give you peace. The more you honor me, the more I will bless you."

The priest had the statue repaired, and the Carmelites enshrined it in their restored church. As was customary in Catholic churches at the time, the statue was always dressed in elaborate robes. Replicas of the Infant of Prague can be found in churches, homes, and schools across the globe, and in most cases the tradition of dressing the statue continues.

Feast day: Third Sunday in May.

SANTO NIÑO (HOLY CHILD) DE ATOCHA. During the thirteenth century the Moors conquered the village of Atocha (now a neighborhood of Madrid, Spain) and imprisoned all the men without food or water. The women invoked the help of the Blessed Virgin, and that night a little boy entered the prison with a basket of food and a jug of water. The prisoners scrambled for something to eat and drink, yet the basket never emptied and the jug never ran dry. Night after night the child returned until at last the prisoners were freed. By then, the people of Atocha had concluded that the mysterious child was the Child Jesus. The Santo Niño is venerated as the patron of prisoners, but since Our Lord appeared at Atocha as a child, he is also revered as the guardian of children.

Feast day: December 15.

DIFFICULT IN-LAWS

ST. ELIZABETH OF HUNGARY (1207-1231). At age four Elizabeth, daughter of the king and queen of Hungary, was betrothed to an eleven-year-old German prince named Ludwig. It was hoped that the marriage (which was scheduled to take place ten years later) would bring peace to the two neighboring realms.

For members of Ludwig's family who did not want an alliance with Hungary, little Elizabeth became a focus of resentment.

Elizabeth was naturally religious, and as she matured she made an effort to cultivate the virtues of humility and patience. Elizabeth's spontaneous gestures of reverence irritated her mother-in-law. Once, when she prostrated herself before a crucifix, her mother-in-law snapped at her, "Get up! You look like a tired old mule." Elizabeth's sister-in-law believed that humility was unbecoming in a princess. "You might as well be a housemaid," she told her.

In 1227 Ludwig joined a crusade to the Holy Land. He left behind his five-year-old son Hermann; his three-year-old daughter Sophia; and Elizabeth, who was pregnant with their third child. Ludwig never reached Palestine — he died of an epidemic in camp in Italy. News of Ludwig's death arrived the day Elizabeth gave birth to her daughter Gertrude.

Elizabeth's brother-in-law, Henry, the leader of the anti-Hungarian faction in court, assumed custody of Hermann and then expelled Elizabeth, Sophia, and the infant Gertrude from the castle. Two of Elizabeth's ladies-in-waiting accompanied her into exile. The refugees spent their first night in a shed because no one in the town was willing to risk Henry's wrath by giving Elizabeth shelter.

Elizabeth's aunt, Matilda, abbess of Kitzingen, gave Elizabeth, her daughters, and her ladies a home in the convent. Eventually Elizabeth settled in Marburg, where she opened a hospital, nursing the sick and the dying herself. In 1231 Elizabeth fell ill and died. When she was declared a saint, her in-laws built a magnificent church in Marburg as a shrine for her relics.

Feast day: November 17.

St. Ludmilla (died 921). In 871 St. Methodius, the great missionary to the Slavic nations of Europe, baptized Ludmilla and her husband Boriwoi. As the duke and duchess of Bohemia (now part of the Czech Republic), they tried to plant the Catholic faith among their people but largely failed. Their son Vratislav married Drahomira, a pagan who accepted baptism but never gave up the old gods and, in fact, led the anti-Christian faction in Bohemia. As Vratislav was dying, he named Ludmilla guardian of his young son, Wenceslaus. Ludmilla raised Wenceslaus to be a faithful Catholic, thereby ensuring that Bohemia's ruling family would remain within the Church. To eliminate Ludmilla's influence over Wenceslaus, Drahomira hired assassins to kill her mother-in-law. The murderers strangled Ludmilla with her own scarf.

Feast day: September 16.

DIFFICULT OR UNFAITHFUL SPOUSES

ST. PHILIP HOWARD (1557-1595). After Henry VIII's break with Rome most members of the Howard family, headed by the Duke of Norfolk, exerted themselves in keeping their lands, wealth, and titles rather than remaining firm in the Catholic faith. They were Protestant under Edward VI; Catholic and contrite under Mary I; then Protestant again under Elizabeth I. One result of this religious inconsistency is that the heir, Philip Howard, grew up contemptuous of religion.

He was a selfish, pleasure-seeking young man. He married a nobleman's daughter, Anne Dacre, but left her at home while he went to Queen Elizabeth's court, where he cheated on his wife and ran himself deeply into debt. To get clear of his creditors he sold off part of Anne's property.

In 1581 Philip went to the Tower of London to hear a prisoner, St. Edmund Campion, debate a panel of Anglican theologians. Although Father Campion was denied reference books and assistants — both of which his opponents had in great number — he defended the Catholic position so well and made such an impression on the spectators that the government ended the debate before it was concluded. One of those whom St. Edmund's arguments had reached was Philip Howard. In the aftermath of the debate he went home, reconciled with Anne, and together they converted to the Catholic faith. Since practicing

Catholicism was illegal in England, they tried to escape to the Continent. But leaving England without the queen's permission was also illegal. Philip, who went first, was caught and sent to the Tower, where he remained for eleven years, forbidden to see Anne or their son.

Shortly before he died he sent Anne a letter. "I call God to witness," he wrote, "it is no small grief unto me that I cannot make recompense in this world for the wrongs I have done you; for if it had pleased God to have granted me longer life, I doubt not but that you should have found me as good a husband . . . by his grace, as you have found me bad before. . . . [God] knows that which is past is a nail in my conscience."

Feast day: October 19.

ST. ELIZABETH OF PORTUGAL (1271-1336). Elizabeth was a Spanish princess who had been named after her great-aunt, St. Elizabeth of Hungary. At age twelve she was married to Dinis, the twenty-year-old king of Portugal. Elizabeth was too young to be a wife, and while he waited for his bride to grow up, Dinis took a series of mistresses. By 1291, when twenty-year-old Elizabeth gave birth to their first child, Dinis had already fathered several illegitimate children. In all he would produce seven (some sources say nine) children out of wedlock. Dinis was not ashamed of his philandering; he acknowledged his illegitimate children and brought all of them to the palace to be raised by Elizabeth, along with the royal princes and princesses. There is no record that Dinis ever repented or even apologized to Elizabeth for his infidelities.

Feast day: July 4.

ST. GUMMARUS OR GOMER (717-774). Gummarus was the son of a noble French family whose parents arranged a marriage for him with a young noblewoman named Guinmarie. They were not well-suited to each other. Gummarus was generous to the needy, gentle, and religious, while Guinmarie was grasping, resentful of every penny her husband gave to the poor, and had no love for God. Nothing he said or did could appease her. While Gummarus was in Germany fighting a war, Guinmarie defrauded the servants of their wages, imposed crippling taxes on their tenants, and let the manor house fall apart rather than pay for repairs. On his return, Gummarus made restitution to his servants and tenants, restored his house, and ordered his wife to leave. No one knows where she went, but Gummarus spent his final years living in peace and solitude as a hermit.

Feast day: October 11.

BLESSED DOROTHY OF MONTAU (1347-1394). Dorothy was a Polish peasant who married a prosperous Czech sword maker named Albrecht. She endured twenty-five years of marriage with a man who abused her verbally and physically. Albrecht died while Dorothy was in Rome on pilgrimage. She returned to Poland, where she entered a convent.

Feast day: October 30 (in some places June 25).

DISAPPOINTING CHILDREN

ST. MATILDA (C. 895-968). Matilda and her husband, Henry, were king and queen of Germany. They had three sons and two daughters. Matilda and Henry were loving parents, but she favored her son Henry over her other children. In 936 King Henry died. In his will he left Matilda several vast estates, and she drew upon these resources to relieve the poor and to build new convents and monasteries. Two of her sons (Otto, the new king, and her beloved Henry) complained that she was squandering the family fortune. They seized control of all of her property, which so humiliated her that she left the castle and took up residence in a distant convent. The boys' mistreatment of their mother caused such a scandal that they were obliged to send a large delegation of bishops and nobles to the convent to plead with Matilda to return home and resume control of her own affairs.

Matilda came back, but her troubles with her children were not over. Henry wanted to be king of Germany. In 953 he formed a conspiracy to assassinate Otto and place himself on the throne. Among the conspirators were Otto's son, Ludolf, and Otto's son-in-law, Conrad. The plot failed, and Otto even forgave his would-be murderers, but Matilda was heartsick that her son Henry would try to kill his brother, and that her grandson would try to kill his father.

For all that she suffered, St. Matilda is the patron of parents burdened with disappointing children.

Feast day: March 14.

St. Monica (332-387). Monica had three children, two sons and a daughter, but St. Augustine was her favorite. She liked to have her boy with her, "as is the way with mothers," he recalled, "but far more than most mothers." Monica was devoutly Catholic, and she raised her children in the faith. But at age seventeen, when Augustine went away to the university at Carthage, he renounced the Catholic faith and joined the Manicheans. This sect believed there were two gods, one good, the other evil, constantly at war with each other for control of the world. At the same time, Augustine took a mistress.

That her son was living an unchaste life pained Monica, but his conversion to the Manichean sect infuriated her. The first time Augustine came home from the university, she locked him out of the house. Years later Augustine retaliated. He decided to move to Rome in hopes of finding a teaching post, and Monica had said she would move there with him, his mistress, and his son. On the day of their departure, Augustine suggested Monica visit a small chapel near the dock while he arranged to have the luggage stowed aboard ship. When Monica finished her prayers she walked to the dock to find that Augustine had sailed without her.

For seventeen years Monica prayed to God to reclaim the soul of her wayward son. Through Monica's prayers, Augustine was converted. He and his son were baptized by St. Ambrose at the Mass of the Easter Vigil in 387. Several weeks later, Monica died.

Feast day: August 27.

DIVORCE

St. HELENA OR HELEN (249-329). Twenty-one-year-old Helena was working in her parent's inn in the town of Drepanum in northern Turkey when she met a Roman soldier named Constantius Chlorus. His father had been a goatherd and his mother the daughter of a freed slave, but Constantius was ambitious, and he believed the army was the best way to rise in Roman society. In 270 Helena and Constantius married, and in 272 they had a son whom they named Constantine.

In the years that followed, Constantius' career advanced. In 288 he was appointed governor of Dalmatia (now part of modern-day Croatia), and in 292 he was given Gaul, Spain, and Britain to govern. At the same time, Emperor Maximian offered his step-daughter to Constantius as his wife. Marrying into the imperial family was an opportunity Constantius could not let pass, so after twenty-two years of marriage he divorced Helena and married the princess. It is this painful event in her life that has made St. Helena patron of the divorced or divorcing.

We possess only one fact about Helena's life between the years 292 and 312: she became a Christian. In 312 her son, Constantine, became emperor after defeating a rival. On the eve of the decisive battle Constantine received a vision of a cross of light with the inscription, "In this sign, conquer." Constantine had a cross mounted on every standard, and as the vision promised, he was victorious. In 313 he issued the Edict of Milan, which freed Christians from persecution. He gave the Lateran Palace to Pope St. Miltiades as a residence for the bishops of Rome, and he built several basilicas for Christian worship, including the Basilica of St. Peter and the Basilica of St. Paul Outside the Walls.

In 326 Helena made a pilgrimage to the Holy Land, where she discovered the True Cross. With funds supplied by her son she erected churches over Christ's tomb, his birthplace in Bethlehem, and atop the Mount of Olives where he ascended into heaven. In 328 Helena returned to Rome with a large fragment of the True Cross, which is enshrined today in the Basilica of the Holy Cross in Jerusalem, built on the foundations of Helena's palace.

Feast day: August 18.

St. Fabiola (died 399). Fabiola was a Roman patrician married to a man whose infidelities were so numerous that her friend, St. Jerome, said of the man, "Not even a prostitute or a common slave could have put up with them." Ultimately Fabiola obtained a civil divorce, then married another man. She was a Christian, and the Church could not recognize her divorce, so she married in a civil ceremony. She had not been married long when her second husband died, and it was at that time that grace touched her heart. She went to confession, did penance, and returned to the sacraments. Then Fabiola took her considerable fortune and founded the first hospital in Rome, where she worked as a nurse. She became one of the most beloved and respected women in Rome; at her death thousands of mourners followed her funeral procession.

Feast day: December 27.

Where Is St. Joseph?

Devotion to the Blessed Mother is as old as the Church, but devotion to St. Joseph is relatively recent. In the early centuries, when the Church was plagued by controversies and heresies regarding the nature of Christ — Was he the Son of God? Was he a special creation of God? Was he a kind of superman? — many bishops felt St. Joseph's place in Our Lord's life would only complicate the situation. Over the centuries there were occasional signs of interest in St. Joseph, but for the most part he was a forgotten man.

That began to change in the fourteenth century, thanks in large part to the visions of St. Bridget of Sweden. She experienced extremely vivid revelations of the birth of Jesus and the home life of the Holy Family. Published accounts of her visions were very popular and initiated new interest in St. Joseph.

In the mid-fifteenth century bishops began petitioning the pope to establish a feast day for St. Joseph, which Pope Sixtus IV granted in 1479. The date he selected was March 19.

In the sixteenth century St. Teresa of Ávila's reformed Carmelites and St. Ignatius Loyola's Jesuits encouraged devotion to St. Joseph. Thanks to the Jesuits, St. Joseph was carried to mission territory in Asia, Africa, and the Americas.

St. Joseph became the guardian of families, the patron of workers, and the patron of a happy death. His name was added to the Litany of the Saints in 1726, and in 1870 Blessed Pope Pius IX named him patron of the Universal Church. Pope Pius XII called upon St. Joseph to join in the struggle against Communism, and he made May Day, May 1, the feast of St. Joseph the Worker. In 1962 Blessed Pope John XXIII inserted Joseph's name into the Roman Canon of the Mass. In Italy the feast of St. Joseph is celebrated as Father's Day.

FAMILIES

THE HOLY FAMILY (FIRST CENTURY). The Church holds up the Holy Family of Jesus, Mary, and Joseph as the model for all families. They knew the hardships of hard work and not having much money. There were moments of great fear and anxiety — when the Holy Family fled to Egypt to save the Christ Child from King Herod (Mt 2:13-18), and when Jesus wandered away from Mary and Joseph without saying where he was going, to spend three days in the Temple in Jerusalem (Lk 2:41-51). Yet they loved and supported each other, and are united together forever in heaven.

Feast day: First Sunday after Christmas.

FATHERS

ST. JOSEPH (FIRST CENTURY). As the foster father of Jesus Christ, and as the man to whom God entrusted the care of his Son, St. Joseph is the logical choice as patron saint of fathers. We see him in the first chapters of St. Matthew's and St. Luke's Gospels going door to door through Bethlehem, trying to find some shelter where Mary can give birth; rising in the middle of the night to take Mary and the Infant Jesus to safety in Egypt; and searching through Jerusalem over three desperate days for the young Jesus who had gone missing.

After Mary and Joseph find Jesus among the learned men in the Temple, St. Joseph is never mentioned again in the New Testament. We can be almost certain that he died before Christ began his public ministry. Certainly, if he had still been alive he would have been with Jesus and Mary at the wedding at Cana.

Feast days: March 19 (St. Joseph, Husband of the Blessed Virgin Mary) and May 1 (St. Joseph the Worker).

ST. JOACHIM (FIRST CENTURY B.C.). Just as God entrusted his Son to St. Joseph, he entrusted the Blessed Virgin Mary to St. Joachim. We do not find St. Joachim or his wife, St. Anne, mentioned in the Gospels; their story has come down to us through an apocryphal work written about the year 150 entitled *The Protoevangelium of James.*

Feast day: July 26.

GRANDPARENTS

STS. ANNE AND JOACHIM (FIRST CENTURY B.C.). As the parents of the Blessed Virgin Mary and the grandparents of Jesus Christ, Sts. Anne and Joachim are the natural choice as patron saints of grandfathers and grandmothers.

Feast day: July 26.

HAPPY MARRIAGES

ST. VALENTINE (DIED 269). According to legend, while Valentine was in prison awaiting martyrdom, he befriended his jailer's young daughter. The day he was taken away for execution he left in his cell a small bouquet of flowers and note to the girl that read, "From your Valentine." From this story arose the custom of couples exchanging gifts on the saint's feast day, which gave rise to St. Valentine being venerated as the patron of sweethearts, engaged couples, and happy marriages.

We do not know much about Valentine except that he was a priest in Rome and was beheaded during Emperor Claudius the Goth's persecution of the Church.

Feast day: February 14.

LARGE FAMILIES

ST. NICHOLAS OF FLÜE (1417-1487). Outside the village of Sachseln in Switzerland, Nicholas and his wife, Dorothy, raised ten children. After twenty-five years of marriage, Nicholas asked his wife and children for permission to retire to a nearby gorge, where he would spend the rest of his life as a hermit. His family was reluctant so see Nicholas go, but they knew he had long been drawn to life of prayer. For the last nineteen years of his life Nicholas lived in a wooden cabin beside a small stone chapel, where a priest said Mass for him daily. He was never entirely alone — his family and neighbors visited him regularly. When he was dying, his wife Dorothy, their ten children, and all their grandchildren crowded into the cabin to see him one last time.

Feast day: March 21.

MOTHERS

BLESSED VIRGIN MARY (FIRST CENTURY). As the mother of the Savior, Mary is the patron of all mothers. She is also the spiritual mother of us all. As he hung dying on the cross, Christ placed his mother in the care of St. John, and gave John to Mary as a second son (Jn 19:26-27). Ever since, the Church has understood that John stands for all of us — that we are all children of Mary.

After Christ's ascension into heaven, the apostles and disciples gathered around Mary in the upper room, the site of the Last Supper and of the Risen Christ's appearances to the apostles. After nine days of prayer — the very first novena — the Holy Spirit descended upon them all, and the Church was born. For this reason, Our Lady is also venerated as the Mother of the Church.

Feast days: January 1 (Mary, Mother of God), March 25 (Annunciation), August 15 (Assumption), September 8 (Nativity), December 8 (Immaculate Conception).

The Novena

The first chapter of the Acts of the Apostles tells us that after Christ ascended into heaven, Our Lady, the apostles, and the other disciples — about one hundred twenty people in all — went back to the upper room, the site of the Last Supper, and "with one accord devoted themselves to prayer" (Acts 1:14). After nine days of prayer the Holy Spirit descended upon them all. This is the probable inspiration for the nine days of prayer Catholics call a novena.

In the early centuries of the Church some Christians prayed for nine days after the death of a loved one (this custom they probably adopted from the Romans, who, after a death in the family, mourned for nine days). In the seventh century, Christians in Spain prepared for Christmas with nine days of Masses in honor of the Blessed Mother. By the year 1000 Catholics in France, Belgium, and the Rhineland in Germany were making novenas to favorite saints.

There is no formal liturgy for a novena and never has been. Yes, in many places a novena takes place in church, with formal prayers read from a little booklet or flyer, followed by Mass or Benediction of the Blessed Sacrament, and perhaps veneration of a relic or a sacred image, but such arrangements have been tacked onto the novena. At its essence, a novena is simply nine days of prayer that anyone can offer any place, at any time of day or night, alone or with others. Although the Church has never given novenas a formal liturgy, it does approve of them because a novena fosters the two qualities essential in the life of prayer: confidence and persistence.

The one novena that has quasi-official status in the life of the Church is the Nine First Fridays. This devotion is based on the visions of St. Margaret Mary Alacoque (1647-1690), who reported that Our Lord promised to save the soul of anyone who attended Mass and received Holy Communion on the first Friday of the month for nine consecutive months. To encourage this devotion, many parishes offer the votive Mass of the Sacred Heart every first Friday.

ST. ANNE (FIRST CENTURY B.C.). According to the apocryphal *Protoevangelium of James*, Sts. Anne and Joachim were a devout, loving couple who had prayed for years to have a child. In old age, when they had despaired of being parents, an angel came to each of them to declare that they would have a daughter who would be "spoken of in all the world." That child, of course, was Mary.

Feast day: July 26.

ST. MONICA (322-387). St. Monica had three children: Augustine, Navigius, and Perpetua. St. Augustine tells us that he was her favorite, that she liked to have him with her at all times. St. Monica is not venerated as a patron of mothers because she played favorites among her children, but because she was as careful about the state of her children's souls as she was about their health and happiness. It was through her prayers that Augustine gave up his sinful life and false religion and returned to the Catholic faith.

Feast day: August 27.

Nursing Mothers

St. Martina (died 228). Martina was the daughter of Roman aristocrats — her father had been consul of Rome. At her parents' death she gave away her wealth to the poor, an act of generosity that attracted the attention of the authorities. Martina was arrested, tortured, and then beheaded. It is said that as her body collapsed on the ground it bled milk, which has led nursing mothers to honor her as their patron saint.

Feast day: January 30.

Orphans

St. Jerome Emiliani (1481-1537). In 1518, the year Jerome Emiliani was ordained a priest, a plague and a famine struck northern Italy. In the wake of the double disaster, countless children were orphaned. Jerome, who had inherited a large fortune, used his money to rent large houses in cities and in the countryside, which he converted into orphanages. It was too big of a job for one man to handle, so Jerome recruited other priests to assist him. In 1928 Pope Pius XI formally named St. Jerome Emiliani patron saint of orphans and abandoned children.

Feast day: February 8.

St. Aurelius (died 852). Aurelius' father was a Muslim, and his mother a Spanish Christian. They both died when he was a baby, so he was raised by an aunt. The Moors were persecuting the Christians of Spain at this time, so Aurelius and his aunt practiced their faith in secret. In time he married a woman named Natalia, a Muslim who had converted to Christianity, and they had two children. The couple spent many hours each week tending the sick and assisting the poor, and as they did so they spoke openly of their Christian faith. They were denounced to the Moorish authorities and executed. St. Aurelius, who was himself an orphan, and whose martyrdom left his children orphans, is the patron saint of children who have lost their parents.

Feast day: July 27.

PREGNANT MOTHERS

ST. GERARD MAJELLA (1726-1755). This model Italian Redemptorist lay brother was close friends with a family named Pirofalo. Once, as he was leaving the family house, one of the Pirofalo girls ran up to Gerard — he had dropped his handkerchief. "Keep it," Gerard said. "Someday you'll find it useful." Years later, after Gerard was dead, this young woman was in labor. The delivery was going badly, so much so that the midwives feared for the lives of the mother and her baby. The woman asked for Gerard's handkerchief. Pressing it to her stomach she prayed to Gerard to help her. Suddenly the danger passed, and she safely delivered a healthy child.

Feast day: October 16.

SINGLE MOTHERS

ST. MARGARET OF CORTONA (1247-1297). Margaret had always been a beautiful, vivacious girl, and at age thirteen she caught the attention of Arsenio, the sixteen-year-old son of the local baron. Arsenio invited Margaret to move into the castle as his mistress, and she accepted. He stated candidly that since he was a nobleman and she was a peasant, he would never marry her, and Margaret accepted this, although in her heart she imagined that in time she could change Arsenio's mind. Yet even after they had a son together Arsenio remained adamant — Margaret's rank made her an unsuitable wife for a future baron.

After living together for nine years, Arsenio was murdered — perhaps by a rival family, perhaps by brigands — and his body dumped in a pit in the forest. It was Margaret who discovered her lover's decomposing corpse, and the shock was the first step in her conversion. For the first time in nine years she worried about the state of her soul, and the state of Arsenio's soul. Had he had time to beg God for mercy? Resolved to start a new life, Margaret took her son and walked to Cortona, where the Franciscan friars found her a place to live, enrolled her son in school, and assigned her two spiritual directors. Margaret was frequently troubled by temptations to return to her old life, but through God's grace she learned to control it.

Feast day: February 22.

STEPPARENTS

ST. LEOPOLD THE GOOD (1073-1136). Leopold was margrave, or ruler, of Austria. He married a widow named Agnes, who had two small children from her first marriage. Agnes and Leopold would have eighteen children together, eleven of whom survived to adulthood. Leopold is the patron of stepparents because as a kind, loving father he made no distinction between his stepchildren and his own children.

Feast day: November 15.

TEENS

ST. ALOYSIUS GONZAGA (1568-1591). In his early teens Aloysius Gonzaga invented a severe program of religious exercises that he believed would prepare him for the religious life. He spent long hours kneeling on the bare stone floor of his room, fasted more often than was called for by the laws of the Church, and deprived himself of sleep so he could spend more time in prayer. As penance for his sins, he would strip off his shirt and whip his back with a leather dog leash. It was the type of overly intense approach that we sometimes see in teenagers. At age eighteen Aloysius joined the Jesuits in Rome, where the director of novices was St. Robert Bellarmine. When Aloysius described his religious regimen, Bellarmine immediately ordered him to give it up and follow the schedule of prayer and self-discipline prescribed in the Jesuit rule. Initially Aloysius thought the Jesuit method was lax, but in time, thanks to Bellarmine's spiritual direction, he recognized the wisdom of it. As he wrote to his brother, "I am a piece of twisted iron; I entered the religious life to get twisted straight."

Feast day: June 21.

St. Philomena (date uncertain). In 1802 excavators working in Rome's Catacomb of Priscilla discovered the tomb of a teenage Christian girl named Philomena. Devotion to this forgotten martyr was one of the religious phenomena of the nineteenth century. Catholics around the world spoke of the favors they had received through the intercession of St. Philomena. Among her most outspoken devotees were St. John Mary Vianney, St. John Neumann, St. Damien de Veuster, St. Peter Julian Eymard, St. Madeleine Sophie Barat, Blessed Bartolo Longo, Blessed Anna Maria Taigi, and Venerable Pauline Jaricot. Teenagers adopted her as one of their patron saints because she was an adolescent at the time of her martyrdom.

Feast day: August 11.

St. John Bosco (1815-1888). In Turin, an industrial city in northern Italy, St. John Bosco opened a complex where orphaned and abandoned boys could keep out of trouble, learn a trade, and in some cases study for the priesthood. He is one of the patron saints of teenage boys because he devoted himself to saving them from a life of poverty and crime.

Feast day: January 31.

St. Stanislaus Kostka (1550-1568). Stanislaus Kostka's teen years were difficult. Technically his family was Catholic, but in fact they were religiously indifferent. Consequently, his parents and brothers found Stanislaus' religious devotion annoying; for his part, he found their religious apathy painful. The situation did not improve when Stanislaus and his brother, Paul, went to study at the university in Vienna. Paul insisted that they rent rooms in the home of a rabidly anti-Catholic Lutheran, who delighted in saying the most scurrilous things about the Mass, the sacraments, Our Lady, and the saints. It was hard for Stanislaus to fit in with his fellow students — he would not join in their bouts of heavy drinking or their nights of chasing women. At age eighteen he left the university and walked to Rome — more than six hundred miles away — to join the Jesuits. In the novitiate he was surrounded by students and faculty who understood and appreciated him. But after only a few months with the Jesuits Stanislaus fell seriously ill and died.

Feast day: November 13.

St. Raphael the Archangel. The Old Testament Book of Tobit, or Tobias, tells how the archangel St. Raphael took on human form to guide and protect a teenage boy named Tobias on his journey to a far-off country. Raphael brought Tobias safely to his destination and safely home again, and along the way defeated a demon who would have killed the boy. Inspired by St. Raphael's watchful care over Tobias, Catholics invoke him to protect teenagers.

Feast day: September 29.

VICTIMS OF ABUSE

St. Rita of Cascia (1381-1447). Rita longed to enter a convent, but as the only child of elderly parents she married so she could care for her mother and father. The traditional story of St. Rita claims that her husband beat her, which has led to her patronage of abused spouses. The story is based on a lengthy Latin inscription painted shortly after her death and installed near her tomb. In recent years, when the inscription was cleaned, it was found that the text read that Rita's husband had a short temper, not that he beat her. Nonetheless, St. Rita continues as the patron of abused and battered women.

Feast day: May 22.

WIDOWS

St. Paula (347-404). Paula was a wealthy Roman patrician who became even wealthier after her husband died and left her a vast fortune. She was thirty-two at the time of her husband's death, and it must have been a happy marriage because Paula fell into a deep depression after he passed away. One of her friends, St. Marcella, who was also recently widowed, introduced Paula to a priest, St. Jerome, the secretary of Pope St. Damasus. St. Jerome became Paula's spiritual director, and when he discovered that she was fluent in Greek he asked her to assist him in translating Greek biblical texts for his great project: a new, accurate Latin version of the Old and New Testaments.

After the death of Pope St. Damasus St. Jerome moved to Bethlehem, and Paula and her daughter Eustochium accompanied him. Drawing upon her great wealth, Paula built a monastery, three convents, and a hospital in Bethlehem. She also continued to translate Greek texts for Jerome. Widows have taken St. Paula, who lived as a widow for twenty-five years, as their patron saint.

Feast day: January 26.

St. Monica (332-387). Monica's husband, Patricius, died in 370 or 371. We do not know the date they were married, but it seems that the marriage lasted about twenty-two years. Although he had a short temper, Patricius treated Monica with affection and respect. And although he was not a Christian and never became one, he never interfered in Monica's practice of her religion, and permitted her to raise their three children in the Catholic faith.

Feast day: August 27.

St. Bridget of Sweden (1303-1373). Bridget was related to the royal family of Sweden. At age fourteen she married a Swedish nobleman named Ulf Gudmarsson. They had four sons and four daughters, all of whom survived to adulthood (which was extremely rare in the Middle Ages). One of the children was St. Catherine of Sweden.

Both Bridget and Ulf were devout Catholics, and one of their greatest pleasures was to go on a pilgrimage together. In

1341 they made the long journey to the tomb of St. James at Santiago de Compostela in Spain. When they returned home in 1343 Ulf was seriously ill, and he died a few months later.

During her first six years as a widow Bridget founded a new community of monks and nuns, the Order of the Holy Savior (better known as the Brigittines). In 1370 she moved to Rome. Her daughter Catherine followed her, and the two women spent their days nursing the sick, assisting the poor, and visiting the shrines of the saints. For the rest of her life Bridget experienced dramatic visions in which she witnessed the great events in the life of Jesus and Mary.

Feast day: July 23.

WIDOWERS

ST. THOMAS MORE (1478-1535). As a young man Thomas More thought he might have a vocation to the monastic life, particularly with the Carthusians. To discern his vocation, he lived for several years at the order's charterhouse in London. Ultimately, More realized that he was meant to be a husband and father. In 1505 he married Jane Colt, the daughter of a well-to-do knight. He was twenty-six and she was sixteen. They had four children and then, after six years of marriage, Jane died giving birth to a stillborn child. The Dutch philosopher Erasmus, one of More's closest friends, visited the couple and tells us that they were very happy together, so Jane's death must have been hard for St. Thomas. Although he is the patron saint of widowers, St. Thomas More did not remain a widower long. About a month after Jane's death he remarried. It may appear that he did not mourn Jane, but his four children needed a mother, his household needed a homemaker, and he needed the love and companionship of a wife.

Feast day: June 22.

CHAPTER 2

Patron Saints
for the Spiritual Life

ALTAR SERVERS

ST. JOHN BERCHMANS (1599-1621). John Berchmans, the son of a shoemaker, began serving Mass when he was a young boy. His first Mass was such a profound experience that he went to his pastor and volunteered to serve several Masses a day. As is often the case, John's devotion to the Mass led to a vocation to the priesthood. He entered the Jesuit seminary, where his superiors were pleased with John's down-to-earth dedication. He had no inclination toward mysticism or ambition to go off to the missions in hopes of dying a martyr; he just wanted to be a faithful Jesuit and a good priest. Even his religious devotions were basic: praying the Rosary; meditating before a crucifix; and, of course, attending Mass. Laypeople were especially fond of John. They sensed that here was a young man of great holiness who was nonetheless completely approachable.

John was also a promising student — so much so that his superiors in what is now Belgium sent him to study at the Jesuit college in Rome. There John attracted a new crowd of friends and admirers among the faculty and students at the college, as well as the Roman laity. At age twenty-two John developed a severe case of inflammation of the lungs. As word spread that he was dying, a throng of visitors lined up outside the college to see him one last time.

Feast day: August 13.

Bible Study

St. Jerome (c. 341-420). In the fouth century most copies of the Bible in circulation among Christians were clumsy, inaccurate translations of the original Hebrew, Aramaic, and Greek texts. Pope St. Damasus commissioned his secretary, Jerome, to produce in Latin (the common language of the people of the Roman Empire) as exact a translation of the ancient biblical texts as possible. The result of twenty-three years of labor was the Vulgate Bible. ("Vulgate" comes from the Latin phrase *"versio vulgata*," which means "common translation.") For fifteen hundred years, St. Jerome's Vulgate has been the official version of the Bible Catholics have read, used for prayer, and studied.

Feast day: September 30.

Bishops

St. Charles Borromeo (1538-1584). Among the many reforms of the Catholic Counter-Reformation was amending, even transforming, the spiritual life of the clergy from top to bottom. By the sixteenth century it was not uncommon for bishops to be worldly, ambitious men who performed the bare minimum of their duties. Some took their revenue and went to live in Paris or Rome or some other cosmopolitan city while a clergyman of lower rank remained in the diocese to do the bishop's job. The Council of Trent called for sweeping reforms, and Charles Borromeo, archbishop of Milan, was one of the new breed of bishops who took their vocation very seriously. He lived in his archdiocese and he ran it — something the Milanese had not seen in decades.

He commanded all priests to keep their vows strictly, to say Mass with reverence, and in their sermons to explain the Catholic faith in simple terms to the congregation. He opened a new seminary to train priests, distributed a new catechism, started schools where little children would receive a religious education, and put a stop to the scandalous conduct of some monks and nuns.

By his forcefulness, dedication, and holiness, St. Charles Borromeo set the standard for Catholic bishops.

Feast day: November 4.

CANON LAWYERS

ST. IVO OF KERMARTIN (1253-1303). Ivo was a Breton who studied canon and civil law at the universities of Paris and Orleans, then returned to his homeland, Brittany, to practice. He represented the poor for free. To save time and money, he urged clients to settle their cases out of court. When he was named a judge of his diocese's tribunal, he refused all bribes — a remarkable thing at a time when "buying" the judge was common practice. After twenty years as a lawyer he studied for the priesthood. In his parish he continued to settle disputes.

Feast day: May 19.

ST. RAYMOND OF PEÑAFORT (1175-1275). Raymond of Peñafort was a Dominican priest who taught canon law in Barcelona. In 1230 Pope Gregory IX invited Raymond to Rome to revise and condense the dozen collections of canon law in existence into a single, comprehensive code. It took him about seven years to complete the task, and when he did Pope Gregory published a decree that Raymond's code should be considered authoritative.

Feast day: January 7.

CATECHISM TEACHERS, CATECHISTS

ST. ROBERT BELLARMINE (1542-1621). By the time Robert Bellarmine was born, the religious unity of Western Europe had been torn apart by the competing doctrines of Luther, Calvin, Henry VIII, and other Protestant leaders. Especially active in defending the Catholic faith and bringing back Protestants to the Catholic Church were the Jesuits, a new religious order. Bellarmine entered a Jesuit seminary at age eighteen and showed himself to be such a gifted theologian that his superiors sent him to teach theology at the University of Louvain (now in modern-day Belgium).

In 1576 Pope Gregory XIII transferred Bellarmine to the Jesuit college in Rome, where he wrote a manual on how to defend Catholic doctrine and answer the attacks of Protestant critics. To give the Catholic laity a better understanding of their faith, he wrote a catechism for adults as well as a simple catechism for children. He also wrote a handbook for catechism teachers, suggesting methods to make their subject interesting and convincing, whether for children or adults.

In recognition of St. Robert Bellarmine's services to the Church, the pope made him a cardinal, appointed him his personal theologian, and made him director of the Vatican Library.

Feast day: September 17.

St. Charles Borromeo (1538-1584). Like St. Robert Bellarmine, Charles Borromeo was concerned about lay Catholics who had a poor understanding of their faith and so were easily persuaded to leave the Church by dynamic Protestant preachers. He issued a catechism in his Archdiocese of Milan, and established the Confraternity of Christian Doctrine (CCD) to give children a solid foundation in the essentials of the faith.

Feast day: November 4.

Chastity

St. Maria Goretti (1890-1902). The lovely, pious daughter of Italian tenant farmers, Maria Goretti was only twelve when a neighbor, twenty-year-old Alessandro Serenelli, began making sexual advances. Maria rebuffed him. One day, when the Gorettis and Serenellis were working in the fields and Maria was alone watching her baby sister, Alessandro appeared and tried to rape her. When Maria fought him off, he pulled out a knife and stabbed her fourteen times. Maria died of her wounds two days later, but not before she had forgiven Alessandro. St. Maria Goretti is venerated as martyr for chastity.

Feast day: July 6.

CHOIR BOYS

ST. GREGORY THE GREAT (C. 540-604). As pope, Gregory I was devoted to enhancing the beauty and solemnity of the Mass. He was especially committed to the style of chant that had developed in Rome, which he encouraged the churches in other lands to adopt. Roman chant is better known as Gregorian chant, in his honor. Throughout the Middle Ages boys were taught Gregorian chant in monastery schools. They sang it either in distinct boys' choirs or with the monks' choirs.

Feast day: September 4.

DEACONS

ST. STEPHEN (DIED C. 35). In the years immediately after Our Lord's ascension into heaven Jewish converts to Christianity who had been born outside the land of Israel complained that their poor were not being carried for as generously as poor Jewish Christians who had been born in Israel. To settle the matter the apostles selected seven men, ordained them deacons, and charged them to see that alms were distributed without any form of discrimination. (The word "deacon," by the way, comes from the Greek words for "minister" or "servant" and "action" or "activity.")

Feast day: December 26.

ST. MARINUS (FOURTH CENTURY). During a period of anti-Christian persecution Marinus, a stonemason and lay preacher, consoled Christians who had been condemned to work in the quarries. St. Gaudentius, the bishop of Rimini, ordained him a deacon. Later he retired to a cave in Monte Titano, where he spent the rest of his life as a hermit. The town that grew up near the cave became the tiny Republic of San Marino.

Feast day: September 4.

The Martyrdom of St. Stephen

Chapters six and seven of the Acts of the Apostles tell us that Stephen was "a man full of faith and of the Holy

Spirit." His zeal extended beyond caring for the poor to bringing more converts into the Church. To this end he engaged in debates with members of Jerusalem's four synagogues for Greek-speaking Jews. Unable to get the better of Stephen in those arguments, his opponents arraigned him before the court of the Sanhedrin, where witnesses testified falsely that Stephen had blasphemed God. When the high priest asked Stephen, to reply he answered with a lengthy speech that concluded, "You stiff-necked people, uncircumcised in heart and ears, you always resist the Holy Spirit. As your fathers did, so do you. Which of the prophets did not your fathers persecute?"

The court erupted with cries of anger, threats, and denunciations, but Stephen appeared oblivious to the uproar. Raising his voice above the tumult he shouted, "Behold, I see the heavens opened, and the Son of man standing at the right hand of God."

That was too much for the Sanhedrin and the spectators. They dragged Stephen outside the walls of Jerusalem, stripped off their coats (which they left in the custody of a man named Saul — the future St. Paul), and stoned Stephen to death. "Lord Jesus, receive my spirit," he prayed. "Lord, do not hold this sin against them."

DIOCESAN PRIESTS

St. THOMAS BECKET (c. 1120-1170). A Londoner and a member of the middle class, Thomas Becket realized early in life that the easiest way to rise in the world was to enter the Church and serve the king. He was ordained a deacon but he was more interested in satisfying the demands of his king, Henry II, than in serving the Church, and he became a vain, selfish, even heartless man. When the archbishop of Canterbury died Henry insisted that he would accept no new archbishop other than Becket.

In a matter of days Becket was ordained a priest, then consecrated archbishop, and during those ceremonies something unexpected happened: God's grace touched his heart, and he turned away from his vain, pleasure-seeking life and gave himself to the business of God and the Church. Henry had thought that with Becket as archbishop, he would have the Church in England under his thumb, but it was not playing out that way.

The tension came to a head when Henry demanded that priests accused of crimes should be tried in civil courts. Becket replied that the state could not sit in judgment over the Church and that accused priests must be tried in ecclesiastical courts. At that moment, Henry realized that Becket was not his puppet archbishop.

A blizzard of indictments on false charges and even death threats followed, so Becket fled to France. He lived in exile for six years until representatives of the pope and the king of France negotiated a truce that would permit him to return to England. Back in Canterbury he excommunicated several bishops who had been too willing to sacrifice the liberty of the Church to satisfy the king. When Henry learned of the excommunications he exclaimed, "Will no one relieve me of this troublesome priest?"

Taking the hint, four knights set out for Canterbury. They found Becket in the cathedral, at the altar steps, about to say vespers with his monks. The knights demanded that Becket submit to the king, but the archbishop refused. Drawing their swords they murdered Becket in his own cathedral.

St. Thomas Becket is a champion of the Church, and particularly of diocesan priests, whose rights and independence from government interference he gave his life to protect.

Feast day: December 29.

First Communicants

St. Tarsicius (third century). Tarsicius was a Roman acolyte who was given the Blessed Sacrament to take to imprisoned Christians (the guards were less likely to be suspicious of a child than an adult). Slipping his hands beneath his tunic he kept the Host concealed. As he passed a group of pagan men and boys they called out to him, asking what he was hiding. Tarsicius did not reply and kept walking. The men and boys followed him, but he would not reveal what he was carrying. At that, their mood turned ugly, and they attacked Tarsicius with clubs and rocks. He collapsed on the ground, face down to protect the Blessed Sacrament. When he was dead the mob rolled him over and searched his clothes, but the Host had vanished. St. Tarsicius' love and reverence for the Blessed Sacrament is offered as a model to First Communicants.

Feast day: August 15.

BLESSED IMELDA LAMBERTINI (1322-1333). Until 1910, Catholic children did not receive their First Communion until they were fourteen. At age nine Imelda Lambertini, the daughter of a noble family, entered the convent school of the Dominican sisters in Bologna, Italy. She developed an intense longing for the Blessed Sacrament and tried to persuade the convent's chaplain to permit her to make her First Holy Communion early. As gently as he could, the chaplain told Imelda she must wait until she was mature enough to understand the great privilege she would receive in the Eucharist. During the next two years Imelda's eagerness for full communion with Christ only intensified. On Ascension Thursday, 1333, after attending Mass in the convent chapel, she went to pray before the tabernacle. Suddenly the nuns saw a Host appear above Imelda's head. The chaplain came out of the sacristy to investigate the cause of the excitement, and he saw the mystical Host, too. Taking the vision as a sign from God, he went to the tabernacle, removed a ciborium, and gave Imelda Communion. Overcome with joy, Blessed Imelda Lambertini died that same day.

Feast day: May 13.

HERMITS

ST. PAUL THE HERMIT (C. 230-342). Paul came from a wealthy Egyptian Christian family. According to his biographer, St. Jerome, when Paul was twenty-two Emperor Decius began persecuting Christians. Paul hid in the house of a friend, then fled into the desert, where he made his home in a cave. By the time the persecution ended, Paul had found that a life of solitude and prayer appealed to him, so he remained in the desert. Some sources declare that he was the first Christian hermit, but that claim is difficult to prove. He lived alone for ninety years, surviving on fruit, vegetables, water, and a loaf of bread, which a raven brought him daily. Toward the end of his life St. Anthony of the Desert found him. (When the dinner hour arrived, the raven flew down as usual, but this time with two loaves.) Anthony was present the day Paul died; it is said that because Anthony was too elderly to bury his friend, God sent a lion to dig a grave with its paws.

Feast day: January 15.

St. Giles (eighth century). The life of St. Giles is tangled with colorful legends. It seems likely that he was a hermit who lived in a forest in southern France, where he attracted a large number of disciples. Reluctantly, he left his hermitage, built a monastery, and served as abbot. The most popular story told about St. Giles says that every day a female deer came to his cave so he could milk her. One day the deer was being pursued by hunters when it ran by Giles. As the doe leaped through a barrier of brush, one of the hunters fired an arrow after her. As they crashed into the clearing the hunters found the deer safe in Giles' arms, and the arrow lodged in his chest.

Feast day: September 1.

Holy Death

St. Joseph (first century). After the twelve-year-old boy Jesus is found in the Temple (Lk 2:41-52), the Gospels never mention Joseph again. It has been assumed that he died before Christ began his public ministry because whenever Mary is mentioned during the three years Jesus preached and performed miracles, she is always alone. Joseph would have died with Jesus and Mary at his side — the holiest death imaginable. We pray to St. Joseph that at the moment of our death, he will come with Jesus and Mary to console us and lead us to heaven.

Feast days: March 19 (St. Joseph, Husband of the Blessed Virgin Mary) and May 1 (St. Joseph the Worker).

LAITY

ST. FRANCES OF ROME (1384-1440). Frances was twelve years old when she married a fellow member of Rome's nobility. They lived happily together for forty years and had three children, but they also endured banishment and the confiscation of their property. In addition to running her household and raising her children, Frances fed the hungry, clothed the naked, and even collected firewood from her estates outside the city so the poor would have fuel. And she was ready at any hour of day or night to leave her home to tend the sick. For her fidelity to her vocation as a wife and mother, and her personal acts of charity and compassion, St. Frances of Rome is venerated as the patron of the laity.

Feast day: March 9.

LAY BROTHERS

ST. GERARD MAJELLA (1726-1755). Gerard Majella's mother used to say that her son was "born for heaven." He was so devout that after he made his First Communion at age fourteen his parish priest received permission from his bishop to give Gerard Communion every other day — a rare privilege at the time when, out of a profound sense of unworthiness, Catholics rarely received more than a few times a year. He was twenty-three when priests from a new religious order, the Redemptorists, came to his hometown to preach a mission. Impressed by their zeal, Gerard asked to be admitted as a Redemptorist lay brother. In the novitiate he excelled in all his studies. The founder of the Redemptorists, St. Alphonsus Liguori, was so impressed that he permitted Gerard to take his vows ahead of all his classmates.

Alphonsus considered Gerard the glory of the Redemptorists. He brought serious sinners to repentance and encouraged young women to enter the religious life. People in the neighborhood claimed that Gerard was a miracle-worker. A desperately poor family said that through Gerard's prayers, their meager supply of grain lasted until the next harvest. Fishermen who were caught in a violent storm told how Gerard appeared and brought their boat safely to harbor. And the parents of a boy who had fallen off a cliff testified that Gerard raised their son from the dead.

Feast day: October 16.

LECTORS

ST. SABAS THE LECTOR (DIED 372). Sabas was the lector of a parish church in what is now Romania. When the barbarian Goths attacked the town, Sabas was among those taken prisoner. In thanksgiving for their victory, the Goths sacrificed to the their gods. When Sabas refused to eat the sacrificial meat, the Goths killed him.

Feast day: April 12.

MISSIONARIES

ST. FRANCIS XAVIER (1506-1552). Francis Xavier met St. Ignatius Loyola at the University of Paris. In 1534, Xavier became one of the first members of the Society of Jesus, the Jesuits.

In 1541 Xavier became the first Jesuit missionary, sailing from Lisbon for the Portuguese colony in India — a thirteen-month-long voyage during which Xavier was usually seasick. Upon arrival Xavier discovered that he would have as much work to do among the Portuguese Catholics as among the Indian Hindus. Many of the colonists were inhuman, rapacious men who brutalized their Indian slaves, abandoned their Indian mistresses and the children they had fathered with them, and ruthlessly exploited the people of India as well as the country's resources. In addition to preaching repentance to the Portuguese

Catholics (without much success), Xavier also visited prisoners, taught the faith to lepers and slaves, and composed little songs for children based on the essentials of Catholicism.

From India he sailed to Indonesia, where he met three Japanese Christians who urged him to visit their country. In Japan Xavier was deeply impressed by the courtesy and sophistication of the Japanese, and the converts he made there were the foundation of what would become in another generation a thriving Japanese Catholic community.

As happy as he was in Japan, Xavier longed to go to China. En route he fell seriously ill and was put ashore on a barren island off the Chinese coast. There St. Francis Xavier died.

It is estimated that during his career in Asia he baptized forty thousand people. In 1904, Pope St. Pius X formally named St. Francis Xavier the patron saint of missionaries.

Feast day: December 3.

St. Thérèse of Lisieux (1873-1897). The Little Flower was not a missionary — once she took her vows as a cloistered Carmelite nun she never set foot outside her convent. Nonetheless, the intensity of devotion to this young saint, including her worldwide popularity, was one of the religious phenomena of the twentieth century. Like St. Philomena in the nineteenth century, many groups wanted Thérèse as their patron, including priests in the foreign missions. In response, in 1923 Pope Pius XI officially declared St. Thérèse patron of missionary priests.

Feast day: October 1.

Mocked for Their Religion

Blessed Kateri Tekakwitha (1656-1680). Tekakwitha's father was a Mohawk warrior, and her mother was a Huron Christian who had been taken captive in a Mohawk raid. In the 1640s the family's village, Ossernenon, in New York's Mohawk Valley, had been the site of the martyrdom of three Jesuits: St. René Goupil, St. Isaac Jogues, and St. John de la Lande.

Tekakwitha was four years old when a smallpox epidemic took the lives of her father, mother, and baby brother. Although she contracted the disease, too, Tekakwitha survived. Relatives took in the little orphan.

In 1675 a Jesuit missionary, Father Jacques de Lamberville, settled in the Mohawk village. No one harmed him, but no one converted to Catholicism either — except twenty-year-old Tekakwitha. On Easter 1676 Father Lamberville baptized Tekakwitha, who took the Christian name Kateri — Mohawk for "Catherine." Her conversion enraged Kateri's family and fellow Mohawks. Her aunts beat her on the slightest pretext, and children threw stones at her when she walked through the village. On one occasion a warrior threatened to hack her to death with his tomahawk. Seeing that his only convert's life was in danger, Father Lamberville urged her to go to the Huron Christian village of Kahnawake on the St. Lawrence River near Montreal. It was a journey of two hundred miles, and it took Kateri three months to reach her destination by foot.

Kahnawake was the refuge she had been longing for. By chance, almost immediately she met a woman who had known her mother. Anastasia Tegonhatsihonga invited Kateri to live with her. In this Christian village she attended Mass daily, and returned to the chapel in the afternoon for vespers. Her saintliness was so apparent that at Mass, when it was time for Communion, Hurons jostled one another for the privilege of kneeling beside Kateri at the altar rail. After three happy years in Kahnawake, Kateri succumbed to an undiagnosed illness. Father Pierre Cholenc, one of the Jesuit priests assigned to the village, was with her at the end. Moments after her death he saw the smallpox scars which had marred her face vanish. He wrote, "Suddenly [her face] became in a moment so fair and beautiful that, noticing the change, I cried out in surprise."

Feast day: July 14.

The Lily of the Mohawks

One of Blessed Kateri Tekakwitha's titles is "Lily of the Mohawks," a reference to her commitment to virginity. Even before she converted to the Catholic faith Kateri had resolved not to marry. Her decision perplexed her family. In Mohawk society, everyone married, and in the Mohawk religious tradition there was nothing comparable to the life of a Christian nun. As a result, Kateri's decision confused and offended her family and her fellow Mohawks.

We do not know her reasons. Perhaps she was excessively self-conscious about her personal appearance — the smallpox scars that marred her face. Or perhaps she couldn't bear the thought of her own children dying in an epidemic, as her baby brother had. Or perhaps this was the first sign of God's grace moving in Kateri and drawing her to him.

After her conversion Kateri discovered that, among Catholics, consecrated virginity was not only considered normal but was greatly admired.

St. Bernadette Soubirous (1844-1879). Bernadette Soubirous' parents made a comfortable living operating a mill in Lourdes, France, until they lost their business through mismanagement and laziness. By the time Bernadette was fourteen the family was in such desperate straits they could only afford to live in a dank, unhealthy cellar that had once been the town jail.

On February 11, 1858, while collecting firewood at a nearby grotto known as Massabeille, Bernadette received a vision of the Blessed Virgin Mary — the first of eighteen. Reaction among the people of Lourdes to news of the apparition was mixed. Many of Bernadette's friends were excited, but her family was not certain what to make of her story. At school Bernadette's teacher, Sister Marie Thérèse Vauzous, openly mocked her, and the chief of police had Bernadette detained and tried to force her to admit that she was a fraud; Father Dominique Peyramale, Bernadette's pastor, rebuked her harshly for causing such a commotion. But after Bernadette, directed by Our Lady, uncovered a spring at the grotto, and people who bathed in the spring reported miraculous cures, much of the hostility against Bernadette dissipated. Instead of an object of scorn, she became a celebrity. Crowds of strangers tried to give her money and lavish gifts, asked for her blessing, and pleaded with her to touch their rosaries. Bernadette refused to do any of these things, and to escape the unwanted attention entered the convent of the Sisters of Charity of Nevers, where the mistress of novices was her old nemesis Sister Marie Thérèse — who still thought Bernadette was a convincing actress who had fooled the world.

Shortly after Bernadette took her final vows in 1878 she contracted tuberculosis of the bone, an incurable and extremely painful disease. Her last words were, "Holy Mary, Mother of God, pray for me, a poor sinner, a poor sinner." To the end of her life, Sister Marie Thérèse refused to believe that St. Bernadette's visions were authentic.

Feast day: April 16.

The Message of Lourdes

Between February 11 and July 16, 1858, the Blessed Mother appeared eighteen times to St. Bernadette Soubirous. During the apparitions, Mary rarely spoke — and when she did, her messages were brief.

"I do not promise to make you happy in this world," she told Bernadette, "but in the next."

"Go to the spring, drink of it, and wash yourself there." Ever since Bernadette uncovered this spring, millions have drunk the water and bathed in it, and many miraculous cures have been reported.

"Go, tell the priests to come here in procession and build a chapel here." This request of Our Lady is fulfilled

every day, when pilgrims walk in procession to the basilica near the grotto.

In her final message to Bernadette, the Lady identified herself, saying, "I am the Immaculate Conception."

MONKS

ST. ANTHONY OF THE DESERT (C. 251-356). Anthony was twenty years old when he sold all his property, distributed the proceeds to the poor, and traveled into the desert of Upper Egypt to live as a hermit. Disciples lived near him, so he founded two monasteries for them — the first of the Christian world. Occasionally, he was persuaded to leave the desert and return to society. During the Arian crisis Anthony's friend, St. Athanasius, brought him to Alexandria to preach a public sermon against the heresy.

The monastery St. Anthony built in 361 near the Red Sea is still open — it is the oldest surviving Christian monastery in the world.

Feast day: January 17.

ST. BENEDICT (C. 480-550). Long before St. Benedict was born there were monks who lived in the deserts of the Middle East and Egypt. The monastic rule in many of these communities was excessively harsh: little sleep, little food or water, inadequate clothing or blankets, and long periods of solitude. Benedict believed that such strict practices were not only unhealthy, but were counterproductive to the goal of the monastic life: a closer union with God and a deeper understanding of his will. So Benedict's Rule offered a common-sense approach: a regular routine of prayer, work, study, and rest; healthy food and drink; clothing and bedding appropriate to the season and the climate; and no excessive penances. As a result, St. Benedict has been acclaimed as "the Father of Monks."

Feast day: July 11.

Major Monastic Orders for Men and Women

BENEDICTINES: Founded around 549 in Italy by St. Benedict and his twin sister, St. Scholastica, the Benedictines are the first monastic order founded in Western Europe.

CARMELITES: The monastic branch of the Carmelite order began on Mount Carmel in the Holy Land in the 1190s. In 1593, St. Teresa of Ávila and St. John of the Cross introduced a strict, reformed branch known as the Discalced (meaning barefooted) Carmelites.

CARTHUSIANS: In 1084 in the French Alps, St. Bruno created a community of hermit monks and nuns who live very austere lives in almost total silence. The Carthusians are the only religious order in the Catholic Church founded in the Middle Ages that has never needed to be reformed because the members of the order never departed from their rule of life.

CISTERCIANS: In reaction to what he regarded as the comfortable lives of Benedictine monks and nuns, St. Robert of Molesme founded the Cistercians in France in 1098. The new rule called for long hours of prayer, meditation, and manual labor.

POOR CLARES: St. Francis and St. Clare of Assisi founded this order of nuns in 1212. After Clare's death, the nuns took her name for their community. St. Clare was committed to a life of absolute poverty. Her nuns owned nothing and had no income other than donations.

TRAPPISTS: A French priest, Armand Jean le Bouthillier de Rancé, founded the Trappists in France as a return to the original austerity of the Cistercians.

VISITATION NUNS. St. Jane Frances de Chantal and St. Francis de Sales founded the order of Visitation nuns in France in 1610. The nuns have both contemplative and active lives, usually operating a school for girls.

MYSTICS

ST. JOHN OF THE CROSS (1542-1591). A love for the contemplative life led John to join the Carmelites. While studying theology
at Spain's University of Salamanca he met St. Teresa of Ávila,
who insisted that he join her movement to restore the Carmelite
nuns and friars to the original austere principles of their order.
When he was not assisting Teresa in her work, John wrote mystical works, often drawing upon his own experiences during meditation. Among his most famous mystical works are *The Ascent of
Mount Carmel* and *The Dark Night of the Soul.*

Feast day: December 14.

NUNS

BLESSED VIRGIN MARY (FIRST CENTURY). By her perpetual virginity, her complete obedience to the will of God, and her life of
poverty and humility, Mary is the model and mother of all nuns.
She participated in the mysteries of our salvation — and like a
true contemplative, she pondered them in her heart.

Feast days: January 1 (Mary, Mother of God), March 25
(Annunciation), August 15 (Assumption), September 8 (Nativity), December 8 (Immaculate Conception).

ST. BRIGID OF KILDARE (c. 450-525). St. Patrick had established
a few communities of nuns, but Brigid spread convent life across
Ireland. She began at Kildare about the year 468 with seven
women. That convent became the motherhouse for the many
communities Brigid established throughout her life.

Feast day: February 1.

ST. GERTRUDE THE GREAT (1256-1302). From the age of five
Gertrude was raised at the Benedictine Abbey of St. Mary of
Helfta in the German province of Saxony. She was a model
Benedictine who combined religious devotion with intellectual
achievement. She mastered philosophy and theology and had

a deep love for the Bible and the writings of the Fathers of the Church. She was also among the first to promote devotion to the Sacred Heart of Jesus.

Feast day: November 16.

St. Scholastica (c. 480-543). As the founder of the first order of nuns in Western Europe, Scholastica is the mother of all communities of religious women. For centuries her Benedictines were virtually the only order of nuns in the West, and her Rule has been the inspiration and model for religious orders ever since.

Feast day: February 10.

Orthodoxy (in belief or practice)

St. Athanasius (c. 295-373). Athanasius was about eighteen years old when Emperor Constantine issued the Edict of Milan, which put an end to the persecution of Christians in the Roman Empire. Almost immediately the Church faced a new crisis: an Egyptian priest named Arius denied the Church's doctrine of the Blessed Trinity and asserted that Jesus Christ was not the equal of God the Father and God the Holy Spirit, nor was he eternal like them, nor was he begotten by God. Instead, according to Arius, God had created Jesus just as he had created Adam, only he had given Jesus superhuman powers. This heresy took root and spread across the empire thanks to several emperors who approved Arius' teaching and countless weak bishops who did little or nothing to oppose it.

Athanasius, patriarch of Alexandria, was the champion of orthodox doctrine. He was not alone. Pope Liberius in Rome, St. Ambrose in Milan, and St. Hilary in Poitiers, among others, fought the heresy. But because Egypt was the place where Arianism began it was especially virulent there. Five times the Arians succeeded in having Athanasius driven out of Alexandria, but he always returned and never wavered in his opposition to the false teaching.

Feast day: May 2.

PENITENT SINNERS

ST. MARY MAGDALENE (FIRST CENTURY). At least since the sixth century Christians have believed that Mary Magdalene was a prostitute, or at least a sexually promiscuous woman whom Christ had converted. But the Gospels do not say that about Mary: St. Luke's Gospel tells us that Christ cast seven devils out of Mary Magdalene, but there is no suggestion that she was a notorious sinner.

It was Pope St. Gregory the Great who assumed that Mary Magdalene, Mary of Bethany (the sister of Martha and Lazarus), and the anonymous sinful woman who poured scented oil over Jesus, washed his feet with her tears, and dried them with her hair were all the same person. A tradition developed later that Mary was also the woman caught in adultery, whom Christ saved from being stoned to death. This misconception has led to St. Mary Magdalene being venerated as the patron of penitents.

Feast day: July 22.

PERSECUTED BY THE CHURCH

ST. JOAN OF ARC (1412-1431). In the long history of the Church, no faithful Catholic suffered more at the hands of so-called representatives of the Church than Joan of Arc. This scrupulously Catholic young woman fell into the hands of a corrupt Church tribunal of French clerics who pushed aside all notions of justice in order to prove their loyalty to their English overlords. Given a mission by God to drive the English invaders from France — and assisted by visions of St. Michael the Archangel, St. Catherine of Alexandria, and St. Margaret of Antioch — this illiterate teenage peasant girl led the army of France to victory after victory. When she was captured in 1430, Pierre Cauchon, bishop of Beauvais and a Frenchman firmly under the thumb of the English, falsely accused Joan of witchcraft, idolatry, and heresy.

Joan's trial was a mockery of justice. She had no lawyer arguing her defense; she was not permitted to call any witnesses to testify on her behalf; and no churchmen were allowed to explain the difficult questions of law and theology put to her during the trial. Joan had never been to school, but she understood that this court was a travesty, that her judges betrayed and distorted the Catholic faith, so she asked repeatedly to be taken to Rome for an impartial trial before the pope. Her request was denied.

In the end, Joan's judges described her visions as diabolical, and the theology faculty of the University of Paris weighed in with the opinion that everything Joan had said about her mission was poisonous to Christian souls. Bishop Cauchon's court handed down the decision the English wanted to hear: Joan was a heretic, a sorceress, a schismatic, and an apostate who deserved to be burned.

On May 30, 1431, Joan was taken to the marketplace in Rouen and bound to a stake. She begged for a cross, and while Father Isambart de la Pierre ran to the nearby Church of the Holy Savior to fetch a processional crucifix, an English soldier took a stick, snapped it into pieces, and made a cross for Joan. She took it from his hand, kissed it, then slipped it under her gown between her breasts. As the flames rose around her, Joan cried, "Jesus! Jesus!" and Father Isambart held the cross as high as he could so she could see it in her final agony.

Twenty-five years after Joan's death her mother Isabelle and her brothers Jean and Pierre petitioned Rome to revisit the case. In 1456 Joan's case was heard once again, this time in Paris' Cathedral of Notre Dame. An enormous crowd of Joan's friends and supporters filled the church as witness after witness testified that Joan was pious, orthodox, and as true a daughter of the faith as the Catholic Church had ever known.

Feast day: May 30.

St. Mary MacKillop (1842-1909). Between 1850 and 1860 the population of Australia had tripled, and many of the immigrants were poor, illiterate, unskilled laborers. There were not enough hospitals to care for the sick, enough schools to educate the children, enough charitable institutions to shelter orphans and the elderly. To meet these pressing needs Father Julian Tenison-Wood, a charismatic, imaginative priest of the Diocese of Adelaide, and twenty-four-year-old Mary MacKillop founded a new religious order, the Sisters of St. Joseph of the Sacred Heart. Together they wrote the sisters' Rule of Life, which called for the independence of the sisters from local bishops. The nuns were to be governed by their mother superior, and if an issue could not be resolved within the order they would appeal to Rome. Such independence of action was virtually unheard of for nuns or laywomen in nineteenth-century society. A nun was expected to submit to the authority of her bishop, just as a laywoman was expected to submit to authority of her husband or father.

Initially, the bishop of Adelaide, Laurence Sheil, had given his approval to the new order, but by 1871 he had had second thoughts. "Every convent will be under the control of the local pastor," he wrote to Mother Mary. "No authority to appeal to except myself. There will be no Sister Guardian, no head but myself." Sister Mary wrote back, "Such an arrangement would be quite opposed to the Rule. I could not in conscience remain under those changes."

Acting through an envoy, Bishop Sheil informed Mother Mary that she had been assigned to a distant convent. Mother Mary replied that she would not leave Adelaide until she had met with the bishop.

The day after Mother Mary refused to leave, Bishop Sheil, accompanied by four priests, arrived unexpectedly at the convent and ordered the entire community to assemble. Once the sisters were all gathered together, Bishop Sheil, vested in cope and miter, his crosier in his hand, called Mother Mary forward and commanded her to kneel. Then he said, "Sister Mary of the Cross, Superior of the Institute of St. Joseph, on account of your disobedience and rebellion, I pronounce on you the awful sentence of excommunication. You are now Mary MacKillop, free to return to the world, a large portion of the wickedness of which you have, I fear, brought with you into this Institute."

The sisters screamed and wept, but Mother Mary remained perfectly calm. Rising from her knees she walked out of the convent. In the days that followed, all but two of forty-nine sisters of the Adelaide convent also left. Dressed as laywomen, they found shelter with friends. Meanwhile, sympathetic priests filed an appeal for Mother Mary with Rome. Five months later, as Bishop Sheil lay on his deathbed, he revoked the excommunication.

Although St. Mary MacKillop never again suffered excommunication, her troubles with bishops continued for the rest of her life. Nonetheless, her order flourished. At the time of her death there were seven hundred fifty Sisters of St. Joseph in Australia and New Zealand, operating dozens of charitable institutions, and teaching twelve thousand children.

Feast day: August 8.

What Is Excommunication?

Excommunication is a canonical penalty whereby a Catholic is excluded from the Church. It can be incurred automatically for certain offenses or imposed by competent authority. Among the reasons for excommunication are apostasy, heresy, or schism; committing sacrilege against the Blessed Sacrament; physically assaulting the pope; and having an abortion. A criminal or sinful priest granting absolution to an accomplice or a bishop ordaining a man a bishop without authorization from the pope are also offenses subject to excommunication.

Excommunicated Catholics are barred from the sacraments. If the excommunicated person repents, only the local bishop can grant absolution. In extremely grave cases absolution must come from the pope.

Pilgrims

St. James the Greater (first century). Since the ninth century the tomb of the apostle St. James in Compostela, Spain, has been a popular destination for pilgrims. To emphasize the point, in the Middle Ages it became customary to depict St. James in the garb of a pilgrim: walking staff, sturdy boots, cloak, and wide-brimmed hat bearing a cockle shell, the emblem of St. James. According to legend, a family was walking to the shrine along the seashore when a giant wave crashed on the beach and carried off a little boy. The parents pleaded with St. James to restore their son to them. A moment later a second wave struck the beach and deposited the child at his parents' feet. He was draped in seaweed and cockleshells.

Feast day: July 25.

St. Benedict Joseph Labre (1748-1783). It was Benedict Joseph Labre's dream to enter the monastic life, but he had an eccentric personality that made him unsuitable for community life. After being rejected by one religious order after another, he made a vow to spend his life as a perpetual pilgrim. He visited all the great shrines of France, Spain, and Italy, until he finally settled in Rome. He slept in the ruins of the Colosseum and went to Mass daily at the nearby Church of St. Mary dei Monti. Then he spent the day on a mini-pilgrimage, making his own personal circuit of Roman churches.

Feast day: April 16.

St. Foy or Faith (died 286). Pilgrims from northern Europe en route to Compostela usually took the road that led to Conques, where the relics of St. Foy were enshrined. For these pilgrims a visit to her church to see the relics of the child-martyr encased in a golden statue became a memorable part of the journey, and so they began to invoke St. Foy as their patron.

Feast day: October 6.

Poor Souls in Purgatory

St. Odilo of Cluny (c. 962-1049). In the early Church at every Mass priests read the names of departed members of the parish so the congregation could pray for the repose of their souls. By the sixth century Benedictine monks offered Mass for all the deceased members of their order on a day shortly after Pentecost Sunday. About the year 1030 Odilo, abbot of the great Benedictine Abbey of Cluny in France, commanded his monks to pray for the souls of all the faithful departed on November 2. The custom spread to other lands until it became a universal practice of the Catholic Church.

Feast day: May 11. (Commemoration of All Souls: November 2. The Church has dedicated the entire month of November to the souls in purgatory. Catholics are urged to offer additional prayers and sacrifices for them.)

St. Nicholas of Tolentino (1245-1305). Nicholas of Tolentino was a priest of the Augustinian order in Italy. One day he had a vision of a fellow Augustinian who had just died, Father Pellegrino of Osimo. He told Nicholas of the sufferings he and the other poor souls in purgatory endured and begged him to offer Masses for them. With the permission of his superior, for the next week Nicholas said a Requiem Mass every day, and offered his Divine Office and all of his other prayers for the relief of the poor souls. At the end of the week Father Pellegrino and a host of souls dressed in dazzling white robes appeared to Nicholas to thank him and say that they had been released from purgatory and were going to heaven.

Feast day: September 10.

Popes

St. Peter (died c. 67). "And I tell you, you are Peter, and on this rock I will build my Church, and the gates of Hades shall not prevail against it. I will give you the keys of the kingdom of heaven, and whatever you bind on earth shall be bound in heaven, and whatever you loose on earth shall be loosed in heaven" (Mt 16:18-19). These words that Jesus spoke to St. Peter gave him and his successors spiritual authority over all Catholics and established the papacy. Rome became the city of the popes because that is where Peter taught and was martyred on Vatican Hill. His tomb lies directly below the high altar of St. Peter's Basilica.

Feast days: June 29 and February 22 (Chair of St. Peter).

St. Catherine of Siena (1347-1380). Catherine of Siena lived at a time when the popes had despaired of bringing a halt to the violence and political upheavals in Italy and moved to the peace and security of the city of Avignon in southern France. An unforeseen result of this move was that the popes came under the thumb of the kings of France. Meanwhile, Rome was falling into ruins, and thousands of inhabitants were leaving the city to escape the gangs of robbers who prowled the streets and especially preyed on pilgrims. Catherine believed that the only way to secure the independence of the papacy and restore Rome was for the Holy Father to return to the Eternal City.

In 1376, the twenty-nine-year-old member of the Dominican Third Order traveled to Avignon to convince Pope Gregory XI to move the papacy back to Rome where it belonged. Gregory had been considering the move, but he was a timid man who worried what the king of France would do if he left Avignon, and feared that his enemies might try murder him in Rome. But Catherine was adamant. "Courage, Father," she said, "be a man! I say to you that you have nothing to fear. But if you neglect to do your duty, then indeed you have cause to fear. It is your duty to come to Rome; therefore come." On January 17, 1377, Gregory XI entered Rome — the first pope to reside there in sixty-eight years.

Feast day: April 29.

The Doctors of the Church

From time to time the pope formally declares a saint a Doctor of the Church. This title is granted to a saint whose writings have advanced the Catholic Church's understanding of the mysteries of God. As of 2011, the Doctors of the Church are:

St. Albert the Great

St. Alphonsus Liguori

St. Ambrose

St. Anselm of Canterbury

St. Anthony of Padua

St. Athanasius

St. Augustine

St. Basil

St. Bede the Venerable

St. Bernard of Clairvaux

St. Bonaventure

St. Catherine of Siena

St. Cyril of Alexandria

St. Cyril of Jerusalem

St. Ephrem the Syrian

St. Francis de Sales

St. Gregory the Great

St. Gregory Nazianzen

St. Hilary of Poitiers

St. Isidore of Seville

St. Jerome

St. John Chrysostom

St. John of the Cross

St. John Damascene

St. Lawrence of Brindisi

St. Leo the Great

St. Peter Canisius

St. Peter Chrysologus
St. Peter Damian
St. Robert Bellarmine
St. Teresa of Ávila
St. Thérèse of Lisieux
St. Thomas Aquinas

PRIESTS

ST. JOHN MARY VIANNEY (1786-1859). In 1818 John Mary Vianney's bishop assigned him to the parish of Ars, a village that had not had a priest for years. The people had become irreligious, and some were even hostile to religion — they cursed him in the streets and pelted his house with filth. Yet every morning at dawn Vianney went to the church, knelt before the tabernacle, and prayed, "My God, here is all — take all, but convert my parish."

The first eighteen months were especially difficult as Vianney battled the villagers' habitual drunkenness and lewd behavior, while at the same time he tried to bring them back to Mass and the sacraments. Slowly, he made progress in Ars, and inspired by the priest's success, his bishop sent him to preach missions in other troubled parishes. It was during these missions that Vianney developed a reputation as an insightful, compassionate confessor. It has been estimated that during the last years of his life, he heard the confessions of approximately eighty thousand penitents who traveled to Ars from all over Europe and even from the United States.

After forty-one years of tireless parish work, Vianney collapsed, too weak even to leave his bed. As word spread that he was dying, penitents lined up outside his room to make one last confession. The crowd in the street sent in baskets of holy medals for him to bless. Twenty priests formed a procession to carry the Blessed Sacrament to Vianney for the last time. "How kind the good God is," Vianney said. "When we are no longer able to go to him, he comes himself to us."

In 1929 Pope Pius XI declared St. John Mary Vianney the patron of parish priests. In 1986, Blessed Pope John Paul II traveled to Ars to conduct a religious retreat for priests and seminarians: he based his retreat on the life and work of St. John Vianney.

Feast day: August 4.

RELIGIOUS RETREATS

ST. IGNATIUS LOYOLA (1491-1556). There is no set format for a religious retreat. Some are directed by a priest or religious; others are private, in which the individual retreatant follows his or her own routine of prayer and meditation. For nearly five hundred years most retreats have been modeled on the *Spiritual Exercises* of St. Ignatius Loyola. Ignatius developed this method by examining his own life: he had been a hotheaded, vain young nobleman, eager for glory in battle and not overly concerned about his spiritual life. His conversion began when he examined his actions and his motives and realized that he had not been trying to submit to the will of God. The *Spiritual Exercises* challenges the retreatant to examine his or her actions, and then offers a practical method for shaking off the sinful old life and drawing ever closer to God.

Feast day: July 31.

RELIGIOUS VOCATIONS

ST. ALPHONSUS LIGUORI (1696-1787). Alphonsus Liguori was a member of the Italian nobility and a successful lawyer who gave up his rank and his career to become a priest. Although there were tens of thousands of priests in southern Italy at this time, many of them did no parish work: they served as church bureaucrats or lived comfortably off their inheritances. In 1732 Alphonus founded the Congregation of the Most Holy Redeemer, or Redemptorists, to reverse this trend. Members traveled from town to town, teaching the catechism, preaching, hearing confessions, and leading the people in religious devotions — all to give parishioners a better understanding of their Catholic faith and a deeper love for God, the Blessed Mother, and the saints. St. Alphonsus Liguori's order of zealous, dynamic priests and brothers spread across Europe and in 1839 arrived in the United States.

Feast day: August 1.

RIGHT-TO-LIFE MOVEMENT

OUR LADY OF GUADALUPE. On the morning of December 9, 1531, Juan Diego, a Nahua Indian, was walking to Mass. As he passed Tepeyac Hill he heard music, so he left the path that led to the church and climbed the hill. Near the summit he encountered a beautiful young woman, dark-skinned like himself and his fellow Indians. She spoke to him in Nahuatl — his own language: "I am the ever-virgin Holy Mary, Mother of the true God. I am your merciful mother, to you and to all the inhabitants of this land." Then Mary instructed Juan Diego to go to the bishop of Mexico City and tell him that she wanted a chapel built on Tepeyac.

Bishop Juan de Zumárraga listened to Juan Diego's message but asked for proof. So once again the Blessed Mother appeared to Juan Diego and directed him to the summit of Tepeyac Hill, where he would find Castillian roses growing six months out of season. He was to collect them in his tilma, or cloak, and carry them to the bishop. When he was in the presence of the bishop Juan Diego said, "You asked for a sign. Now look." He opened his tilma, and the roses cascaded to the floor. But more remarkable was the image of Mary, as she had appeared to Juan Diego, imprinted on his tilma.

Some historians who have studied the image of Our Lady of Guadalupe (as this apparition of the Virgin has come to be known) have observed that in the picture Mary is wearing her belt high, just below her breasts, as Indian women did when they were pregnant. Because Our Lady appeared to Juan Diego bearing the Infant Jesus in her womb, members of the right-to-life movement have taken her as their patron saint.

Feast day: December 12.

SACRISTANS

ST. GUY OF ANDERLECHT (C. 950-1012). Guy was a field hand in what is now Belgium. When the workday was done he spent hours in the parish church. The pastor noticed Guy's piety and hired him as sacristan. It was Guy's ideal job: he lived in a small room attached to the church, and spent his days caring for the house of God.

Feast day: September 12.

ST. THEODORE THE SACRISTAN (SIXTH CENTURY). St. Gregory the Great tells us that Theodore was the sacristan of St. Peter's Basilica in Rome. As he went about his work, he often saw angels in the church, and on one occasion St. Peter appeared to him.

Feast day: December 26.

SEMINARIANS

ST. CHARLES BORROMEO (1538-1584). Charles Borromeo believed that well-trained, intelligent, holy priests were essential to reforming the Church and reversing the damage caused by the Protestant Revolt. He opened a new seminary in his Archdiocese of Milan and placed three Jesuits in charge of the education and formation of the seminarians.

Feast day: November 4.

ST. LAWRENCE (DIED 258). St. Lawrence was a deacon at the time of his martyrdom, and it is assumed that if he had lived he would have completed his studies (although there were no formal seminaries in the third century) and been ordained a priest.

Feast day: August 10.

THEOLOGIANS

ST. JOHN THE EVANGELIST (FIRST CENTURY). John is believed to have been the youngest of Christ's apostles, and the Lord's personal favorite — the Beloved Disciple. While the Gospels of Matthew, Mark, and Luke are full of episodes from the life of Jesus and Mary and accounts of miracles and parables, the emphasis in the Gospel of John is theology, with Our Lord frequently identifying himself and describing his mission in theological language. "I am the bread of life," he says. "I am the good shepherd.... I am the light of the world.... I am the resurrection and the life.... Before Abraham was, I am." And, of course, John's Gospel begins with the magnificent prologue, "In the beginning was the Word," a sublime hymn to the divinity of Jesus Christ.

Feast day: December 27.

St. Thomas the Apostle (first century). Thomas spoke with Jesus, heard him teach, witnessed his miracles, saw him risen from the dead, and touched him. When the Risen Christ appeared to doubting Thomas, he said, "You have believed because you have seen me. Blessed are those who have not seen and yet believe" (Jn 20:29). Theologians, of course, are among those who have not seen, yet believe, and they declare with St. Thomas, "My Lord and my God!" (Jn 20:28).

Feast day: July 3.

St. Augustine of Hippo (354-430). After his conversion to the Catholic faith and his consecration as bishop, Augustine spent the rest of his life explaining and defending Catholic doctrine. Of his many works, the two most influential today are his *Confessions* and *City of God*. *Confessions* is Augustine's autobiography, the story of how God's grace drew him away from a life of sin to repentance and redemption. *City of God* sees the world divided between the citizens of the City of Man and the citizens of the City of God — the city to which all Christians are called to belong. It is said that after St. Paul, no one has had more influence on Christian theologians than St. Augustine. He is the most quoted theologian in the *Catechism of the Catholic Church*.

Feast day: August 28.

St. Thomas Aquinas (1224/25-1274). Thomas Aquinas studied philosophy and theology under St. Albert the Great at the University of Paris. Because he was overweight and never spoke in class, his fellow students called Aquinas "the dumb ox." One day Albert proposed a difficult theological problem and asked two students — one being Aquinas — to solve it. The first student presented what he believed to be an unassailable argument. Then it was Aquinas' turn: carefully, step by step, he took his opponent's argument apart and offered an entirely different solution to the problem that was so clear and convincing everyone in the class marveled. "You call him 'the dumb ox,'" Albert said to the class. "Someday his bellowing will be heard around the world."

Aquinas' theological works drew upon the methods of classical Greek philosophy to explain Christian doctrine and reveal the truths of the faith. His system, especially in the *Summa Theologica* and the *Summa contra Gentiles*, is so brilliant it has been studied by theologians for eight hundred years and earned St. Thomas the title "Doctor of the Church."

Feast day: January 28.

To Drive Away the Devil

St. Cyriacus (died 303). The only facts we possess about St. Cyriacus are that he was a Roman deacon who was martyred with twenty-four Christians on the Ostian Way outside the walls of Rome. According to legend he cast out a demon who possessed the daughter of the king of Persia, which led to the conversion of the entire royal family; and he also exorcized a demon from the daughter of the Roman emperor Diocletian, which led to the conversion of the young woman and her mother the empress. St. Cyriacus is one of the Fourteen Holy Helpers, a group of patron saints who are considered especially effective against common ailments and difficulties.

Feast day: August 8.

St. Benedict (c. 480-550). During the years when Benedict was living alone in the cave at Subiaco, the devil appeared to him in the form of a woman Benedict had known before he entered the religious life. Lust nearly overcame him, but through prayer and God's grace he resisted the temptation. Since the fifteenth century Catholics have worn the St. Benedict medal as a sign of their confidence in the prayers of St. Benedict to strengthen them against temptation. On one side of the medal is an image of St. Benedict and on the other side is a cross. The medal bears several Latin inscriptions and abbreviations, including "*Vade Retro Satana, Nunquam Suade Mihi Vana — Sunt Mala Quae Libas, Ipse Venena Bibas*" ("Begone, Satan, do not suggest your vanities to me — evil are the things you offer, drink your own poison").

Feast day: July 11.

St. Michael the Archangel. Two hundred years before the birth of Jesus Christ, the people of Israel revered Michael the Archangel as their heavenly protector. The prophet Daniel assured his fellow Jews that whenever they were in danger, "At that time shall arise Michael, the great prince who has charge of your people" (Dn 12:1). By the late first century, Christians venerated St. Michael as the defender of the Church, especially against the powers of darkness. Two thousand years later Catholics still pray to St. Michael to "thrust into hell Satan and all the evil spirits who prowl about the world for the ruin of souls."

Feast day: September 29.

To Make a Good Confession

St. Padre Pio (1887-1968). Padre Pio is renowned as the Italian Capuchin friar who for fifty years bore on his hands, feet, and side the stigmata, the wounds Christ suffered on the cross. Padre Pio's Capuchin superiors and officials at the Vatican tried to keep him out of the public eye, but crowds came anyway to the Capuchin monastery at San Giovanni Rotondo. They hoped to be in the congregation when Padre Pio said Mass or to catch a glimpse of the bloodstained bandages that covered his hands and feet. Those who went to confession to Padre Pio discovered that his spiritual counsel was profound, and they claimed that he could read souls, disclosing to the penitent sins he or she had been afraid to confess. By 1948 so many people came to confess to Padre Pio that the Capuchins insisted that penitents must make a reservation. In 1967 the Capuchins estimated that, on average, Padre Pio heard twenty-five thousand confessions a year, and brought countless souls back to God.

Feast day: September 23.

UNITY OF THE WESTERN AND EASTERN CHURCHES

STS. CYRIL (DIED 869) AND METHODIUS (DIED 885). These two Greek brothers both entered the priesthood — Cyril as a diocesan priest, Methodius as a monk. Together they carried the Gospel to the pagan Slavic tribes in Eastern Europe. With the permission of Pope Hadrian II, they celebrated the Eucharist in Slavonic, the Slavs common language, rather than in Greek or Latin, the traditional liturgical languages of the East and West. German missionaries, who were jealous of the brothers' success, spread false rumors that they taught unorthodox doctrine and that the Slavic nations would all go into schism, but an ecclesiastical investigation cleared the pair of these charges. Furthermore, Methodius was elevated to archbishop. In addition to his new duties as a bishop, Methodius worked on translating the Bible into Slavonic, a task he had nearly completed at the time of his death.

While Sts. Cyril and Methodius carried out their mission before the beginning of the East-West schism in 1054, most of the people in the lands where they labored now belong to the Orthodox Church. The two brothers are invoked for the reunification of the Orthodox with the Catholic Church.

Feast day: February 14.

CHAPTER 3

Patron Saints
for Ailments

ACNE AND SKIN INFLAMMATION

ST. ANTHONY OF THE DESERT (c. 251-356). There is no incident in the life of St. Anthony that suggests why he should be invoked against skin ailments, but during the Middle Ages Catholics in Europe began to ask his intercession to cure rashes, inflammations, and acne. At the time, pork fat was a common folk remedy for inflammation, so St. Anthony was often depicted with a pig standing beside him.

Feast day: January 17.

AIDS

ST. ALOYSIUS GONZAGA (1568-1591). As part of his training for the priesthood at the Jesuit seminary in Rome, once a week Aloysius Gonzaga was sent to work at one of the city's hospitals. Aloysius was a young man with tremendous will power, but the unhygienic hospitals, the disgusting wounds, and the incurable diseases all nauseated him. But in time he began to see the suffering Christ in these suffering people.

In January 1591 an epidemic swept through Rome. Every Jesuit priest, brother, and seminarian was assigned hospital duty. Aloysius went out into the streets, collecting the sick and the dying, and carrying them to the Jesuit hospital. Washing, feeding, and nursing the sick was exhausting work, and then he, too, contracted the disease and died of it.

For the compassion he showed to victims of an incurable disease, St. Aloysius Gonzaga is the patron of those who suffer from AIDS.

Feast day: June 21.

ALCOHOLISM

ST. MONICA (331-387). When Monica was an adolescent girl her parents would send her to the cellar to bring up the wine. It became her habit to drink a cup as she carried the wine to the house. One day one of the servants saw her draining a cup of wine and called her "a little tipler." Monica was so humiliated that she stopped drinking wine entirely.

Feast day: August 27.

ST. MATTHIAS (FIRST CENTURY). The Acts of the Apostles 1:15-26 tells us that the eleven apostles decided to replace the traitor Judas (who had hanged himself on Good Friday) so that their number would be twelve again. One of the Lord's disciples, Matthias, was chosen. According to tradition St. Matthias preached the Gospel in Ethiopia and was martyred there. He may have written one or more letters, but none have survived the centuries. Yet a third-century Egyptian theologian, St. Clement of Alexandria, quotes a single sentence attributed to Matthias: "We must combat our flesh, set no value on it, and concede to it nothing that can flatter it." This call for self-control is the basis of St. Matthias being invoked against alcoholism.

Feast day: May 14.

ALZHEIMER'S DISEASE AND OTHER FORMS OF DEMENTIA

ST. DYMPHNA (SEVENTH CENTURY). Dymphna's father became mentally unstable after the death of his wife, so much so that he became convinced that Dymphna was her mother. To escape these attentions, Dymphna and her chaplain, Gerebernus, fled from her home in Ireland to what is now Gheel, Belgium. Her father hunted them down and killed them both.

When the remains of Sts. Dymphna and Gerebernus were discovered in the ninth century, many people who suffered from mental illness were healed after praying at the tomb. Gheel became a center of pilgrimage, as well as a place where the mentally ill were treated.

Feast day: May 15.

AMPUTATIONS

ST. ANTHONY OF PADUA (1195-1231). One day a young man of Padua, Italy, named Leonardo got into a terrible argument with his mother that ended with Leonardo kicking her and storming out of the house. When he regained control of his temper he felt terrible about what he had done and went to confession to St. Anthony. In an unguarded moment Anthony said to Leonardo, "That foot deserves to be cut off." Leonardo, who appears to have been impulsive in the extreme, ran from the church, took the first axe he came upon, and chopped off his foot. When word reached Anthony he rushed to the scene, lifted the severed foot from the ground, and reattached it to Leonardo's leg.

Feast day: June 13.

APPENDICITIS

ST. ERASMUS OR ELMO (DIED C. 303). The dreadful martyrdom endured by Erasmus, (he was disemboweled by his executioners) has led to him being invoked against all stomach pains, including appendicitis.

Feast day: June 2.

ARTHRITIS AND RHEUMATISM

ST. JAMES THE GREATER (FIRST CENTURY). After Pentecost James the Greater preached the Gospel in Jerusalem where he fell victim to Herod Agrippa's persecution of the Church. There is a story that as James was being taken to execution outside the city, he and his guards passed a man crippled with arthritis or rheumatism lying beside the road. The man begged James to heal him. "In the name of Jesus Christ," James said, "in whose name I am being led to execution, stand up and bless your Creator." The man leaped to his feet immediately, and as James was led away to martyrdom, the former cripple ran to the Temple to offer thanks to God.

Feast day: July 25.

St. Alphonsus Liguori (1696-1787). Alphonsus Liguori, a member of the Italian nobility, founded the Redemptorist order of priests, laybrothers, and nuns. He became a noted preacher, and served as bishop of Sant' Agata de' Goti. In 1767, at age 71, he was diagnosed with arthritis in his hip and spine. Some of the attacks were so severe that he was confined to his bed, and they plagued him for the rest of his life.

Feast day: August 1.

St. Killian (died c. 689). Killian was an Irish monk who with eleven fellow monks traveled as a missionary to Bavaria, Germany, where he converted a great many people, including the duke, Gozbert. As tactfully as possible, Killian explained to the duke that his current marriage was illicit and that he had to send the woman away. Geilana, the woman in question, had Killian murdered, along with two of his companions, Colman and Totnan. The murderers dumped the missionaries' bodies in a common grave where, decades later, they were discovered by St. Boniface. In 752 the relics were enshrined in the cathedral of Wurzburg. Many pilgrims who suffered from arthritis or rheumatism were cured after praying at St. Killian's tomb.

Feast day: July 8.

Asthma

St. Bernadette Soubirous (1844-1879). By age six Bernadette had developed asthma. Her sister Toinette later recalled that Bernadette "had a bad chest, she ate very little." Sickly all her life,

St. Bernadette is venerated as the patron of the chronically ill, especially those suffering from asthma.

Feast day: April 16 (February 18 in France).

Autism

St. Ubaldo Baldassini (c. 1100-1160). Ubaldo Baldassini's mother is the link between the saint and autism: she suffered from a developmental disorder, which has led to her son being invoked for all those diagnosed with autism.

Ubaldo was born and raised in Gubbio, a hilltop town near Assisi. He became bishop of his hometown and was loved and respected for his dedication to his people and the Church. One of his first acts as bishop was to reform the clergy, who were failing to fulfill their religious obligations. Ubaldo was also a renowned peacemaker among the feuding families of Gubbio. When Emperor Frederick Barbarossa was ransacking the countryside, Ubaldo rode out to meet the emperor and persuaded him to leave the region in peace.

Feast day: May 16.

Birth Complications

St. Ulrich (890-973). As bishop of Augsburg in Germany, Ulrich was tireless. He revived the zeal of his parish priests, visited all the parishes in his diocese to learn about the spiritual condition of his people, and nursed the sick in the hospital. He built churches, but he also built fortresses to protect his diocese from barbarian invasions. During the Middle Ages, pregnant women reported that they had easy deliveries after drinking from St. Ulrich's chalice.

Feast day: July 4.

Breast Cancer and Breast Diseases

St. Agatha (died c. 250). Agatha was a Christian in the Sicilian city of Catania. The governor of Sicily, Quintianus, tried to seduce her, and when she rejected him he had her arrested and tortured. The torturers sliced off Agatha's breasts, but St. Peter appeared to the martyr and restored them. This element of St. Agatha's martyrdom has led to her patronage against breast cancer and all other breast diseases.

Feast day: February 5.

BURNS

ST. JOHN THE EVANGELIST (FIRST CENTURY). According to tradition, when John was a very old man he was arrested in Ephesus, where he was bishop, and taken to Rome. The emperor Domitian condemned John to be plunged into a cauldron of boiling oil. Instead of being scalded to death, John emerged from the cauldron unharmed. In Rome a small church beside the Latin Gate stands on the site of the miracle.

Feast days: December 27 and May 6 (St. John Before the Latin Gate).

CANCER

ST. PEREGRINE LAZIOSI (1260-1335). Peregrine Laziosi was a Servite priest who suffered from an open sore on his leg that would not heal. A surgeon examined it, diagnosed it as cancer, and told Father Peregrine the leg would have to be amputated. The night before surgery Peregrine limped to the chapter room of his monastery, sat at the foot of a life-size crucifix, and began to pray. He drifted off to sleep and dreamed that Christ came down from the cross and touched his wounded leg. When Peregrine awoke, he found his leg completely healed.

Feast day: May 1.

The Chapter Room or House

Abbeys and some cathedrals have a room or separate building where the monks or the cathedral clergy meet to discuss administrative and business matters that effect the entire community. The room tends to be large and furnished only with benches along the walls so all the members of the community can see one another. It also features a large throne-like chair in the center for the abbot, abbess, or bishop.

The name "chapter house" comes from the tradition of beginning each meeting by reading aloud one chapter from the community's book of rules.

St. Ezekiel Moreno y Diaz (1848-1906). Ezekiel Moreno y Diaz was a Spanish Augustinian priest who served as a missionary, first in the Philippines and then in Colombia, where he was named bishop of the diocese of Pasto. St. Ezekiel became one of the saints invoked against cancer because during the process that led to his canonization, the miracles attributed to his intercession involved the miraculous healing of cancer patients.

Feast day: August 19.

CHILDHOOD DISEASES

St. Pharaildis (c. 650-c. 740). Pharaildis came from a devout Flemish family: her mother and three of her sisters were saints. Her aunt was St. Gertrude of Nivelle. Although she had planned to enter a convent, her parents forced her into marriage. Pharaildis' husband was violent and abusive, but she outlived him. During her widowhood Pharaildis uncovered a spring whose water cured sick children.

Feast day: January 4.

COUGHS

St. Quentin (died 287). The son of a Roman senator, Quentin left his home to preach the Gospel in Gaul (modern-day France). At the town known today as Saint-Quentin, he was arrested and horribly tortured. At one point his executioners poured a stinging concoction of lime, vinegar, and mustard down his throat, which has led to St. Quentin being invoked against coughs.

Feast day: October 31.

DIABETES

St. Paulina of the Agonizing Heart of Jesus (1865-1942). Paulina was a child when her family, along with one hundred of their fellow townsfolk, emigrated from Italy to Brazil. In 1890 Paulina founded the Congregation of the Little Sisters of the Immaculate Conception, an order dedicated to caring for the sick and the elderly. Paulina expanded her work to include sheltering orphans and elderly freed slaves (slavery was not abolished in Brazil until 1888). Paulina suffered from diabetes, and during the last four years of her life the disease compelled her to give up her responsibilities as superior of her order.

Feast day: July 9.

St. Rafael Arnaiz Baron (1911-1938). Rafael Arnaiz Baron was an architecture student who gave up his studies to enter the Trappist Abbey of St. Isidore in Duenas, Spain. He suffered from acute diabetes, and died of the disease four years after he joined the Trappists.

Feast day: April 26.

DISABILITIES

St. Germaine Cousin (c. 1579-1601). Germaine Cousin was the child of modestly comfortable peasants in the town of Pibac, France. She was born with a withered right arm and an incurable inflammation of the skin. After birth she developed scrofula, a form of tuberculosis that causes hideous swellings at the neck. When Germaine was only a few years old her mother died. Her father married a widow with young children of her own. Germaine's stepmother could not abide the sight of her: she forced her to take her meals under the stairs, made her sleep in the barn, and refused to let her to play with her stepbrothers and stepsisters. About the time she was ten Germaine was sent from the house every day to tend the family's flock of sheep.

She spent her days in silent communion with God. Her rosary never seemed to be out of her left hand. Every day she attended Mass, but none of her sheep wandered off while she was in church, nor was the flock ever attacked by a wolf.

Toward the end of her life Germaine's father tried to make amends with her, but she was uneasy joining a family that had excluded her. She kept to her familiar routine, with one exception: she slept in the house, under the stairs. That is where Germaine died in her sleep at age 22.

Feast day: June 15.

BLESSED MARGARET OF CASTELLO (1287-1320). Margaret came into the world with a host of disabilities: she was blind, she had curvature of the spine, her left arm was misshapen, and her right leg was shorter than her left. When she was six her parents took her to a shrine at Castello, hoping their child would be healed. When a miracle did not occur, they left her at the shrine. Some kind women of the town cared for Margaret and found a childless couple to adopt her. In Castello, Margaret found herself a member of a loving extended family.

As she grew she spent more and more of her time with the sick and the sorrowing, and even with prisoners. She became Castello's most beloved citizen. At her death, the entire town attended Margaret's Requiem Mass. The priest planned to bury Margaret's body in the parish cemetery, but the congregation insisted that she must have a tomb inside the church with other distinguished residents of the town. As priest and people argued, a crippled girl limped up to Margaret's coffin. The moment she touched it, the child's legs were healed. In light of the miracle, the priest relented and buried Margaret inside the church.

Feast day: April 13.

Requiem Mass

*Before 1969, when Pope Paul VI introduced the Novus Ordo
(New Order) of the Mass, a Catholic funeral was known as
a Requiem Mass. The name comes from the opening line
of the Introit, or Entrance Antiphon, for the Mass: "Requiem aeternam dona eis, Domine," "Eternal rest grant unto
them O Lord." Since 1969 a Catholic funeral Mass is known
as the Mass of Christian Burial.*

ST. SERAPHINA (DIED 1253). Seraphina was a pretty child who grew up in the town of San Gimignano, near Florence, Italy. In her teens she contracted an undiagnosed illness that left her an invalid. Unable to walk or care for herself and often in great pain, she offered her sufferings to Christ. After six years of patient suffering, Seraphina died. It is said that when her body was lifted off the board that had been her bed, a mass of white violets blossomed from the wood.

Feast day: March 12.

EARACHES AND LOSS OF HEARING

ST. CORNELIUS (DIED 253). Cornelius' name comes from "*cornu*," Latin for "horn." In art he is often shown holding a horn, or ear trumpet, which in centuries past people who suffered from hearing loss used to amplify sound.

Cornelius was a member of one of Rome's most distinguished noble families. He was elected pope in 251, at a time when the Church was once again being torn apart by the issue of the *lapsi*, Christians who during persecution renounced their faith to save their lives but later wished to return to the Church. Hardliners demanded that the *lapsi* be banned from the Church, but Pope Cornelius insisted that lapsed Catholics who were contrite and agreed to do penance could return to the sacraments.

In 252 the Roman authorities exiled Cornelius to Civita-veccha, where he died of abuse and neglect. Roman Christians venerated him as a martyr.

Feast day: September 16.

EPIDEMICS

ST. ROCH (DIED 1378). Roch was a pilgrim who came to the Italian city of Piacenza just as it was suffering an outbreak of bubonic plague, also known as the Black Death. He could have fled the city (as many of the inhabitants had), but instead he remained and nursed the sick. When he contracted the disease he left Piacenza and traveled deep into a nearby forest, where he would not infect anyone else. Every day a dog brought Roch a fresh loaf of bread, and eventually he recovered. St. Roch is almost always depicted with a plague sore on his leg.

Feast day: August 16.

ST. SEBASTIAN (DIED C. 300). In the fourteenth century, when the Black Death ravaged Europe, Catholics likened the epidemic to a volley of arrows that struck down victims at random. Because St. Sebastian had been martyred by being shot through with arrows, he was invoked against the disease.

Feast day: January 20.

EPILEPSY

ST. VITUS (DIED C. 303). As a boy Vitus was converted to Christianity by his tutor, Modestus, and his nurse, Crescentia. A few years later all three were arrested and martyred by being thrown into cauldrons of boiling oil. In Germany during the late Middle Ages it was the custom to dance before a statue of St. Vitus on his feast day. The dancing often became frenzied, so that the dancers appeared to be suffering from an epileptic seizure. For many years epilepsy was known as "St. Vitus' Dance."

Feast day: June 15.

BLESSED GERARD OF LUNEL (1275-1298). Gerard was only eighteen when he and his brother left home to live as hermits in a cave. Their reputation for sanctity attracted a great many visitors who sought their spiritual advice or asked for their prayers. To escape this unwelcome attention they set out on a pilgrimage to Jerusalem. Gerard died at Montesanto, Italy, and was buried there. Many epileptics who prayed at his tomb were cured, so Blessed Gerard became their special patron.

Feast day: May 6.

EYE DISEASES

ST. LUCY (DIED C. 304). There are three possibilities why Lucy is invoked against eye ailments. Her name comes from the Latin word "*lux*," which means "light." It is said that in the course of her martyrdom the executioners blinded her. And another story tells of a young pagan who, hoping to convince her to give up her Christian faith and marry him, complimented Lucy on the beauty of her eyes. She plucked them out and gave them to the young man. St. Lucy was executed in her hometown, Syracuse, on the island of Sicily, by being stabbed in the neck with a dagger. She lived long enough for a priest to bring her Holy Communion for the last time.

Feast day: December 13.

ST. ODILIA OF ALSACE (C. 660-720). Odilia was born blind. During her baptism, as the priest anointed her with sacred chrism, some of the oil ran into her eyes and she was healed. As a young woman Odilia entered a convent, where she developed a reputation as a saint. It is said that when her father killed her brother, she raised him from the dead.

Feast day: December 13.

ST. ODILIA OF COLOGNE (FIFTH CENTURY). St. Odilia is believed to be one of the eleven thousand virgin companions of

St. Ursula. They were all martyred together by the Huns at the city of Cologne, Germany. In 1287 St. Odilia appeared to John of Eppa, a brother of the Crosier order, with the message that she would be the protectress of the Crosiers and the patron of everyone who suffers from eye trouble.

Feast day: July 18.

ST. RAPHAEL THE ARCHANGEL. In the Old Testament Book of Tobit, or Tobias, young Tobias catches a monstrous fish (Tb 6:1-5). The archangel Raphael, who is traveling in human form with the young man, tells him to save the fish's liver. Later, Raphael instructs Tobias to apply the fish liver to the eyes of his blind father. Young Tobias does as the angel commands, and his father's sight is restored.

Feast day: September 29.

The Book of Tobit, or Tobias

This Old Testament book was written sometime between 300 and 100 B.C. It describes the world of Jews who had moved from Israel, their ancestral homeland, and settled elsewhere in the Middle East. The narrative reads like a novel, although the Catholic Church teaches that the main characters in the Book of Tobit are historical.

This is the only book of the Bible in which an archangel plays such a dominant role. It is also our only source of information about St. Raphael the Archangel.

FOOD POISONING

ST. JOHN THE EVANGELIST (FIRST CENTURY). There is a legend that the Roman authorities tried to execute John by forcing him to drink poison. He made the sign of the cross over the drink, and the poison took the form of a serpent and slithered out of the cup.

Feast day: December 27.

St. Benedict (c. 480-550). A community of monks invited Benedict to become their abbot. He agreed, but once he arrived at the monastery Benedict found that the monks had grown lax. Benedict's attempts to restore discipline met with stiff resistance, but he persisted. To rid themselves of this troublesome abbot, they poisoned his wine. Benedict made the sign of the cross over it, and the cup shattered.

Feast day: July 11.

Headaches

St. Acasius (died 303). Acasius was a centurion in the Roman army stationed in what is now northern Turkey. He was arrested during a roundup of Christians. Before he was beheaded, torturers twisted thorn branches around his head, which led to St. Acasius being invoked against headaches.

Feast day: May 8.

St. Hugh of Grenoble (1053-1132). Hugh came from a devout family. His mother was renowned for her generosity to the poor. His father, after serving as a soldier, became a Cistercian monk. His uncle, Blessed Hugh, was abbot of the monastery of Bonnevaux. Hugh was only twenty-seven years old when Pope St. Gregory VII named him bishop of Grenoble, France. He served for fifty-two years. He reformed the clergy; introduced new religious communities, including the newly formed Carthusian monks; revived the religious devotion of the people of his diocese; and opened new institutions to help the sick, the poor, and the helpless. Throughout his adult life St. Hugh suffered from chronic headaches.

Feast day: April 1.

Heart Disease

St. John of God (1495-1550). In 1538 John of God opened a small hospital for the poor in Granada, Spain. He washed and nursed the sick, prepared their meals, and scrubbed the floors and washed the bed linens. He also led the sick in daily prayers, and brought in priests to hear his patients' confessions and say Mass in the hospital. In time other men joined him, and he founded a new community of nursing brothers. St. John of God is the patron of the sick, especially those suffering from heart disease.

Feast day: March 8.

INFERTILITY

ST. ANNE (FIRST CENTURY B.C.). Anne and her husband, Joachim, had been married for many years, yet they never had a child. Finally, when the couple were elderly, God sent an angel to them with the message that they would have a daughter, the Blessed Virgin Mary.

Feast day: July 26.

ST. FELICITY OF ROME (DIED 165). During the reign of Emperor Lucius Verus, Felicity, a wealthy widow, was arrested with her seven sons. The magistrate had her sons executed, one by one before her eyes, then he ordered Felicity beheaded. St. Felicity is invoked against infertility because she had a large family.

Feast day: November 23.

ST. GERARD MAJELLA (1726-1755). St. Gerard was initially invoked by women who were having a difficult pregnancy or delivery. Soon, he was also being invoked by women who were having a difficult time conceiving a child.

Feast day: October 16.

LEPROSY, OR HANSEN'S DISEASE

ST. DAMIEN DE VEUSTER (1840-1889). Damien de Veuster was the son of Belgian farmers. He joined the Congregation of the Sacred Hearts of Jesus and Mary, popularly known as the Picpus Fathers, and volunteered for missionary work in the Hawaiian

Islands. After working among the native Hawaiians for several years, Father Damien asked to be assigned to the leper colony on the island of Molokai. He served not only as their chaplain, but also as their nurse and as a good neighbor who helped the lepers build small homes for themselves. After twelve years on Molokai Father Damien developed the symptoms of leprosy. By that time two priests, two lay brothers, and several Franciscan nuns joined his ministry on Molokai. They nursed Father Damien until his death in 1889.

Feast day: May 10.

ST. LAZARUS (FIRST CENTURY). The Gospel of St. Luke records Christ's parable about an unnamed rich man who did nothing to help a poor man named Lazarus, who begged at the rich man's door. The Gospel doesn't state specifically that Lazarus suffered from leprosy, but only mentions that his body was covered with open sores. These have been interpreted to be the result of leprosy. Devotion to St. Lazarus began among Eastern Christians and spread to the West during the Crusades. In Jerusalem a band of knights founded the Order of St. Lazarus to help lepers.

Feast day: June 21.

Leprosy: A Dreaded Disease

Leprosy, or Hansen's disease, a contagious disease that has been dreaded and feared for thousands of years, is now easy to treat. Every year the number of reported cases declines. The World Health Organization reports that in 2010 there were 211,903 cases of leprosy, down almost 33,000 cases from 2009.

In the long centuries when there was no cure, people had a real horror of the disease and drove out of their communities anyone infected with it. The disease attacks the skin, and can eat away fingers and toes. It also affects the eyes, causing blindness, and spreads to the respiratory system, which brings about the death of the patient.

*In 1873 Gerhard A. Hansen, a Norwegian physician,
identified the bacterium that causes leprosy, but it wasn't
until the late 1940s that an effective treatment was found.*

MALARIA

ST. MACARIUS THE YOUNGER (DIED C. 401). Macarius the Younger had a successful business in Alexandria, Egypt, where he sold candy and sweet pastries. In 335 he closed his shop and traveled into the desert to live as a hermit. These early hermits and monks imposed strict penances on themselves as punishment for their sins, but also to extinguish all desire for food, drink, rest, and comfort, in order to focus entirely on conversation with God. One time Macarius left his hermitage and spent six months in a swamp, where he was attacked day and night by swarms of mosquitoes. Because of this penance, St. Macarius the Younger is invoked against malaria.

Feast day: January 2.

MISCARRIAGE

ST. CATHERINE OF SWEDEN (1331-1381). The beautiful daughter of St. Bridget of Sweden, Catherine lived with her mother in Rome, where they spent their days nursing the sick poor, visiting Rome's many churches, and calling upon noble Roman families to win their support for their nursing apostolate. It appears that St. Catherine is invoked against miscarriage because her mother bore eight healthy children, all of whom reached adulthood, which was very unusual in the Middle Ages,

Feast day: March 24.

RESPIRATORY AILMENTS

ST. BERNARDINE OF SIENA (1380-1444). A dynamic preacher, Bernardine attracted large crowds — so big that usually he was compelled to preach outdoors because there was no church large enough to hold the congregation. Bernardine had a strong voice that could carry to the edge of any crowd. Because he had such strong lungs, he is invoked against respiratory ailments.

Feast day: May 20.

SNAKEBITE

ST. PAUL (DIED C. 67). About the year 60 St. Paul was under arrest and being transported by ship to Rome for trial (the complete story is found in Acts 27-28). Near Crete the ship was overtaken by a violent storm that blew it off course, ultimately wrecking it off the island of Malta. St. Paul, some fellow prisoners, their guards, and the crew — 276 men in all — survived the wreck. On shore they were discovered by some Maltese who built a fire for them. Paul was collecting firewood when he was bitten by a poisonous snake. He shook the snake into the flames but remained unharmed.

Feast days: June 29, January 25 (conversion), February 10 (shipwreck).

ST. PATRICK (C. 390-C. 461). The best-known story about St. Patrick tells how he drove the snakes out of Ireland. It is true that there are no snakes of any kind in Ireland, but centuries before Patrick was born Roman visitors to the island reported that Hibernia (as they called Ireland) was completely without snakes. In recent times the snakes are taken as a metaphor for the false religion that St. Patrick banished from Ireland.

Feast day: March 17.

Holy Legends

Over the centuries many legends have grown up around the saints. Whoever first told these stories was not so much manufacturing lies as trying to convey a message about the holiness and kindness of the saint, and God's love for him or her. In that way, the story of St. Patrick driving the snakes out of Ireland is on par with the

American legend of George Washington and the cherry tree.

Legends, whether secular or sacred, can teach us important lessons. For example, the cherry-tree legend teaches the importance of honesty. Similarly, the legend of St. George slaying a dragon assures us of the triumph of good over evil, of holiness over the power of the devil.

STOMACH TROUBLE

ST. TIMOTHY (DIED 97). St. Paul wrote two epistles to Timothy, addressing him as "my true child in the faith." Both letters are part of the New Testament. Timothy must have suffered from a chronic stomach ailment, because Paul advises him, "No longer drink only water, but use a little wine for the sake of your stomach and your frequent ailments" (1 Tim 5:23). Timothy was stoned to death by a mob he had provoked by condemning the worship of the god Dionysus.

Feast day: January 26.

STROKE

ST. ANDREW AVELLINO (1521-1608). Andrew Avellino was a lawyer employed by the archbishop of Naples. At one point the archbishop sent him to a convent where the nuns had stopped keeping their vows. The nuns rebelled against the archbishop's order to reform, and the nuns' lovers attacked Andrew, almost beating him to death. He was nursed by the Theatine priests, and when he recovered Andrew joined the Theatine order. He proved to be a great asset to the Theatines. He was a powerful preacher and sympathetic confessor, and he inspired many young men to enter the community. At age eighty-seven, as he was about to say Mass, he suffered a massive stroke and died.

Feast day: November 10.

THROAT AILMENTS

ST. BLAISE (DIED C. 316). While Blaise was in prison awaiting execution, a Christian woman brought him two tall candles to dispel the gloom of his cell. The next day another woman visited him carrying her little boy who was choking to death on a fish bone that was stuck in his throat. Blaise made a cross from the two candles, laid it against the child's throat, and blessed him. Immediately the bone was dislodged, and the child's life was saved. On February 3 or the Sunday closest to it, Catholics have their throats blessed at church in honor of St. Blaise.

Feast day: February 3.

TOOTHACHE

ST. APOLLONIA (DIED 249). Apollonia, an elderly Christian of the city of Alexandria, Egypt, was attacked by a pagan mob. They beat her face so severely that they broke or knocked out all of her teeth.

Feast day: February 9.

TUBERCULOSIS

ST. THÉRÈSE OF LISIEUX (1873-1897). Early in the morning of Good Friday 1896, Thérèse awoke coughing and spitting up blood. She reported the incident to her mother superior. The young nun said she was not in pain and did not believe she needed a doctor, and the reverend mother did not insist that she seek medical attention. In the months that followed, Thérèse's condition deteriorated, and it became obvious that she had contracted tuberculosis. In spite of being in agony, she was given no painkillers. She died of tuberculosis at age twenty-four.

Feast day: October 1.

ST. GEMMA GALGANI (1878-1903). Gemma Galgani died of tuberculosis on Holy Saturday 1903. She had been sickly all her life and at one point was diagnosed with spinal meningitis. (She attributed her cure of that to the intercession of St. Margaret Mary Alacoque and St. Gabriel Possenti.) In spite of the healing, the religious orders in her hometown of Lucca, Italy, suspected that she would become an invalid and burden for them, so they turned her away when she asked to join their convents. The Passionists permitted her to join their Third Order, which was open to laypeople. St. Gemma is said to have had the stigmata and to have experienced frequent visions of Our Lady, St. Gabriel Possenti, and her guardian angel.

Feast day: April 11.

CHAPTER 4

Patron Saints
for Professions

ACTORS

ST. GENESIUS (DIED C. 300). Genesius was a Roman pagan and a member of a troupe of actors who had received the opportunity of a lifetime: a command performance before Emperor Diocletian. For the occasion they wrote a new piece, a comedy that mocked the Christian sacrament of baptism. Genesius would play the part of the convert.

At the performance, as the actor cast as the priest poured water over Genesius' head and recited the words of the baptismal rite, something unexpected happened: Genesius was touched by God's grace and believed absolutely in the Christian faith. Rising, he walked to the apron of the stage and rebuked Diocletian for his cruel persecution of innocent Christians. The audience, thinking the speech was part of the comedy, roared with laughter, but as Genesius continued the emperor realized that the actor was not acting. He ordered Genesius' arrest and condemned him to be tortured to death.

In the torture chamber the executioners offered to spare Genesius' life if he renounced Christianity. "Were I to be killed a thousand times for my allegiance to Christ," he said, "I would still go on as I have begun."

Feast day: August 25.

ACTRESSES

ST. PELAGIA (FIFTH CENTURY). St. John Chrysostom, patriarch of Constantinople and a contemporary of Pelagia, tells us that she was the most famous actress in the Roman Empire. She was also notoriously promiscuous, seducing men who had once been faithful husbands and fathers, and even tempting bishops to forget their vows. One day, by chance, she heard a bishop preaching on the snares of sin and the power of God's mercy to reclaim even the most hardened sinners. Suddenly overwhelmed by all the wicked things she had done, Pelagia wept, confessed to the bishop, and then entered a convent. There, through her prayer and good works, she developed a new reputation as a saint.

Feast day: October 8.

ADVERTISING PROFESSIONALS

ST. BERNARDINE OF SIENA (1380-1444). Bernardine was an Italian Franciscan who lived at a time when the country was being torn apart by petty wars between cities and noble families. He traveled to these "hot spots," where he tried to negotiate peace between the warring parties. Invariably he spoke of Jesus Christ as a loving, compassionate brother who was offended by bloodshed, yet would not turn away anyone who was truly repentant. At the emotional high point of his sermon Bernardine would display a wooden board upon which "IHS" — a monogram of the holy name of Jesus in Greek — was painted in gold. The dramatic gesture never failed to create a profound emotional response in the crowd.

"IHS" became St. Bernardine's logo, or trademark, which led advertising professionals to take him as their patron.

Feast day: May 20.

IHS

The monogram "IHS" is a abbreviation for "Jesus" in Greek. Such abbreviations were common in the early centuries of

the Church. Greek-speaking Christians used the abbrevia-
tion IH for Jesus and the Chi Rho, XP, typically overlapped
like this, ☧, for Christ. St. Bernard of Clairvaux (1090-
1153), who preached devotion to the Holy Name of Jesus,
urged Catholics to venerate the sacred monogram IHS. An
order of priests founded in the 1300s, the Jesuati (not to
be confused with the Jesuits) wore IHS over their hearts.
St. Bernardine of Siena spread this devotion in the fifteenth
century, and it received fresh momentum in the sixteenth
when St. Ignatius Loyola adopted IHS as his personal seal.
The Jesuits then carried devotion to the monogram of Je-
sus across the globe. Today IHS is a common symbol in
Catholic churches and chapels.

AIRLINE PILOTS, CREW, AND PASSENGERS

OUR LADY OF LORETO. According to legend, in 1291, after the last of the crusaders were driven out of the Holy Land, angels transported the house of the Holy Family from Nazareth to what is now Loreto, Italy. A magnificent basilica was built there around the little stone house. In 1920 Pope Benedict XV named Our Lady of Loreto the patron of airline pilots and, over the years, Mary's patronage has been extended to include the entire crew and the passengers.

Feast day: December 10.

ST. JOSEPH OF CUPERTINO (1603-1663). An Italian Franciscan priest, Joseph of Cupertino is said to have not just levitated but moved through the air, usually toward the tabernacle or an image of the Blessed Mother. Because he flew, St. Joseph has become the patron of aviators.

Feast day: September 18.

ANESTHESIOLOGISTS

ST. RENÉ GOUPIL (1608-1642). René Goupil studied medicine in France and took his skills to the New World, where he worked in the hospital in the French colony of Quebec. In 1642 Goupil volunteered to accompany St. Isaac Jogues to his mission among the Huron Indians. About a day's canoe's voyage from Quebec, Jogues, Goupil, and their entire party of Huron companions were captured by Mohawk warriors. The Mohawks burned the Hurons at the stake. They savagely tortured Goupil and Jogues, but kept them alive to serve as slaves at a village called Ossern-enon, in what is now New York's Mohawk Valley. One day a Mohawk warrior saw Goupil teaching a four-year-old boy how to make the sign of the cross. The Mohawk raised his tomahawk and split Goupil's skull.

His medical training and the terrible physical sufferings he endured led anesthesiologists to take St. René Goupil as their patron.

Feast day: October 19.

ARCHAEOLOGISTS

St. DAMASUS (c. 304-384). As pope, Damasus drew upon the resources of the Church to restore and adorn the tombs of the martyrs in the catacombs. He wrote more than sixty metrical epitaphs that were carved on stone tablets and fixed to the saints' tombs. He also improved access to the catacombs through the construction of new stairways and light-and-air shafts.

Feast day: December 11.

St. HELENA OR HELEN (249-329). Helena was more than eighty years old when she went on pilgrimage to the Holy Land. There she excavated the site of Calvary, where Jesus Christ had been crucified, and the Holy Sepulcher, the tomb from which he rose from the dead. During the excavation she found the True Cross and its nails. She moved on to Bethlehem, where she found the cave in which Our Lord was born.

Feast day: August 18.

ARCHITECTS

St. THOMAS THE APOSTLE (FIRST CENTURY). Tradition says that

Thomas carried the Gospel to India where, with his own hands, he built the country's first church. There is a story that an Indian king commissioned Thomas to build him a palace. Thomas took the money the king had given him for the project, distributed it to the poor, and then told the king that he had built him an eternal palace in heaven.

Feast day: July 3.

ST. BERNWARD (C. 960-1022). Bernward was serving as a chaplain at the palace of the Holy Roman emperor when he was appointed bishop of Hildesheim, a diocese in northern Germany that was a frequent target of barbarian raids. As a young man Bernward had studied engineering; now he put his old training to use erecting fortresses, defensive walls around cities and towns, and churches and monasteries. His legacy is the Abbey of St. Michael in Hildesheim, a masterpiece of Romanesque architecture.

Feast day: November 20.

ST. BARBARA (DATE UNCERTAIN). According to legend, Barbara's father locked her in a tower to keep her safe from unsuitable suitors. Once a Christian priest passed Barbara's isolated tower and converted her. When her father sent a work crew to add a second window to the tower, Barbara ordered them to add two windows so she would have three — in honor of the Blessed Trinity.

Feast day: December 4.

ASTRONAUTS

ST. JOSEPH OF CUPERTINO (1603-1663). There are surviving reports from eyewitnesses who saw Joseph Cupertino, an Italian Capuchin friar, rise from the ground and move through the air, usually toward the tabernacle or a statue of the Blessed Mother. Among those who witnessed this phenomenon was a tribunal of the Inquisition investigating Joseph, and Pope Urban VIII, who commanded Joseph's superior to bring him to Rome for a private audience.

Astronauts took St. Joseph Cupertino as their patron because his unhurried movement through the air resembles spacewalking.

Feast day: September 18.

ASTRONOMERS

ST. DOMINIC (1170-1221). At Dominic's baptism his parish priest saw a brilliant star shining over the infant's forehead. Typically, in remembrance of this mystical event, artists depict Dominic with a star over his head, which has led astronomers to take St. Dominic as their patron.

Dominic was a young Spanish priest when he accompanied his bishop on a journey to southern France. There he was shocked by the number of Catholics who had abandoned their faith and joined the Cathars, a puritanical sect so opposed to all things physical that they rejected all seven sacraments because water, holy oil, bread, and wine were essential to their administration. To combat this heresy Dominic founded a new religious order, the Order of Preachers, better known as the Dominicans. As their name suggests, they were especially well-trained orators. Dominic and his new community traveled throughout southern France. But relatively few Cathars responded to them and returned to the Catholic faith, so Dominic invoked the aid of the Blessed Virgin Mary. According to tradition, she appeared to him with the Christ Child in her arms and gave Dominic the Rosary, with the promise that praying the Rosary daily would bring about the conversion of the Cathars. It is true that the Dominicans spread the Rosary devotion across Europe.

Feast day: August 8.

The Dominicans Today

Dominican priests, brothers, and nuns tend to be involved in education, including theology schools at Catholic colleges and universities. Some Dominican priests juggle parish work with their responsibilities in the classroom. Some Dominican sisters are nurses, such as the Hawthorne Dominicans, who care for incurables. And some communities of Dominican sisters are cloistered, devoting their lives to prayer and sacrifice for the good of the world.

BAKERS

ST. HONORIUS OF AMIENS (DIED 653). Legend tells us that when word reached Honorius' family that he had been named bishop of Amiens everyone rejoiced — except his old nursemaid. The elderly lady, who was baking bread at the time, leaned against her baker's peel (the long-handled board she used to bring loaves out of the oven) and declared that she didn't believe it. She added that the boy she had raised was about as likely to become a bishop as her peel was to become a tree. A moment later the peel put down roots and sprouted branches. In memory of the miracle of the baker's peel, bakers have taken St. Honorius as their patron.

Feast day: May 16.

BARBERS

ST. MARTIN DE PORRES (1579-1639). Before Martin de Porres entered the Dominican Priory of the Holy Rosary in Lima, Peru, his father apprenticed him to a barber-surgeon. In the sixteenth century, barber-surgeons cut hair, but they also performed simple surgical procedures such as letting blood, lancing boils, and removing moles and other growths on the skin. When Martin joined the Dominicans he served as the priory's barber and also worked in the infirmary.

Feast day: November 3.

BARTENDERS

ST. AMAND OF MAASTRICHT (C. 584-C. 679). Amand was consecrated bishop of Maastricht in what is now Belgium, but he felt called to carry Christianity to those parts of what is today France and Germany where the faith was unknown. By chance, those regions later became prime producers of beer and wine, which led tavern keepers (or bartenders) to take St. Amand as their patron.

Feast day: February 6.

BOOKSELLERS

ST. JOHN OF GOD (1495-1550). John of God was one of those individuals who had a difficult time finding his place in life. He was a shepherd, a handy man, and a soldier before settling in Granada, Spain, where he opened a little shop and sold holy cards and religious books. Shepherds, handy men, and soldiers have not adopted St. John of God as their patron, but booksellers have.

Feast day: March 8.

BREWERS

ST. WENCELAUS (907-929). Wencelaus was prince of Bohemia, now part of the Czech Republic. For at least one thousand years this region has produced some of the world's finest beer, especially beer from the Bohemian town of Budweis (the inspiration for the American beer, Budweiser). Bohemian brewers took St. Wencelaus as their patron, and his patronage has extended to professional and home beer brewers around the globe.

Feast day: September 28.

BRIDGE BUILDERS

ST. BENEZET (C. 1163-1184). Benezet was a French shepherd who was commanded by God to build a bridge across the River Rhone at Avignon, a project that would increase commerce in the region and aid travelers. The local authorities took no interest in the project, so Benezet called for volunteers. That unskilled peasants would take on such a great venture without the support of the city shamed the bishop of Avignon, who persuaded city officials to employ engineers and supply the funds to build the bridge. Travelers used St. Benezet's bridge for about five hundred years, until a flood destroyed part of it. But the ruins still remain and are an Avignon landmark.

Feast day: April 14.

St. John Nepomucene (c. 1340-1393). King Wenceslaus IV of Bohemia tortured his wife's confessor — John Nepomucene — to learn what she had said in confession, but the priest would not reveal anything. As punishment, Wenceslaus had John wrapped in heavy chains and thrown off a bridge into the Moldau River to drown. The manner of St. John Nepomucene's martyrdom led bridge builders to venerate him as their patron.

Feast day: May 16.

Broadcasters and Telecommunications Workers

St. Gabriel the Archangel. The Gospel of St. Luke tells us that the archangel Gabriel brought to the priest Zechariah news that he and his wife Elizabeth would have a son, St. John the Baptist, and announced to the Blessed Virgin Mary that she would be the Mother of the Savior, Jesus Christ. In the Old Testament Book of Daniel, Gabriel appears to the prophet to explain one of his visions. According to tradition, it was Gabriel who told St. Joseph that Mary was pregnant by the power of the Holy Spirit, who brought the news to the shepherds of Bethlehem that Christ was born, and who warned Joseph to take Mary and Jesus to safety in Egypt. The archangel who brought such important news would naturally be invoked as the patron of broadcasters.

Feast day: September 29.

The Orders of Angels

Concerning the Celestial Hierarchy, *a book written no later than the sixth century, first laid out the belief in the nine orders of angels in heaven. (The book is attributed to St.*

Dionysius the Aeropagite, an Athenian converted by St. Paul, but this is almost certainly a myth. We do not know who wrote Concerning the Celestial Hierarchy*).*

The nine types of angels in order of rank are: sera-phim, cherubim, thrones, dominations, virtues, powers, principalities, archangels, and angels. The author did not make them up. Angels and archangels are often mentioned in the Bible; seraphim and cherubim appear in the works of the Old Testament prophets. St. Paul refers to "princi-pality, and power, and virtue, and dominion" in the Douay translation of Ephesians 1:21 and to "thrones, or domina-tions, or principalities, or powers" in the Douay translation of Colossians 1:16.

BUS DRIVERS

ST. CHRISTOPHER (DIED C. 250). In life St. Christopher carried travelers safely across a raging river. He is the patron of bus driv-ers, who are responsible for getting travelers, commuters, and students safely to their destination.

Feast day: July 25.

BUSINESSMEN

ST. HOMOBONUS (DIED 1197). Homobonus' father had trained him in the family tailoring business in their hometown of Cre-mona, Italy. At his father's death Homobonus inherited the busi-ness. He noticed that many Italian entrepreneurs were getting rich by weaving and selling fine cloth, so Homobonus gave up tailoring and manufactured fabric.

His business was successful and kept him fully occupied, so he attended daily Mass in the evening, on his way home from his shop. And every week he took time out to bring food, clothes, medicine, or money to Cremona's needy.

Homobonus retired at age fifty and devoted himself to char-ity. On November 13, 1197, he was at evening Mass, as usual, when suddenly he raised his arms to make the shape of the cross and fell to the floor. His neighbors hurried over and found that he was dead.

Homobonus, the successful and charitable entrepreneur, is the patron of businessmen.

Feast day: November 13.

BUSINESSWOMEN

ST. MARGARET CLITHEROW (C. 1553-1586). Margaret Middleton learned the basics of running a business from her parents, who were candle makers in York, England. After her marriage to John Clitherow, a butcher, she made their shop one of the most successful enterprises in town.

John and Margaret were both Anglicans, but John's brother William was a Catholic, and it is likely he was the catalyst that brought Margaret to the Catholic Church.

The practice of Catholicism was illegal in England, but Margaret was determined to go to Mass daily and raise her children as Catholics. She hired carpenters to build secret rooms and cupboards, then hired a Catholic tutor for the children and let it be known that Catholic priests would always be welcome in her house. The priests lived in the secret rooms and kept their missal, vestments, and altar furnishings in the secret cupboards. Margaret's Catholicism went undetected for twelve years until an unknown informant reported her to the authorities. As priest-hunters burst into the house, the tutor escaped and the priest hid in his secret room. When the hunters threatened to beat an eleven-year-old boy, a foster child living with the Clitherows, the frightened child revealed that Mass was said in the house daily and then led them to the hidden cupboards and rooms. Margaret was arrested.

In court Margaret refused to enter a plea of guilty or not guilty, a tactic that would prevent her husband, children, and neighbors from being forced to testify against her. The penalty for not cooperating with the court was severe: she was sentenced to be crushed to death.

On March 25 she was staked out on the ground, a heavy wooden door was laid on top of her, and stones were piled on the door until she was dead. The house where St. Margaret Clitherow ran her butcher shop, raised her children, and sheltered priests still stands in York as a shrine to her.

Feast day: March 25.

BUTCHERS

ST. BARTHOLOMEW (FIRST CENTURY). According to tradition the apostle Bartholomew, called Nathaniel or Nathanial in St. John's Gospel, preached in Armenia. He was arrested and condemned to be flayed alive. Since butchers remove an animal's hide before butchering the carcass, they took St. Bartholomew as one of their patrons.

Feast day: August 24.

ST. ADRIAN OF NICOMEDIA (DIED 304). Adrian was one of the guards at the emperor's palace in Nicomedia, now Izmit, Turkey. He was a pagan, but the courage of the Christians as they faced torture and death impressed him, and he asked to be baptized. His conversion led to his own arrest and grisly martyrdom: Adrian's executioners hacked off his limbs.

Feast day: September 8.

CAB DRIVERS

ST. FIACRE (DIED 670). Fiacre was a wandering Irish monk who settled in France on the site of the city of Meaux. He planted a large garden around his hermitage and shared the fruit and vegetables with the poor. He used the herbs to treat the sick. In the nineteenth century in Paris, there was a large cab stand outside the Hotel St. Fiacre. Parisians took to calling the horse-drawn cabs "fiacres," so the cab drivers adopted St. Fiacre as their patron.

Feast day: August 30.

ST. FRANCES OF ROME (1384-1440). Frances was a Roman noblewoman whose generosity and compassion were famous among the poor of the city. When Frances was called out in the middle of the night to tend the sick or the dying, her guardian angel went before her shining a supernatural light that illuminated the unlit city streets. Roman cab drivers have interpreted the light as a kind of mystical headlight and have taken St. Frances of Rome as their patron. On her feast day, cabs line up outside the church where she is enshrined to be blessed.

Feast day: March 9.

CANDY MAKERS

ST. MACARIUS THE YOUNGER (DIED C. 401). As a young man Macarius had a shop in Alexandria, Egypt, where he made and sold candy and pastries. His fellow Christians spoke often about the hermits and monks who had left their comfortable homes to live lives of prayer and penance in the deserts of Egypt. In 335 Macarius closed his sweet shop and traveled to the Red Sea to learn the essentials of monastic life from St. Anthony of the Desert. For forty years Macarius lived in a hut near what is now Aswan. The man who had delighted in making sugary treats ate only vegetables, bread, and water, with a little olive oil, on holy days.

Feast day: January 2.

CAREGIVERS

ST. JOHN THE EVANGELIST (FIRST CENTURY). In the account of Christ's Passion recorded in St. John's Gospel we read that as Jesus was dying on the cross, he committed his mother to the care of his beloved apostle, John. "And from that hour," the evangelist tells us, "the disciple took her to his own home" (Jn 19:27). In 2005, the Friends of St. John the Caregiver was founded to offer assistance to family caregivers. It also encourages devotion to St. John as the patron saint of caregivers. Today, this international

Catholic organization has the support of laypeople, religious, clergy, and bishops.

Feast day: December 27.

CARPENTERS

ST. JOSEPH (FIRST CENTURY). St. Matthew's Gospel tells us that Joseph was a carpenter. When Jesus was teaching in the synagogue of Nazareth, his astonished old neighbors asked one another, "Where did this man get this wisdom and these mighty works? Is not this the carpenter's son?" (Mt 13:54-55). Consequently, all carpenters have St. Joseph as their patron. In 1955 Pope Pius XII made St. Joseph the patron of all laborers and established a new feast day on May 1: St. Joseph the Worker. The new feast was the Church's response to the grandiose May Day parades held in Communist countries. Pope Pius was holding up St. Joseph as a model husband, father, and citizen who fulfilled his obligations and was obedient to the laws of God.

Feast days: March 19 (St. Joseph, Husband of the Blessed Virgin Mary) and May 1 (St. Joseph the Worker).

CEMETERY WORKERS

ST. CALLIXTUS (DIED C. 222). Callixtus was a Christian slave who belonged to a Christian master in Rome. His master, Carpophorus, established a kind of bank for his fellow Christians, and he placed Callixtus in charge of the enterprise. Sadly, Callixtus had no understanding of speculation and was a bit of a thief besides: he stole some of the money and lost the rest through bad investments. In a desperate effort to recover some, Callixtus confronted local Jewish businessmen with whom he had invested part of the bank's funds. This confrontation took place on the Sabbath in one of Rome's synagogues. The disruption of their Sabbath service outraged the congregation, and the dispute spilled out into the street. Callixtus was arrested for disturbing the peace, and when the magistrate learned of his other misdeeds, he sentenced Callixtus to the mines on the island of Sardinia.

Callixtus had not been in the mines long when the emperor, to please his Christian mistress, granted amnesty to all Christian convicts. When Callixtus returned to Rome, Pope Victor took responsibility for him, finding him a small house outside the city, providing him with a stipend, and visiting him often. These visits led to Callixtus' conversion. As a demonstration of his confidence, Pope Victor placed Callixtus in charge of the catacombs, where Christians buried their dead.

Callixtus' conversion was genuine, and in time he was elected pope. He died a martyr, beaten to death by a pagan mob in the Trastevere district of Rome. He was buried in a catacomb on the Appian Way that was named St. Callixtus in his honor. Because he once managed the catacombs, cemetery workers have taken Callixtus as one of their patrons.

Feast day: October 14.

Catacombs

The underground cemeteries known as catacombs are most closely identified with Rome, but they exist elsewhere, too, including Naples in southern Italy, the island of Malta, and Kiev in Ukraine.

The catacombs are long tunnels off of which are small mausoleums or chapels. Most of the dead were placed in niches carved into the tunnel walls. Stone or pottery slabs inscribed with the name of the deceased were placed over the niches.

On the anniversary of a Christian's martyrdom, the Christians of Rome gathered at the saint's grave in the catacomb for Mass.

There is a common misconception that during periods of persecution, the Christians hid in the catacombs. That is not true. Dark and poorly ventilated, suffused with the smell of decomposing corpses, the catacombs would have been a terrible place to try to live. We know that Christians who sought to escape the Roman authorities did not move into their cemeteries, but fled into the mountains or deserts.

St. Anthony of the Desert (c. 251-356). In 342 Anthony went to visit his friend St. Paul the Hermit. He arrived shortly after Paul died. At age ninety-one Anthony was too feeble to dig a grave, so God sent a lion who dug one with its paws. Based on this story, cemetery workers — especially gravediggers — have taken St. Anthony of the Desert as their patron.

Feast day: January 17.

Charitable-Organization Employees and Volunteers

St. Vincent de Paul (1581-1660). Vincent de Paul was a French priest who could never turn away anyone who asked for help. During his more than fifty-year apostolate he established orphanages, homes for the elderly, hospitals, refuges for the blind, asylums for the mentally and emotionally disturbed, shelters for former prostitutes, and ministries to prisoners and galley slaves. Inspired by Vincent's example, in 1833 a group of French laymen founded the Society of St. Vincent de Paul to assist the poor and disadvantaged at the local parish level. Chapters of the society have spread to parishes around the globe.

Feast day: September 27.

St. Elizabeth of Hungary (1207-1231). Elizabeth embarrassed her husband and in-laws by insisting upon caring for lepers in her castle and personally taking food to the poor. There is a story that on one occasion, when Elizabeth's husband saw her smuggling food under her cloak, he tore it open, only to find roses rather than loaves of bread in her arms. After her husband's death Elizabeth founded a hospital in Marburg, Germany, where she served as a nurse.

Feast day: November 17.

CLOCK AND WATCH MAKERS

ST. ELIGIUS (588-660). Before he became bishop of Limoges, France, Eligius trained as a metalsmith. We know that he made splendid gold and silver reliquaries, some of which survived until the eighteenth century, only to be destroyed during the French Revolution. It has been assumed that Eligius was skilled in all kinds of metalwork, and so clock and watchmakers took him as their patron.

Feast day: December 1.

ST. PETER (DIED C. 67). The Gospels of Matthew, Mark, and Luke all recount Christ's prediction to Peter at the Last Supper. Peter had sworn that he would never abandon the Lord, but Jesus told him, "This very night, before the cock crows, you will deny me three times" (Mt 26:34). Of course, it happened exactly as Jesus predicted: Peter, in fear for his life, three times denied that he knew Christ. After the third denial, a cock crowed, heralding the dawn.

Feast days: June 29 and February 22 (Chair of St. Peter).

"Before the Cock Crows"

The other versions of Our Lord's prediction of St. Peter's faithlessness can be found in Mark 14:27-31 and Luke 22:31-34.

CLOWNS AND COMEDIANS

ST. GENESIUS (DIED C. 300). The Roman actor Genesius' conversion came during a farce he was performing before Emperor Diocletian. Because he had been cast in a comedy, clowns and comics have taken St. Genesius as their patron.

Feast day: August 25.

CONSTRUCTION WORKERS

ST. VINCENT FERRER (C. 1350-1419). Vincent Ferrer was a Spanish Dominican who lived during the time of the Western Schism, when the true pope in Rome was challenged by an antipope in Avignon, France. The schism lasted from 1378 until 1417. Vincent was tireless in traveling throughout Spain, France, Switzerland, and Italy, trying to heal the breach and bring Catholics who supported the antipope back to full union with the Church and pope in Rome. It was said that he had the miraculous gift of tongues — that even in multilingual congregations, everyone heard Vincent preaching in his or her own language.

For all he did to build up and restore the Church, St. Vincent Ferrer is the patron of construction workers.

Feast day: April 5.

COOKS

ST. LAWRENCE (DIED 258). As punishment for failing to surrender the treasures of the Church to the Roman authorities and for his refusal to renounce his faith in Christ, Lawrence was sentenced to be roasted on a grill. Just before he died he said to his executioners, "Turn me over. I'm done on this side."

Feast day: August 10.

ST. PASCAL BAYLON (1540-1592). As a Franciscan lay brother Pascal Baylon was put to work as a cook in his friary's kitchen.

He was devoted to Our Lord in the Blessed Sacrament, and was often sent to preach in areas where Calvinists, who denied the Real Presence, were numerous. While he made converts, Pascal was often attacked by angry mobs, one of which beat him so severely that he lost the use of one of his arms.

Feast day: May 17.

DAIRY WORKERS

ST. BRIGID OF KILDARE (C. 450-525). It is said that the cows at Brigid's convent gave a lake of milk every day.

Other miracles of abundance are told about Brigid. When she was a girl still living at home, guests arrived unexpectedly. Brigid's father sent her to the kitchen to cook some bacon. As she stood over the hot pan a starving dog limped in. Filled with pity Brigid fed the dog all the bacon, piece by piece. Then she carried the pan out to the hall where her father was waiting with his guests. When she placed it on the table, the formerly empty pan was brimming with beautifully cooked bacon.

Another story tells of a cask of ale at Brigid's convent that supplied monks at seventeen monasteries with enough ale for the entire octave of Easter.

Feast day: February 1.

DAY LABORERS

ST. GUY OF ANDERLECHT (C. 950-1012). Guy supported himself as a field hand, hiring out to whoever needed help on their farm.

Feast day: September 12.

ST. ISIDORE THE FARMER (C. 1080-1130). Isidore was a tenant farmer who worked his master's land outside Madrid. He rose early every day so he could attend Mass before he went to the fields. While planting or harvesting he prayed quietly to himself. Isidore's fellow tenant farmers claimed that angels plowed the field so he would have more time to pray.

After his death devotion to Isidore was strong in Spain, especially in and around the city of Madrid, but he had never been formally canonized. Then in 1615, King Philip III fell ill with a sickness no physician could cure. Philip prayed to Isidore to intercede for him, and he recovered. Philip wrote of his cure to the pope, who agreed to declare Isidore a saint.

Feast day: May 15.

ST. LUCY (DIED C. 304). According to legend the magistrate in Syracuse, Sicily, condemned Lucy to service in a brothel, but when the guards tried to drag her away they found that she was supernaturally rooted to the ground. They brought in a team of oxen but even that could not dislodge her. The story of the oxen (which were used for plowing) has led to St. Lucy's veneration as patron of day laborers.

Feast day: December 13.

St. Notburga (c. 1265-1313). Notburga was the daughter of poor peasants from the Tyrol district of Austria. She hired herself out as a day laborer to a local farmer, with the understanding that she would be permitted to leave the fields early on Saturdays and the day before holy days to attend vespers in the village church. Notburga and the other field hands were bringing in the farmer's harvest when she heard the church bell ring for vespers. As she set out for the village her employer stopped her and ordered her back to work; he wanted the crop brought in quickly in case the weather turned bad. Notburga reminded the farmer of their agreement, but he was adamant. "We'll let God decide," she said, then she tossed her sickle into the air. Instead of falling to the ground it hung suspended in the air. As the farmer marveled, Notburga continued on her way to church.

Feast day: September 14.

Dentists

St. Apollonia (died 249). In 249 the pagan inhabitants of Alexandria, Egypt, rioted against their Christian neighbors. Christians were attacked on the streets, dragged from their homes and places of business, and ordered to sacrifice to the gods. The mob took those who refused outside the city and threw them into an enormous bonfire.

Apollonia was an elderly Christian who was so severely beaten that all her teeth were broken. At the edge of the bonfire the rioters demanded that she renounce Christianity. Apollonia asked for a moment to consider, and when her captors released her she leaped into the flames.

Feast day: February 9.

DIETICIANS

ST. MARTHA (FIRST CENTURY). Martha lived in Bethany with her sister Mary and their brother Lazarus. Jesus was a friend of the family and a frequent guest in their home. On one occasion Martha was bustling about cooking, setting the table, making everything perfect, while Mary sat at Jesus' feet listening attentively to everything he said. Frustrated, Martha said to Jesus, "Lord, do you not care that my sister has left me to serve alone? Tell her then to help me." Our Lord answered, "Martha, Martha, you are anxious and troubled about many things; one thing is needful. Mary has chosen the good portion, which shall not be taken away from her" (Lk 10:40-42).

Martha, the careful cook, is venerated as the patron of dieticians.

Feast day: July 29.

DIPLOMATS

ST. GABRIEL THE ARCHANGEL. Like a diplomat from heaven, Gabriel carried to the Blessed Virgin Mary a message from God — that he had chosen her to be the Mother of the Savior.

Feast day: September 29.

DOCK WORKERS AND LONGSHOREMEN

ST. NICHOLAS OF MYRA (DIED C. 350). According to legend Nicholas was sailing to the Holy Land when a violent storm threatened to sink the ship. As the sailors and his fellow pilgrims ran about in panic, Nicholas prayed and the storm ceased. From this miracle, sailors and dock workers took St. Nicholas as their patron.

Feast day: December 6.

Doctors (Physicians)

Sts. Cosmas and Damian (died c. 287). Cosmas and Damian were Arab twin brothers who traveled to Antioch in Syria to study medicine. They opened a practice in what is now Iskendrun, Turkey, where they treated patients free of charge. As they tended their patients, they instructed them in the basics of the Christian faith. Word of this indiscretion reached the authorities, who arrested them, along with their three younger brothers, and had them all beheaded.

Feast day: September 26.

St. Raphael the Archangel. In the Old Testament Book of Tobit, or Tobias, Raphael instructs Tobias to save the liver of a giant fish he has caught. Later, when the boy and the archangel have returned to the house of Tobias' parents, Raphael instructs him to rub his blind father's eyes with the fish liver. Immediately the old man's sight was restored.

Feast day: September 29.

St. Luke the Evangelist (first century). In St. Paul's letter to the Colossians he refers to his disciple, "Luke the beloved physician" (Col 4:14). St. Luke's patronage of doctors is based on this phrase.

Feast day: October 18.

St. Pantaleon (died c. 305). Although a Christian, Pantaleon was selected by the emperor Maximian as his personal physician. At the imperial court Pantaleon lost his faith, and may have even worshipped the gods of Rome. When he came to his senses, he sought out a priest, who heard his confession and restored him to the Church.

Pantaleon gave up his practice at the palace and treated patients free of charge. Diseases he could not cure with medicine he cured by prayer. When he was arrested, he challenged pagan priests to a trial: who would cure a paralyzed man, the gods of Rome or Jesus Christ? The pagan priests invoked their gods, but nothing happened. Then Pantaleon spoke the Holy Name of Jesus and the paralytic stood up and walked.

The executioners nailed Pantaleon to a tree, then cut off his head.

Feast day: July 27.

St. Joseph Moscati (1880-1927). Joseph Moscati combined a busy medical practice with intense medical research. He operated a hospital for incurables, studied the use of insulin in the treatment of diabetes, and served on the boards of several medical societies. During World War I he opened a hospital for wounded soldiers and treated about three thousand of them personally. A devout man, he watched for an opportunity to mention the faith to his patients. Under Moscati's influence, an untold number returned to the Church.

Feast day: April 12.

Domestic Workers

St. Zita (1212-1272). Zita was twelve years old when the wealthy Fatinelli family of Lucca, Italy, hired her as a housemaid. As the newest and youngest member of the household she was given all the tedious tasks the other servants didn't want. Whenever she felt dejected by the drudgery she offered her work up to God, and that revived her spirits.

Zita was devout. She rose early every morning to attend Mass at the Church of St. Frediano, next door to the Fatinelli's house. If she had spare time during the day, she retired to her room in the attic to pray. Once, after placing loaves of bread in the oven, she went to her room, where she became so caught up in her prayers she forgot about the bread. She ran down to the kitchen, but instead of finding burned loaves in the oven she found perfectly baked bread cooling on the table: while Zita prayed, angels had watched the bread.

Impressed by Zita's goodness, her honesty, and her diligence, the Fatinellis placed her in charge of their household and even made her governess of their children.

Feast day: April 27.

EDITORS

ST. JOHN BOSCO (1815-1888). John Bosco had his school and shelter for boys in the city of Turin, which was one of the industrial centers of Italy. Don Bosco ("Don" is the title for priests in Italy) kept up with the latest technology and introduced it to his job-training school so that when his boys reached adulthood they would be able to make a good living. He started a publishing company and became familiar not only with the editorial side of the business, but also the manufacturing and distribution. This patron of editors was the founder of the Salesian Paper Mill, Printing Works, Bindery and Bookshop.

Feast day: January 31.

ENGINEERS

ST. FERDINAND III OF CASTILE (1198-1252). During the Middle Ages, Spain was divided into several kingdoms; Ferdinand III was king of Castile. At least half the country was in the hands of the Moors, so for most of his reign Ferdinand fought to reclaim Spanish territory from the invaders. But Ferdinand was not only a warrior king; he was also a great builder. He built hospitals, churches, monasteries, and the University of Salamanca. He also rebuilt the cathedral of Burgos and converted the Great Mosque in Cordoba into a Catholic cathedral.

Feast day: May 30.

BLESSED MIGUEL PRO (1891-1927). One of the results of the Mexican Revolution of 1910-1920 was the adoption of harsh anti-Catholic legislation that exiled members of religious orders, closed churches, and banned priests from saying Mass and administering the sacraments. Miguel Pro, a Mexican Jesuit, started a clandestine ministry to Catholics in Mexico City. Dressed as a businessman, he visited houses and apartments, saying Mass, hearing confessions, baptizing babies, and performing marriages. He was caught in 1927 and executed by firing squad. Before the soldiers fired, Blessed Miguel extended his arms, as Christ did on the cross, and cried, *"Viva Cristo Rey!"* ("Long live Christ the King!"). Miguel Pro's father was a mining engineer, so engineers have taken the martyr as one of their patrons.

Feast day: November 23.

FARMERS

ST. ISIDORE THE FARMER (C. 1080-1130). Isidore and his wife Maria were tenant farmers who worked for a nobleman outside Madrid, Spain. Some of the other tenant farmers complained to their master that Isidore shirked his responsibilities, running off to daily Mass and taking time out during the day to pray. When the master came to the field he found that Isidore was indeed at church — but he also saw angels plowing the field. And at every harvest, the land Isidore worked produced three times as much grain as any other field.

Feast day: May 15.

ST. WALSTAN OF BAWBURGH (DIED 1016). Walstan was a prince who gave up his inheritance to travel to the shrines of Europe. When he returned to England from his lengthy pilgrimage, he worked as a field hand. His master was impressed by Walstan's diligence and presented him with a pregnant cow, which gave birth to twin calves. It is said that when Walstan died, the calves drew the cart bearing his body to church.

Feast day: May 30.

ST. BOTULPH (C. 610-680). Botulph was an English Benedictine monk who founded the monastery of Ikanhoe in East Anglia. The land he purchased was rough country, but Botolph and his monks cleared it, drained the marshes, and transformed the wilderness into productive farmland.

Feast day: June 17.

FINANCIAL PROFESSIONALS

ST. MATTHEW (FIRST CENTURY). Accountants, bankers, financial advisers, and all others involved in finance (including tax collectors) have the apostle Matthew as their patron saint.

Matthew was collecting taxes in the town of Capernaum when Jesus entered the customs house and said to him, "Follow me" (Mt 9:9). At once Matthew left his bags of coins and piles of ledger books and joined the band of apostles.

Matthew's Gospel is addressed particularly to his fellow Jews. He filled it with quotations from the prophets to prove that Jesus Christ is the long-awaited Messiah. According to tradition St. Matthew preached in Ethiopia, where he was martyred as he said Mass.

Feast day: September 21.

FIREFIGHTERS

ST. FLORIAN (DIED 304). Firefighters took St. Florian as their patron because, according to legend, he once extinguished a fire raging through a town with a single bucket of water.

Feast day: May 4.

FISH DEALERS

ST. ANDREW (FIRST CENTURY). All four Gospels recount the miracle of Christ multiplying loaves and fishes to feed five thousand. It is St. John's Gospel that tells us it was Andrew who brought to Our Lord the boy who had five loaves and two fishes (Jn 6:9). For his part in this miracle, and his work as a fisherman, St. Andrew is venerated as the patron saint of fish dealers.

Feast day: November 30.

FLORISTS

St. DOROTHY (DIED 311). Dorothy was on her way to execution when a pagan lawyer named Theophilus mocked her. "Bride of Christ! Send me some fruit and flowers from your bridegroom's garden." A moment later a child appeared beside Dorothy with a basket of rare fruit and exquisite flowers. "Give them to Theophilus," Dorothy said.

Feast day: February 6.

St. ROSE OF LIMA (1586-1617). Rose lived in a hermitage in her parents' garden. She tended the flowers, and during a period when the family was in dire financial straits, she sold her flowers in the market of Lima, Peru.

Feast day: August 23.

St. THÉRÈSE OF LISIEUX (1873-1897). As Thérèse was dying of tuberculosis she promised her sister Carmelites to intercede for them. She said that from her prayers, miracles would descend like a shower of roses from heaven.

Feast day: October 1.

FUNERAL DIRECTORS

St. JOSEPH OF ARIMATHEA (FIRST CENTURY). St. Mark's Gospel calls Joseph of Arimathea "respected" and a secret follower of Our Lord who went to Pontius Pilate and requested the body of Jesus. With Nicodemus, another secret disciple, he took the Lord's body down from the cross, wrapped it in linen, then laid it in the rock-cut tomb he had prepared for himself.

Feast day: March 17.

GAS STATION ATTENDANTS

St. ELIGIUS (588-660). Eligius was a goldsmith, but in the Middle Ages workers in all metal trades, including blacksmiths, took him as their patron. Since blacksmiths make horseshoes, the stable hands and everyone involved with horses also considered Eligius their saint. In the twentieth century, when horse-drawn vehicles were replaced by cars and trucks, St. Eligius made the transition to patron of gas station attendants.

Feast day: December 1.

HAIRSTYLISTS

ST. MARY MAGDALENE (FIRST CENTURY). In St. Luke's Gospel we read of a sinful woman who wept before Jesus, washing his feet with her tears and drying them with her hair. For many centuries is has been assumed that this unnamed woman was Mary Magdalene. Consequently, artists have depicted Mary with long, luxurious, usually red hair. This prominent attribute led hairstylists to choose St. Mary Magdalene as their patron.

Feast day: July 22.

HIGHWAY CONSTRUCTION WORKERS

ST. JOHN THE BAPTIST (FIRST CENTURY). It is a verse from the Old Testament that led to John the Baptist becoming the patron of highway construction workers. The prophet Isaiah foretold that, before the Messiah revealed himself, a messenger would appear in the wilderness, crying, "Prepare the way of the LORD, make straight in the desert a highway for our God" (Is 40:3). That messenger foretold by Isaiah was St. John.

Feast days: June 24 (nativity) and August 29 (beheading).

Feast Days

Typically, a saint is commemorated on the day he or she died. Some saints have more than one feast day. For example, St. John the Baptist's birth as well as his death are listed on the Church's liturgical calendar. St. Francis of Assisi also has two feast days: October 4, the anniversary of his death; and September 17, the commemoration of the day Francis received the stigmata.

HOSPITAL ADMINISTRATORS AND STAFF

ST. CAMILLUS DE LELLIS (1550-1614). Camillus de Lellis' decision to open a hospital in a rough neighborhood of Rome created a rift between him and his spiritual director, St. Philip Neri. Camillus had been a violent man, a mercenary and a con artist, who only recently had repented. Philip Neri believed that Camillus was still immature in the spiritual life and that he was exposing himself to temptation. But Camillus could not be dissuaded. He did open his hospital, and he founded a male nursing order to help him tend the sick. Furthermore, he did not return to his old, sinful life.

Feast day: July 14.

ST. JOHN OF GOD (1495-1550). After years of drifting from job to job, John of God finally found his vocation running a small hospital in Granada, Spain. Initially he did all the work himself: nursing, cooking, and cleaning. John had been a bit eccentric in the past, so no one in Granada was willing to volunteer to work with someone they considered unstable. In time John's goodness and reliability convinced his neighbors that his peculiar days were behind him, and they offered to assist him.

Feast day: March 8.

HOTELKEEPERS

ST. THEODATUS (DIED C. 304). Very few facts about St. Theodatus have come down to us. He was an innkeeper in Ancyra (now modern-day Ankara, Turkey). The local authorities discovered he was a Christian after he buried the bodies of seven martyred women. For this work of mercy, Theodatus was beheaded.

Feast day: May 18.

JEWELERS, GOLDSMITHS, SILVERSMITHS, AND METALWORKERS

ST. ELIGIUS (588-660). Eligius' parents noticed that he had a talent for design and so apprenticed him to one of the goldsmiths who worked for France's royal mint. Once he mastered his art, Eligius traveled to Paris where he offered his services to King Clothaire II. The king commissioned a throne from Eligius, supplying him with gold and jewels. With the valuables the king gave him, Eligius made two thrones and secured for himself the position of court goldsmith.

Abbots brought Eligius new commissions: he fashioned shrines for the relics of St. Denis, St. Genevieve, and St. Martin of Tours. After entering a monastery, Eligius devoted his art to making beautiful sacred vessels for the Church.

Feast day: December 1.

ST. DUNSTAN (909-988). Dunstan was the son of Anglo-Saxon nobles whose lands were near Glastonbury Abbey, which according to legend had been founded by St. Joseph of Arimathea and as such was the birthplace of Christianity in England. As a young man Dunstan became a monk at Glastonbury. During his novitiate, the monks in charge of the abbey's various workshops were delighted to discover that Dunstan had many talents: he could play the harp, embroider, paint lovely illustrations for manuscripts, and was a skilled goldsmith.

Dunstan was also blessed with good judgment. After the king met him, he was called to court to serve on the royal council. He became bishop of Worcester, then archbishop of Canterbury — the most important see in England. The pope named Dunstan his legate, or representative, in England.

Feast day: May 19.

JOURNALISTS

ST. MAXIMILIAN KOLBE (1894-1941). Maximilian Kolbe was a Polish Franciscan who founded the Immaculata Movement to revive religious fervor among lukewarm or fallen-away Catholics. Near Warsaw he established a large religious complex called Niepokalanow, or City of the Immaculate. Kolbe started a magazine, *Knights of the Immaculate*, which during his lifetime reached seven hundred fifty thousand subscribers.

In 1939, when the Nazis invaded Poland, Kolbe's City of the Immaculate sheltered two thousand Jewish and one thousand Catholic refugees. In 1941 he was arrested along with the refugees he had tried to protect; Kolbe was sent to Auschwitz. In July 1941 several prisoners escaped from the death camp. In retaliation, the Nazis selected ten prisoners at random for execution. One of the men chosen was Francis Gajowniczek, a husband and father. Kolbe offered to take Gajowniczek's place. The officer in charge asked why he would do such a thing. "He has a family," Kolbe replied. "And I am a Catholic priest." The officer shrugged, and Kolbe took the place of Gajowniczek.

The Nazis locked the ten men in a punishment bunker, where they were left without food or water. Two weeks later Father Kolbe was found still alive. He was executed with an injection of carbolic acid.

Feast day: August 14.

JUDGES

ST. IVO OF KERMARTIN (1253-1303). In the late Middle Ages, Bretons sang a little song about Ivo: "St. Ivo was a lawyer but not a thief, which is a rare thing." For several years he practiced civil and canon law in Brittany, then he was named to the diocesan court as judge. Lawyers, their clients, and Ivo's fellow judges were astonished that he refused to accept bribes.

Feast day: May 19.

LAWYERS

ST. THOMAS MORE (1478-1535). Thomas More's father was a London lawyer (and eventually a judge), so it was natural that he would follow his father's profession. He studied at the law school known as the New Inn, and when he was called to the bar (the old-fashioned term for earning a law degree), he was offered a position as a lecturer on the law at another school, Furnival's Inn.

More was scrupulously honest with clients and colleagues. In court his arguments were eloquent and forceful. Yet he did not let his profession dominate his life. He doted on his extended family. He devoted several hours each day to Mass, prayer, and meditation. And he was a writer, best known in his day and in ours for *Utopia*, his vision of an ideal society.

Feast day: June 22.

LIBRARIANS

St. Jerome (c. 341-420). Jerome immersed himself in ancient texts to create his authoritative translation of the Bible. His research and wide reading led librarians to adopt him as their patron.

Feast day: September 30.

St. Catherine of Alexandria (died c. 305). Catherine spent hours reading and studying in Egypt's great Library of Alexandria. Her conversion to Christianity also began there with a dream of the Virgin and Child.

Feast day: November 25.

LOCKSMITHS

St. Peter (died c. 67). When Christ named Peter the first pope, he said, "I will give you the keys of the kingdom of heaven, and whatever you bind on earth shall be bound in heaven, and whatever you loose on earth shall be loosed in heaven" (Mt 16:19). Typically, in art, St. Peter is shown carrying two keys, one gold, the other silver, which has led locksmiths to take him as their patron.

Feast days: June 29 and February 22 (Chair of St. Peter).

St. Baldomerus (died c. 650). During the Middle Ages in France locksmiths venerated as their patron St. Baldomerus, a locksmith in the city of Lyon, who gave up his trade to enter a monastery.

Feast day: February 27.

LUMBERJACKS

ST. SIMON (FIRST CENTURY). The Gospels refer to Simon as either "the Canaanite" or "the Zealot," which indicates that he came from the region near Gaza, and that before he became one of Christ's apostles he belonged to the Zealot party, a political organization that called for the overthrow of the Roman occupation of Israel.

Tradition says that, together, St. Simon and St. Jude carried the Gospel to Persia, where Simon was martyred by being sawn in half — which has led lumberjacks to take him as their patron.

Feast day: October 28.

MECHANICS

ST. CATHERINE OF ALEXANDRIA (DIED C. 305). According to tradition, Catherine's executioners attempted to martyr her by tearing her apart on a large spiked wheel. The moment she touched the wheel, however, it shattered. Since the wheel is a basic mechanism in countless machines, St. Catherine has become the patron of mechanics.

Feast day: November 25.

MINERS

ST. ANNE (FIRST CENTURY B.C.). Miners took St. Anne as their patron for metaphorical reasons: her daughter, the Blessed Virgin Mary, is like silver, and her grandson Jesus Christ is like pure gold.

Feast day: July 26.

NURSES

ST. CAMILLUS DE LELLIS (1550-1614). Camillus de Lellis would not have been anyone's idea of a nurse: a former mercenary and con man, he was a hulking, six-feet-six-inch giant. Once, when he was down on his luck, he had taken a job as an orderly at the San Giacomo Hospital in Rome. San Giacomo was typical of hospitals of the time: an untrained staff (Camillus being a prime example), no sanitation, poor food, and a high death rate among the patients. Once he turned his life around, Camillus opened a hospital in a poor neighborhood of Rome. There he instituted a revolutionary approach to the care of patients: the wards, bedding, and patients were kept scrupulously clean; patients received healthy meals; and those suffering from contagious diseases were quarantined. The volunteers who joined Camillus in his work became a new order of nursing priests and brothers. In 1930, Pope Pius XI named St. Camillus de Lellis the patron of nurses.

Feast day: July 14.

ST. ALEXIUS (DIED EARLY FIFTH CENTURY). Alexius was the son of a wealthy Roman family who gave up his riches and privileges. He traveled to Syria, where he lived in a hut beside a church. Whatever food or money he received he shared with the poor, and he nursed the sick. In the thirteenth century a group of men came together in what is now Belgium and Rhineland Germany to serve the sick and the dying. They took St. Alexius as their patron; this nursing order is known as the Alexian Brothers.

Feast day: July 17.

Lay Brothers

Most male religious orders offer candidates a choice: they can train to be lay brothers or they can train to be priests. Brothers and priests are bound by the same vows of poverty, chastity, and obedience, but a brother is not ordained and therefore cannot offer Mass, hear confessions, or administer any of the other sacraments.

OBSTETRICIANS AND MIDWIVES

ST. RAYMOND NONNATUS (1204-1240). *"Nonnatus"* is Latin for "not born." Raymond was delivered by cesarean section. For this reason he is patron of obstetricians and midwives.

Feast day: August 31.

PARK SERVICE WORKERS

ST. JOHN GUALBERT (C. 993-1073). John Gualbert was abbot of a small community of monks in Florence, Italy. The noise, dirt, and distractions of the city made the location unsuitable, so the monks began to look for property in the country where they could build a monastery. A community of nuns sold them land about twenty miles from Florence. It was a wasteland of scrub and briar, but John and his monks cleared the land, planted trees, and established a forest, which they managed and used as a renewable source of building material for the community as well as for their lumber business.

Feast day: July 12.

PAWNBROKERS

ST. NICHOLAS OF MYRA (DIED C. 350). The most famous story of St. Nicholas tells of a widowed merchant who had fallen on hard times. With no dowry for his three daughters, they would find no husbands, and to support themselves they might be driven to a life as prostitutes. Nicholas heard of the family's desperation. One night he walked to their house and threw a bag of gold through an open window. Now the eldest daughter had a dowry. The next night he tossed another bag of gold through the window: a dowry for the second daughter. On the third night, just as he threw the third bag of gold into the house the door burst open and out came the family to thank their anonymous benefactor.

In the Middle Ages pawn shops were charitable institutions where the poor could put up personal belongings as collateral for small loans. Pawnbrokers took as their patron St. Nicholas, who had shown compassion to the impoverished family. In art St. Nicholas is often depicted with three bags of gold, or three gold balls — a reference to his act of charity. Pawnbrokers adopted the three gold balls, the symbol of their patron saint, as their professional emblem.

Feast day: December 6.

PERFUME MAKERS

ST. MARY MAGDALENE (FIRST CENTURY). According to tradition, the unnamed sinful woman who poured expensive perfume over Jesus was Mary Magdalene (Lk 7:36-50). Artists have often shown St. Mary Magdalene with an alabaster jar of perfume, so perfume makers took her as their patron.

Feast day: July 22.

ST. NICHOLAS OF MYRA (DIED C. 350). Perfume makers have taken St. Nicholas as one of their patrons because for one thousand years a perfumed oil, or myrrh, has seeped from the saint's tomb in Bari, Italy.

Feast day: December 6.

PHARMACISTS

ST. GEMMA GALGANI (1878-1903). It was Gemma Galgani's father who was the pharmacist, but that connection was good enough for pharmacists in Italy (where St. Gemma is a popular saint) to choose her as their patron. Her life was rich in supernatural events: she was cured of spinal meningitis through the intercession of St. Gabriel Possenti and St. Margaret Mary Alacoque; she saw her guardian angel every day; for two years, every Thursday evening through Friday afternoon she bore on her hands and feet the stigmata. The Church has never ruled on the question of the authenticity of her experiences but canonized her because of the holiness of her life.

Feast day: April 11.

Stigmata

"Stigmata" is the term for the wounds Christ bore on the cross. Typically they appear as wounds in the hands, feet, and side. There have been reports of individuals who bore the wounds of the scourging on their back and shoulders, or the wounds of the crown of thorns on their head. St. Francis of Assisi is the first person to have received the stigmata. The most famous stigmatic of modern times was St. Pio of Pietrelcina.

PHOTOGRAPHERS

ST. VERONICA (FIRST CENTURY). The story of Veronica is not found in the Gospels but in a Christian work written in the fourth century. Nonetheless, for centuries her story has been popular with Catholics. According to tradition, as Christ carried his cross through the streets of Jerusalem, Veronica stepped out of the crowd and wiped the Lord's face with her veil. When she returned home she found imprinted on the veil a perfect portrait of the suffering Jesus. (The name "Veronica" comes from the phrase "*vera ikon,*" meaning "true image.") The story of the miraculous portrait of Christ that appeared on Veronica's veil has led photographers to take her as their patron.

Feast day: July 12.

PLUMBERS

ST. VINCENT FERRER (C. 1350-1419). A tireless, dynamic Dominican preacher, Vincent Ferrer traveled throughout Western Europe for thirty-nine years trying to heal a schism that misled some Catholics to follow antipopes rather than the true successor of St. Peter. For his dedication in restoring the Church, members of all building trades, including plumbers, venerate St. Vincent as their patron.

Feast day: April 5.

POETS

DAVID THE KING (c. 1085-c. 1015 B.C.). David is the shepherd boy who slew the giant Goliath and became king of Israel. We know that he was a talented harpist and singer, and that he wrote some of the psalms (although it is unlikely that he wrote all one hundred fifty, as some sources claim). The psalms are poetic hymns, a cornerstone of the Church's prayer life, prayed at Mass and in the Divine Office.

Feast day: December 29.

POLICE OFFICERS

ST. MICHAEL THE ARCHANGEL. The Old Testament Book of Daniel tells us that by the second century before Christ the Jews regarded St. Michael the Archangel as the guardian of the people of Israel. The first Christians, many of whom were converts from Judaism, took St. Michael with them, venerating him as their heavenly protector against "the wickedness and snares of the devil," to quote the traditional prayer to St. Michael. Like the great archangel, police officers protect us from harm in this world.

Feast day: September 29.

POTTERY MAKERS

ST. SPIRIDON (270-344). Spiridon used a piece of broken pottery to explain the doctrine of the Trinity to a Greek philosopher. Three distinct elements — water, clay, and fire — create pottery; and three Divine Persons — Father, Son, and Holy Spirit — comprise the Trinity.

Spiridon was a shepherd who lived with his wife and daughter on the island of Cyprus. During Emperor Diocletian's persecution of the Church he was arrested, hamstrung, blinded in one eye, and then sent as a slave to the mines in Spain. After Emperor Constantine legalized Christianity in 313, Spiridon was released. He returned to Cyprus, where he, his wife, and daughter agreed to enter the religious life. In time Spiridon became bishop of Cyprus.

Feast day: December 12.

Printers

St. Augustine of Hippo (354-430). One of the most prolific writers the Church has ever known, St. Augustine wrote many sermons, letters, and books, including his autobiography, *Confessions*; a guide to interpreting the Bible; and even a book on music. Printers have taken this busy author as their patron.

Feast day: August 28.

Prison Guards and Jailers

Sts. Martinian and Processus (died c. 67). Tradition tells us that Martinian and Processus were the guards of Sts. Peter and Paul when they were held in the Mamertine prison before their martyrdom. The apostles converted their guards but had no water to baptize them until a spring burst from the floor of their cell. Sts. Martinian and Processus were martyred, and their relics are enshrined beneath an altar dedicated to them in St. Peter's Basilica.

Feast day: July 2.

St. Hippolytus of Rome (died c. 258). From St. Ambrose we learn that Hippolytus was a prison guard converted by St. Lawrence. Hippolytus then converted his elderly nurse, Concordia, and nineteen slaves in his household. They were all arrested together. Concordia was flogged to death, and Hippolytus was torn apart by wild horses, but how the slaves were martyred is unknown.

Feast day: August 13.

Psychiatrists and Psychologists

St. Christina the Astonishing (1150-1224). Christina appears to have suffered from schizophrenia. She threw herself into fire. Saying that she could not endure the smell of people, she climbed to the top of tall trees or took refuge in church steeples. One day she entered her parish church and drenched herself with holy water from the baptismal font; from that day forward her erratic behavior ceased.

Christina had great compassion for persistent sinners. Hoping to bring them to repentance, she called on the most notorious men and women in the region and asked them to contribute money, food, or clothing for the poor and the sick. It was Christina's hope that these acts of charity would be their first step back to living a virtuous life.

Feast day: July 24.

St. Dymphna (seventh century). Dymphna was an Irish princess who bore a striking resemblance to her mother. Her mother's death unhinged Dymphna's father: he thought his daughter was his wife. To escape these unwanted attentions, Dymphna and her chaplain, Gerebernus, sailed to Europe, coming ashore near the present-day town of Gheel, Belgium. But Dymphna's father pursued them. He beheaded Dymphna while his troops killed Gerebernus. The local people buried them together. At the shrine many people who suffered from mental or emotional disorders were cured, which has led to St. Dymphna's veneration as the patron of psychiatrists and psychologists.

Feast day: May 15.

Public Relations Professionals

St. Paul (died c. 67). Like someone in public relations, Paul tried to reach as many people as possible with the message of the Gospel. And he altered his approach depending on his audience. As he tells us in his first letter to the Corinthians, "I have become all things to all men" (1 Cor 9:22)

Feast days: June 29, January 25 (conversion), February 10 (shipwreck).

Ranchers

St. George (died c. 303). Ranchers have taken St. George as their patron because he is almost always portrayed on horseback.

Feast day: April 23.

REALTORS

ST. JOSEPH (FIRST CENTURY). In the late twentieth century a new devotion arose among Catholics in the United States: burying a small statue of St. Joseph on property one wanted to buy or sell. The custom is derived from St. André Bessette, the great promoter of devotion to St. Joseph. It was Brother André's dream to build a shrine church in honor of St. Joseph on Mount Royal in Montreal. He found an ideal location, but the owners of the property would not sell. So Brother André buried St. Joseph medals on the property and prayed to St. Joseph for help. The owners relented, and the great Oratory of St. Joseph was built on the spot.

Feast days: March 19 (St. Joseph, Husband of the Blessed Virgin Mary) and May 1 (St. Joseph the Worker).

Superstition

Wearing holy medals and scapulars. Hanging a crucifix over a bed. Burying statues of St. Joseph on land we want to buy or sell. Some people look at these Catholic practices and cry, "Superstition!" The Church replies that this is not superstition; these sacramentals and acts of devotion are, when used properly, spiritual tools intended to help Catholics grow in holiness.

Here is the difference. Superstitious people perform certain acts, such as wearing a talisman or lucky charm, because they believe it gives them a kind of power or control over the gods or spirits. Catholics wear a holy medal or scapular as a sign of their love for Our Lord, Our Lady, or the saint or angel depicted on it. We ask Jesus, Mary, or the saint to bless and protect us, but wearing the medal does not force any power in heaven to do what we want. Superstitious people strive for supernatural power; Catholics know they have no power over Almighty God, so they pray and petition for help.

Nonetheless, Catholics must be careful not to slip into superstition. For example, it is reported that Mary

promised whoever wore the brown scapular or the Mi-
raculous Medal would not suffer the fires of hell. If anyone
thinks this scapular and this medal are a type of "get-out-
of-hell-free" card, he or she has fallen into superstition. A
persistent sinner who has no penitence cannot slip on a
scapular and expect to get into heaven. We wear the scap-
ular or the medal as we strive to grow in holiness, repent-
ing our sins, and calling upon the Blessed Mother to help
us with her prayers so that at the end of life on earth we
will be welcomed into eternal life.

SAILORS

ST. ERASMUS OR ELMO (DIED C. 303). The bishop of Formiae, a
city south of Rome, St. Erasmus was martyred in a particularly
gruesome manner: the executioner slit open the bishop's stomach, nailed one end of his intestines to a spindle, and turned it.
Sailors took St. Erasmus as their patron because the spindle of
his martyrdom reminded them of the windlass used on ships to
move heavy cargo. Sailors call the electrical phenomenon that
causes balls of light to attach themselves to a ship's mast or rigging before a thunderstorm "St. Elmo's Fire."

Feast day: June 2.

ST. NICHOLAS OF MYRA (DIED C. 350). Among the many miracle
stories told of St. Nicholas, several involve ships. Once, during
a storm, a ship's mast snapped; suddenly Nicholas appeared and
restored it. On another occasion, while sailing on pilgrimage to
the Holy Land, Nicholas stilled a storm that threatened to sink
the ship. And on yet another occasion, when a sailor fell from
the rigging and was killed, Nicholas brought him back to life.

Feast day: December 6.

SCIENTISTS

ST. ALBERT THE GREAT (C. 1200-1280). Albert the Great is best
known as the teacher of St. Thomas Aquinas. But in addition

to his expertise as a theologian and philosopher, Albert had a profound interest in science. "The aim of natural science is not simply to accept the statements of others," he wrote, "but to investigate the causes that are at work in nature." Insisting that "experiment is the only safe guide" in scientific inquiry, he looked upon the whole world as his laboratory. St. Albert the Great wrote forty books on various branches of the sciences.

Feast day: November 15.

SCULPTORS

FOUR CROWNED MARTYRS (DIED C. 305). Claudius, Nicostratus, Symphorian, and Castorius were sculptors who worked in a stone quarry in Pannonia (now part of modern-day Hungary and Serbia). Emperor Diocletian attempted to commission from them a statue of Asclepius, the god of medicine, but the four Christian sculptors declined to create an idol. For their impudence, the emperor had each of them flogged, sealed in a lead chest, and thrown into the Danube River to drown.

Feast day: November 8.

SHEEP FARMERS

ST. CUTHBERT (DIED 687). As a teenager, Cuthbert watched over his father's sheep. One night, while guarding the flock, he saw the soul of St. Aidan ascending to heaven. This vision inspired him to become a monk. At age seventeen he entered Melrose Abbey in southern Scotland. Cuthbert had a delightful personality that charmed all of the monks. They also discovered that he had a genius for administration, and in 664, when Cuthbert was only thirty, they elected him abbot.

In 685 Cuthbert was consecrated abbot and bishop of Lindisfarne, an ancient island monastery off England's northeast coast. At that time the Church in England had decided to give up its native liturgical customs and calendar and adopt the Roman style of saying Mass and praying the Divine Office. The monks of Lindisfarne resisted. Fearful that this could lead to schism, the bishops of England sent Cuthbert to gently persuade them to adopt the Roman liturgy. During the last two years of his life, Cuthbert accomplished this, thereby keeping peace and unity in the Church.

Feast day: September 4.

SHOEMAKERS

STS. CRISPIN AND CRISPINIAN (DIED C. 285). Crispin and Crispinian were brothers who had a shoemakers shop in what is now Soissons, France. As they waited on customers they explained their Christian faith — and they made many converts, which brought them to the attention of the authorities. They were horribly tortured to force them to renounce Christ; when that failed, the magistrate had the brothers beheaded.

Feast day: October 25.

SOCIAL WORKERS

ST. LOUISE DE MAURILLAC (1591-1660). After her husband died, Louise de Maurillac moved to Paris where she met St. Vincent de Paul. Vincent had established hospitals, orphanages, shelters for the elderly, and even a ministry to galley slaves, but he did not have enough volunteers to serve in all of these charitable institutions. Louise supplied the solution: she recruited hardy young women from the working class who were accustomed to long, busy days. Rather than be confined to a convent — which was the typical life of nuns in the seventeenth century — Louise's sisters would leave their convent every day to go wherever they were needed. These sisters became the Daughters of Charity. In 1960 Blessed Pope John XXIII named St. Louise de Maurillac the patron of social workers.

Feast day: March 15.

ST. JOHN REGIS (1597-1640). John Regis was a French Jesuit who spent his life traveling from parish to parish to revive and strengthen religious life among Catholics and bring Huguenots back to the Catholic Church. He opened homes for penitent prostitutes and helped them begin new lives. Many young women found it difficult to make a living in the country and considered moving to the cities. John believed the cities were full of temptations and evil influences, so he established cottage industries, such as lace-making and embroidery, where young women could support themselves without leaving their families and friends.

Feast day: December 31.

SOFTWARE DEVELOPERS, INFORMATION TECHNOLOGY PROFESSIONALS, AND OTHER WORKERS IN THE COMPUTER INDUSTRY

ST. ISIDORE OF SEVILLE (560-636). In the 1990s, Catholics working in the new online industry selected St. Isidore as their patron saint. During his career as bishop of Seville, Isidore had compiled a twenty-volume encyclopedia of all existing knowledge. The Catholic webmasters interpreted Isidore's magnum opus as the world's first database.

Feast day: April 4.

STATESMEN AND POLITICIANS

ST. THOMAS MORE (1478-1535). Thomas More's friends knew him to be intelligent, good-humored, a man of integrity, a gifted lawyer, and a devout son of the Catholic Church. About the year 1516 Henry VIII and Cardinal Thomas Wolsey began consulting More on matters of state. In 1529, when Cardinal Wolsey died, the king named More lord chancellor of England — the second-most-powerful post in England. More was also the first layman to serve as chancellor.

More's appointment came during a difficult time: Henry had become infatuated with a young woman at his court, Anne Boleyn, but before he could marry Anne he needed the pope to annul his marriage to his queen, Catherine of Aragon. When the pope declared that Henry and Catherine's marriage was valid, the king broke with Rome and declared himself supreme head of the Church in England. After the archbishop of Canterbury declared Henry and Catherine's marriage null and void, the king married Anne Boleyn.

More resigned his office without making any public statement about the king's marriage or his schismatic church. When he refused to take the Oath of Supremacy, renouncing his allegiance to the pope and recognizing Henry as head of the English Church, More was imprisoned in the Tower of London and later beheaded. On the scaffold More said to the crowd of spectators, "I die the king's good servant, but God's first."

In 2000, in recognition of St. Thomas More's fidelity to the faith and personal integrity, Pope John Paul II formally named him patron of statesmen and politicians.

Feast day: June 22.

STONE MASONS

FOUR CROWNED MARTYRS (DIED C. 305). Stone masons have taken as their patrons Sts. Claudius, Nicostratus, Symphorian, and Castorius, who worked in a stone quarry.

Feast day: November 8.

ST. STEPHEN (DIED C. 35). St. Stephen, the first martyr, was stoned to death, which has led stone masons to take him as one of their patrons. The complete story can be found in Acts 6-7. St. Stephen's dying words were, "Lord Jesus, receive my spirit. Lord, do not hold this sin against them."

Feast day: December 26.

ST. PETER (DIED C. 67). The name Peter comes from the Greek word for "rock." Christ gave Simon this name, then declared, "You are Peter, and on this rock I will build my Church" (Mt 16:18).

Feast days: June 29 and February 22 (Chair of St. Peter).

TAILORS

ADAM AND EVE. In the Garden of Eden, Adam and Eve were naked. After God expelled them from Eden, they became the first humans to make clothing.
Feast day: December 24.

ST. HOMOBONUS (DIED 1197). Homobonus operated his family's tailor business in Cremona, Italy, until he changed careers and became a cloth merchant. Instead of competing with other tailors, he then had tailors for his clients.
Feast day: November 13.

ST. MARTIN OF TOURS (C. 316-397). In the most famous act of his life, Martin acted like a tailor: he cut his cloak in half to clothe a poor man.
Feast day: November 11.

TOUR GUIDES

ST. BONA OF PISA (1156-1207). During the Middle Ages making pilgrimages to shrines was a popular activity. Pilgrims often traveled in groups for safety and for the pleasures of social interaction, and were led by an experienced pilgrim who knew the route. Bona of Pisa made her first pilgrimage — to the Holy Land — when she was fourteen. After returning home she traveled to the shrine of St. James in Compostela, Spain. After visiting Compostela several times, Bona became a pilgrimage leader; she led groups of pilgrims to the shrine of St. James at least eight times.
Feast day: May 29.

TRANSLATORS

ST. JEROME (C. 341-420). To produce the most accurate Latin translation of the Bible, Jerome turned to the oldest surviving texts. This required him to learn Greek and Hebrew, both of which he mastered (although St. Paula, who was fluent in Greek, assisted him).
Feast day: September 30.

VETERINARIANS

ST. BLAISE (DIED C. 316). Two legends reveal Blaise's connection with animals. During a period of anti-Christian persecution he took refuge in a mountain cave. The region was filled with wild animals, but around Blaise they were perfectly tame. On the day Blaise was arrested, as he was being led to prison, he and his guards saw a wolf running with a small pig in its mouth; a poor woman was pursuing the animal. Taking pity on the woman, Blaise commanded the wolf to release the pig. To everyone's astonishment, the wolf dropped the pig and scurried into the forest.

Feast day: February 3.

WINEMAKERS

ST. ARMAND (DIED C. 584). Armand was a missionary monk who introduced Christianity in the region of Bourges, France (famous for its fine Sancerre wine), and Navarre in northern Spain (home to fine Garnacha wine). Devotion to St. Armand was strong in these regions, and local winemakers took him as their patron.

Feast day: February 6.

ST. VINCENT OF SARAGOSSA (DIED 304). Word play is the source of St. Vincent's patronage of winemakers: in French, "wine" is *vin*, and in Spanish and Italian "wine" is *vino*.

Feast day: January 22.

ST. URBAN OF LANGRES (DIED C. 390). Urban was bishop of Langres, France. Once, when his life was in danger, he took refuge out in the countryside, where the owner and workers of a vineyard sheltered him. During his stay, Urban converted all the winemakers in the region.

Feast day: April 2 (January 23 in Langres).

ST. MORAND (DIED C. 1115). Morand took his monastic vows at the great Abbey of Cluny in France. Later he founded a monastery at Altkirch, France, which he dedicated to St. Christopher. It is said that during Lent he survived on a single bunch of grapes.

Feast day: June 3.

WRITERS

ST. FRANCIS DE SALES (1567-1622). First as a wandering preacher and then as bishop of Geneva, Francis de Sales wrote small pamphlets that explained basic Catholic doctrine. Catholics who had not been especially well educated in their faith and Calvinists who had left the Church were his target audience. But Francis' runaway best-seller was *Introduction to the Devout Life*. He wrote it as a manual for laypeople who wanted to grow in holiness but had obligations such as earning a living, raising a family, and running a household. The book made Francis' publisher a fortune (Francis refused to accept royalties). Ever since it was first published in 1609 the book has been translated into many languages and has never gone out of print.

Feast day: January 24.

CHAPTER 5

Patron Saints
for Education

CATHOLIC SCHOOLS, COLLEGES, AND UNIVERSITIES

ST. THOMAS AQUINAS (1224/25-1274). As a young Dominican friar Thomas Aquinas studied for a doctorate at the University of Paris, at the time the finest school of theology in Western Europe. He went on to teach theology in Rome, Naples, Paris, and other cities. St. Thomas Aquinas is especially invoked that Catholic schools will provide their students with an authentic Catholic education.

Feast day: January 28.

ST. URSULA (DATE UNCERTAIN). According to tradition, Ursula was a British princess who, with her eleven thousand virgin companions, was massacred by the Huns at present-day Cologne in Germany. Since 1535, the year St. Angela de Merici founded her Institute of St. Ursula for the education of girls, St. Ursula has been venerated as a patron of Catholic schools.

Feast day: October 21.

CATHOLIC SCHOOLS IN AMERICA

ST. ELIZABETH ANN SETON (1774-1821). Born in New York City and raised in the Episcopal Church, Elizabeth Ann Seton converted to the Catholic faith in 1805. At the time she was a widow with five children. With the approval of Bishop John Carroll of Baltimore (America's first Catholic bishop), she founded a new religious order, the Sisters of Charity of St. Joseph. They established themselves in Emmitsburg, Maryland, and on February 22, 1810, opened the first parochial school in the United States. Mother Seton chose the date carefully: it was the feast of the Chair of St. Peter and George Washington's birthday.

Feast day: January 4.

LEARNING

ST. AMBROSE (C. 339-397). Like all Roman boys of good families, Ambrose received an education in philosophy, rhetoric, mathematics, and the Greek and Roman classics. But unlike his fellow students, Ambrose was exceptional: an original thinker, an eloquent speaker, and a very persuasive debater. His friend St. Augustine (whom Ambrose succeeded in converting to the Catholic faith) marveled that Ambrose was the only literate man he knew who could read without moving his lips. Ambrose used his intellectual gifts not only to draw souls to Christ, but also to defend the Catholic faith against the Arian heretics.

Feast day: December 7.

The Arian Heresy

About the year 319 an Egyptian priest named Arius began to teach that Jesus Christ was not the eternal and divine Son of God but a creature, a kind of superman made by God and sent into the world. In 325, three hundred bishops gathered at Nicaea in what is now Turkey. There they studied Arius' teaching and concluded it was heretical. To set forth the doctrine of the Church they composed a definition of the Holy Trinity that became known as the Nicene Creed. (It is the creed from the First Council of Constantinople in 381, called the Nicene-Constantinople Creed, that is used today as the profession of faith in the liturgy.)

ST. ACCA (C. 660-742). This English Benedictine abbot had three passions: the Bible, theology, and sacred music. He introduced

Gregorian chant to his Abbey of St. Andrew in Hexham, England, and encouraged other English monasteries and churches to adopt this Roman style of liturgical music, too. At a time when books were rare, Acca had a large personal library of biblical commentaries and theological works, all of which he studied intently. Along with his friend St. Bede the Venerable, he made northern England one of the intellectual and cultural centers of the Christian world.

Feast day: October 20.

St. Margaret of Scotland (c. 1045-1093). As queen, Margaret brought her convent education and her personal library to Scotland. Books, like schools, were rare in Scotland in the eleventh century, so Margaret invited Benedictine monks to found abbeys in her kingdom and open schools and libraries for the improvement of the Scottish people.

Feast day: November 16.

Blessed Nicholas Albergati (1375-1443). When Nicholas Albergati joined the Carthusians he expected to live an anonymous life of prayer and study in his monastery, but in 1418 the pope commanded him to become archbishop of Bologna, Italy. Nicholas had a subtle mind, and was frequently called upon to settle disputes between the pope and the Holy Roman Emperor. At the Council of Ferrara-Florence, Albergati drew upon his command of the Greek Fathers to persuade the Greek Orthodox patriarch and bishops to reunite with the Catholic Church. The patriarch and the bishops consented, but tragically, the Greek Orthodox faithful rejected the union.

Feast day: May 9.

LIBRARIES

St. Jerome (c. 341-420). In 382 Pope St. Damasus commissioned his secretary, Jerome, to prepare a new, accurate Latin translation of the Bible based on the best available texts. For the rest of his life Jerome labored on this massive project, hunting down ancient Aramaic and Greek texts, and learning Hebrew so he could read the Torah and other sacred Jewish books.

Feast day: September 30.

St. Catherine of Alexandria (died c. 305). Tradition tells us that Catherine was a well-educated young woman who spent many hours reading and studying in the Library of Alexandria, Egypt, one of the greatest libraries of the ancient world. One day while reading she dozed off and dreamed of a beautiful woman holding an even more beautiful little boy on her lap. Pointing to Catherine, the mother asked her son, "Would you like to marry her?" "Oh no," said the boy. "She is so ugly."

Catherine awoke in tears, which attracted the attention of an elderly man who was browsing through the shelves. He asked her why she was crying, and Catherine told him of her dream. "The woman you saw," the gentleman said, "was the Blessed Virgin Mary, and the little boy was her son, Jesus Christ. He said you are ugly because you are still a pagan and your soul has not been cleansed in baptism." Catherine asked what she could do to be beautiful for Christ. "I am a Christian priest," the old man said, "I will instruct you."

After Catherine's baptism she dreamed again of Mary and the Christ Child. "Now would you like to marry her?" Mary asked Jesus. "Oh yes," he replied, "because now she is beautiful." Then Jesus put a ring on Catherine's finger, and when she awoke she was wearing it.

Since this lovely legend is set in the Library of Alexandria, St. Catherine is venerated as a patron of libraries.

Feast day: November 25.

PHILOSOPHERS

St. Justin Martyr (c. 100-165). As a young man Justin was an avid student of Greek and Roman philosophy, but ultimately he found all of them unsatisfactory. By chance he met an el-derly Christian who explained the Gospels to him. "I discovered that his was the only sure and useful philosophy," Justin would write later. He asked to be baptized, then opened the world's first Christian philosophical school in Ephesus. In 150 he relocated his school to Rome, where he published several books that drew upon classic Greco-Roman philosophy to prove that the Christian faith was true. When Emperor Marcus Aurelius began persecut-ing Christians, Justin and six of his pupils were arrested. A prefect ordered them to sacrifice to the Roman gods. "No one in his right mind gives up piety for impiety," Justin replied. The prefect con-demned Justin and his student to be flogged and then beheaded.

Feast day: June 1.

St. Catherine of Alexandria (died c. 305). At Catherine's trial the magistrate brought in fifty pagan philosophers to dis-pute with her and prove that the gods of Rome were true and that Christianity was a false religion. Catherine not only won the debate, but she also converted all fifty to Christianity. Enraged, the magistrate had the philosophers burned alive.

Feast day: November 25.

St. Albert the Great (c. 1200-1280). Albert is best remem-bered as the man who taught theology and philosophy to St. Thomas Aquinas. But Albert was an accomplished man in his own right, and in a variety of fields, including philosophy. In the thirteenth century the works of the ancient Greek philoso-pher Aristotle were introduced to Western Europe by way of Spain, where Christian scholars, working in collaboration with their Jewish and Muslim colleagues, translated Arabic editions of Aristotle into Latin. Albert believed that Aristotle's appeal to human reason to discover what was true could be used to defend and prove the truths of Christian doctrine.

Feast day: November 15.

Public Schools

St. Martin de Porres (1579-1639). Martin de Porres was born in Lima, Peru, the illegitimate son of a freed African slave and a Spanish gentleman. Because Martin was born dark-skinned like his mother, his father did not acknowledge him. The family lived in poverty until Martin was eight, when at last his father relented and took responsibility for his mistress and their children (by that time, Martin had a sister). His wretched childhood taught Martin compassion. When he joined the Dominicans, Martin's kindness extended to the hungry, the sick, the abandoned, and the dying. A generous donor gave him a large house in Lima, which Martin used as an orphanage. In the orphanage he opened a school so the children would be able to support themselves once they were old enough to go out into the world.

Feast day: November 3.

Science and Mathematics Students

St. Albert the Great (c. 1200-1280). In Albert's day, books on natural history were more works of fiction than scientific texts, with fanciful accounts that said barnacle geese hatched out of trees and lion cubs were stillborn, coming to life three days later when their father roared over them. Albert was in the forefront of the scientific method, using direct observation of the world and its creatures rather than musty old "authorities." He wrote approximately forty books on the sciences.

Feast day: November 15.

Students and Scholars

St. Brigid of Kildare (c. 450-c. 525). Brigid's father was a pagan Irish chieftain, and her mother was a Christian slave in the chieftain's household. Brigid grew up at a time when Catholicism was relatively new in Ireland. After taking the vows of a nun and founding a convent at Kildare, Brigid started a school — the first Catholic school in Ireland. Here the students were taught Christian doctrine, the Greek and Roman classics, and Irish music and poetry. In her convent scriptorium, Brigid's nuns copied Christian and ancient Greek and Roman texts, which were then disseminated to other schools and religious houses throughout Ireland.

Feast day: February 1.

ST. NICHOLAS OF MYRA (DIED C. 350). There are two versions of the story of Nicholas raising three boys from the dead. One describes them as small children, but another version says they were students on their way to Athens to study theology. The theology-students version is the origin of St. Nicholas being venerated as the patron of students and scholars.

Feast day: December 6.

ST. CASSIAN OF IMOLA (DIED C. 250). Cassian taught school at Imola, a town in northeastern Italy. He was denounced as a Christian and commanded to sacrifice to the Roman gods. Cassian refused, and the magistrate sentenced him to an especially gruesome death: he was stripped and tied to a stake, then his students were brought in, given knives and clubs, and ordered to execute their teacher. Some used their sharp-pointed iron styli to cut letters and numbers into Cassian's flesh.

Feast day: August 13.

ST. BENEDICT (C. 480-550). Virtually every monastery founded by Benedict, his disciples, and their successors contained a scriptorium where books were copied so that both Christian and classical learning would be preserved. The next step was the establishment of abbey schools, where boys were given what we would consider a grammar school education. For most of these children, the abbey school was as far as they would go, but a few went on to one of medieval Europe's great universities, such as Oxford, Paris, or Bologna.

Feast day: July 11.

The Benedictines

In 529 at Monte Cassin, Italy, St. Benedict founded the first monastery of monks who became known as Benedictines. About the same time his twin sister, St. Scholastica, founded the first convent of Benedictine nuns. In contrast to the hermits, monks, and nuns of the East, many of whom deprived themselves of adequate food, clothing, rest, and recreation, the Benedictines followed a balanced daily routine of prayer and work.

Early on they became the guardians of Western civilization, collecting, copying, and distributing ancient Roman and Greek works as well as Christian texts. They also opened schools for children in their monasteries and convents.

TEACHERS AND TUTORS

ST. JOHN BAPTIST DE LA SALLE (1651-1719). John Baptist de La Salle was serving as one of the clergy assigned to the cathedral of Rheims when he was approached by a layman named Adrian Nyel, who wanted to open a free school for the city's poor children. De La Salle, who had inherited a large fortune, offered to purchase a house for the teachers and pay their salaries. Soon it was apparent to de La Salle that most of the teachers were ineffectual. He began to implement new teaching methods, including a question-and-answer format, so children would think rather than just repeat back what a teacher had told them. He also called for individualized attention for students who were not grasping the material. And he founded a new teaching order, the Brothers of the Christian Schools, or Christian Brothers. St. John Baptist de La Salle's innovative teaching methods can be found in most public, private, and Catholic schools today.

Feast day: April 7.

ST. FRANCIS DE SALES (1567-1622). In 1602 the pope named Francis de Sales bishop of Geneva. It was an unenviable assignment

— the diocese had been rigidly Calvinist since 1533 when John Calvin and his followers expelled the bishop, all the clergy and nuns, and outlawed the practice of the Catholic faith. Bishop de Sales was forbidden to enter the city, let alone say Mass in the cathedral. To reach his people he published pamphlets that explained Catholic doctrine in simple terms. He traveled to every village and town of his diocese, teaching the faith and bringing many Calvinists back to the Church. Since he had no seminary, he instructed candidates for the priesthood personally.

Feast day: January 24.

St. Ursula (date uncertain). St. Angela de Merici's teaching sisters, the Ursuline nuns, took St. Ursula as their patron in 1535. St. Urusla is especially venerated as the teacher of schoolgirls.

Feast day: October 21.

St. Marguerite Bourgeoys (1620-1700). Marguerite Bourgeoys left a comfortable home in France to establish schools for French and Indian children in Canada. She founded a new order of teaching sisters, the Congregation of Notre Dame. The sisters opened several schools in Canadian towns and Indian villages, and operated a vocational school where girls learned how to run a household.

Feast day: January 12.

Test Takers

St. John Mary Vianney (1786-1859). As the son of a French peasant family John Mary Vianney received very little education. He wanted to be a priest, and in spite of his lack of schooling, Father Charles Balley admitted Vianney to the preparatory seminary he operated out of his rectory. Vianney found all of the classes difficult, especially Latin. He made a pilgrimage on foot to the tomb of St. John Regis to ask for the saint's help in his studies.

Vianney's grades improved sufficiently for Father Balley to send him to the minor seminary; there Vianney had trouble with philosophy and, as always, Latin. During the summer break Father Balley tutored Vianney so he would be prepared for an oral examination in the fall. When classes resumed Vianney appeared reasonably well-prepared for his test, but the moment he entered the examination room he froze. He could not remember a thing he had been taught. Once again Father Balley intervened, assuring the examiners that Vianney would be a good priest, and suggesting they test him in the familiar setting of his rectory, and in French rather than Latin. The examiners agreed, and this time Vianney passed. After Vianney's ordination to the priesthood, the archbishop of Lyon appointed him Father Balley's curate. No other pastor in the archdiocese would have him.

Feast day: August 4.

ST. JOSEPH OF CUPERTINO (1603-1663). Joseph of Cupertino was an illiterate Italian peasant when he joined the Capuchins (a branch of the Franciscan order). He wanted to be a priest, and although he learned to read and write, he never excelled in his studies. As the day of his examination approached, he prayed to God that he would be asked only those handful of questions to which he knew the answer. That is what happened in the examination room, and Joseph was ordained.

Feast day: September 18.

The Capuchins

In 1525 a group of Franciscan priests and brothers formed a new branch of their religious order that placed special emphasis on contemplation. Today Capuchins can be found serving as prison and hospital chaplains, staffing soup kitchens and homeless shelters, working as missionaries around the globe, serving parishes, and teaching in university classrooms.

St. Philomena (date uncertain). In the nineteenth century, when devotion to St. Philomena was at its highest, she was invoked for a host of causes, including impossible situations. Desperate students asked for her intercession when passing a test seemed impossible.

Feast day: August 11.

CHAPTER 6

Patron Saints
for the Military

ARMIES

St. Maurice (died c. 287). Maurice was the *primicerius*, or first officer, of a legion of more than six thousand men — all of them Christians from the city and region of Thebes in Egypt. About the year 287 Emperor Maximian sent the Theban Legion to Switzerland to put down a rebellion. Before the battle, Maximian called upon his troops to sacrifice to the Roman gods, an act Maurice and the Theban Legion refused to do. As punishment Maximian ordered two decimations, in which one out of every ten men was killed, but still Maurice and his men would not worship false gods. His patience exhausted, Maximian ordered the rest of the army to massacre the Theban Legion. St. Maurice, as the commander of this great army of martyrs, has become the patron of all armies.

Feast day: September 22.

ARTILLERY

St. Barbara (date uncertain). Barbara and her family were pagans, but after a chance encounter with a Christian priest she asked to be baptized. She kept her newfound faith secret until her father sent stonemasons to add a second window in her chamber. Barbara asked them to add two so she would have three windows, in honor of the Blessed Trinity. When her father learned of Barbara's conversion, he took his sword and cut off her head. The moment she died, fire fell from heaven, killing Barbara's father. When gunpowder and artillery were introduced to Europe in the fifteenth century, the first artillerymen, recalling the fire that had consumed Barbara's father, adopted her as their patron saint.

Feast day: December 4.

BATTLE

ST. MICHAEL THE ARCHANGEL. "St. Michael the Archangel, defend us in battle" is how the best-known prayer to the captain of the heavenly host begins. St. Michael is the patron saint of battles because in that great, decisive battle in heaven he cast Lucifer and his rebel angels into hell.

Feast day: September 29.

Prayer to St. Michael

"St. Michael the Archangel, defend us in battle; be our defense against the wickedness and snares of the devil. May God rebuke him, we humbly pray. And do you, O prince of the heavenly host, by the power of God thrust into hell Satan and all the evil spirits who prowl about the world for the ruin of souls. Amen."

Before the liturgical changes authorized by Pope Paul VI, this prayer was one of several recited by the priest, altar boys, and congregation after Mass. It is still recited when the traditional Latin Mass, also known as the Extraordinary Form of the Mass, is celebrated. The prayer is also a popular private devotion.

CAVALRY

ST. GEORGE (DIED C. 303). George was a Christian martyred at Lydda (now modern-day Lod in Israel). His heroism in the face of what is said to have been an agonizing death attracted the devotion of his fellow Christians. The Byzantine army took him as its patron saint, and soon it was said that he had been a soldier. The legend of St. George slaying a dragon to rescue a maiden added a new dimension to his story — the knight on horseback. During the First Crusade (1096-1099), soldiers from Western Europe heard a great deal about George and returned home with stories of him, including how at the Battle of Antioch in 1098, he had ridden down from heaven and scattered the Saracens. The dragon legend and the miraculous appearance at Antioch led cavalrymen to adopt St. George as their patron.

Feast day: April 23.

St. Martin of Tours (c. 316-397). Although for most of his life Martin served as a priest and bishop, as a young man he was conscripted into the Roman army and assigned to Amiens in France. One especially cold night, as he was riding through the city back to camp, he saw a beggar, dressed in rags, shivering violently beside the road. Martin drew his sword, cut his thick woolen army cloak in two, and gave half to the beggar. That night Christ appeared in Martin's tent: he was surrounded by angels, and wearing the half-cloak. "Look," Our Lord said to the angels, "Martin is not even baptized, yet he wrapped me in his own cloak." For sixteen centuries, in sculpture, painting, stained glass, and on holy cards, St. Martin has been depicted on horseback performing his best-known act of charity.

Feast day: November 11.

Conscientious Objectors

St. Marcellus the Centurion (died 298). In the early Church many Christian men served in the Roman legions, but there was a strong school of thought that Christians ought to be pacifists. Late in the third century a Christian named Marcellus, who had achieved the rank of centurion (similar to captain), was stationed near Tangier in North Africa. During the annual celebration of the emperor's birthday, he tried to keep his distance, but when he was commanded to participate in pagan ceremonies in the emperor's honor, Marcellus refused. Then he stood before the standard of his legion, cast aside his sword and staff of office, and declared that as a Christian he could no longer in conscience keep the oath he had sworn to serve the emperor as a soldier. His superiors gave him every chance to repudiate his actions, but Marcellus had made up his mind. He was condemned as a Christian and a disloyal soldier and beheaded. Interestingly, the actual transcript of St. Marcellus' trial has survived the centuries.

Feast day: October 30.

FORTIFICATIONS

ST. BARBARA (DATE UNKNOWN). According to legend, Barbara was so beautiful that her father was afraid she would run off with an unsuitable man. To keep her safe until he found the right husband for her, he built an impregnable tower and locked her inside. St. Barbara, whose home was a fortress, is the patron of all military fortifications and defensive works.

Feast day: December 4.

MILITARY CHAPLAINS

ST. JOHN OF CAPISTRANO (1386-1456). John of Capistrano was a vigorous sixty-seven-year-old Franciscan priest when he found himself commander of a peasant army. The Ottoman Turks had invaded Hungary with sixty thousand men; arrayed against them were fifty thousand Hungarians, about half of them Father John's poorly armed, inexperienced farmers and villagers. In July 1453 the Turks had the Hungarians besieged at Belgrade. On July 22 Father John was standing on the city walls when he saw the Turks massing for an attack. Climbing down, he grabbed a horse and rode out to warn some Christians skirmishers to retreat to the safety of the city. Suddenly, he was surrounded by two thousand Hungarian knights who had come out to protect him. Now Father John changed his tactics and called for a charge against the Turks. Inspired by the Franciscan's daring, the Hungarian general, Janos Hunyady, rallied his men and led them out of the city in an attack on the Turkish artillery. The double surprise attacks panicked the Turks — they ran from the battlefield. For his heroism, St. John of Capistrano is venerated as the patron of military chaplains.

Feast day: October 23.

Naval Officers

St. Francis of Paola (1416-1507). Francis of Paola founded a branch of the Franciscans known as the Minim Friars, meaning they considered themselves the least of the Franciscan friars. Once Francis asked a boatman to carry him and several of his friars across the strait that separates Messina in southern Italy from Sicily. The boatman refused, so Francis took off his cloak, spread it on the water, attached one end to his staff to make a sail, and then invited his friends to step aboard. This miraculous voyage inspired naval officers to take St. Francis of Paola as their patron saint.

Feast day: April 2.

The Minims

St. Francis of Paola founded this austere branch of the Franciscans in 1435. As penance they abstained from all meat, except in cases of illness; as a sign of their commitment to poverty they went barefoot and begged for their support. There are a few Minim houses still in existence: most are in Italy, and there is one each in Mexico, Brazil, and the Czech Republic.

Pontifical Swiss Guards

St. Sebastian (died c. 300). Sebastian was a Praetorian, an elite soldier who guarded the Roman emperor. He kept his Christian faith secret and used his rank to visit imprisoned Christians and encourage them to be faithful. When it was revealed that Sebastian was a Christian, Emperor Diocletian took it as a personal betrayal. He sentenced Sebastian to be shot to death with arrows by his fellow Praetorians, but Sebastian survived the ordeal and was nursed back to health by a Christian woman named Irene. Once he had recovered his strength he confronted Diocletian and reproached him for his cruelty to innocent Christians. Initially astonished to see his bodyguard alive, Diocletian regained his composure and ordered his guards to beat Sebastian to death on the spot. Since 1506 the Swiss Guards have protected the popes. In 1527, when German and Spanish troops sacked Rome, one hundred forty-seven Swiss Guards gave their lives to cover Pope Clement VII's retreat to the safety of Castel Sant'Angelo.

Feast day: January 20.

St. Maurice (died c. 287). Just as Maurice and his companions laid down their lives for Christ, the Swiss Guards are ready to sacrifice their lives in defense of Christ's Church and his vicar on earth, the pope.

Feast day: September 22.

St. Martin of Tours (c. 316-397). Martin, who served in the Roman legions, was a model soldier and a model Christian, an example the Swiss Guards try to emulate.

Feast day: November 11.

St. Nicholas of Flüe (1417-1487). Nicholas of Flüe fought in a series of wars, some between rival Swiss canons and others against French and Austrian invaders of Switzerland. Several times he saved civilians from rampaging troops; and in his old age, when Switzerland was on the brink of civil war, Nicholas negotiated a peaceful settlement. As a soldier and one of

Switzerland's most popular saints, it is natural that the Swiss Guards have taken St. Nicholas of Flüe as one of their patrons.

Feast day: March 21.

SAILORS

ST. ERASMUS OR ELMO (DIED C. 303). The bishop of Formiae, a city south of Rome, St. Erasmus was martyred in a particularly gruesome manner: the executioner slit open the bishop's stomach, nailed one end of his intestines to a spindle, and turned it. Sailors took St. Erasmus as their patron because the spindle of his martyrdom reminded them of the windlass used on ships to move heavy cargo. Sailors call the electrical phenomenon that causes balls of light to attach themselves to a ship's mast or rigging before a thunderstorm "St. Elmo's Fire."

Feast day: June 2.

BLESSED JOHN ROCHE (DIED 1588). John Roche was an Irish boatman working in London in the household of a gentlewoman, St. Margaret Ward. In 1588 Margaret and John helped a priest, Father Richard Watson, escape from Bridewell Prison. During the escape Father Watson fell, breaking an arm and a leg. To throw off the priest's pursuers, Roche exchanged clothes with him. Father Watson escaped to safety, but both John Roche and Margaret Ward were captured and hanged.

Feast day: August 30.

ST. NICHOLAS OF MYRA (DIED C. 350). There are two stories of St. Nicholas that led to sailors adopting him as their patron saint. The first tells of a sailor who, during a storm, lost his footing in the rigging and fell into the sea. St. Nicholas drew the sailor out of the water and placed him safely on the deck of his ship. The second story also involves a storm, one so violent that the ship's mast began to crack. Suddenly St. Nicholas appeared, grasped the mast, and made it whole.

Feast day: December 6.

St. Peter Gonzalez (1190-1246). A Spanish Dominican priest who was the confessor of St. Ferdinand, king of Castile, Peter Gonzalez also spent a good deal of time away from the court and down by the docks, where he befriended the sailors. Once he had won their trust, he urged them to keep away from taverns and brothels, to go to confession, and to return to the practice of their faith. St. Peter Gonzalez is especially popular among Spanish and Portuguese sailors.

Feast day. April 14.

Our Lady, Star of the Sea. The Blessed Virgin has been invoked under the title "Star of the Sea" (*Stella Maris* in Latin) at least since the ninth century. It is a metaphor in which she is the constant, guiding star for Christians overwhelmed by the sea of troubles that is day-to-day life. St. Bernard of Clairvaux (1090-1153) preached beautifully on this topic: "If the winds of temptation arise; if you are driven upon the rocks of tribulation look to the star, call on Mary; if you are tossed upon the waves of pride, of ambition, of envy, of rivalry, look to the star, call on Mary. Should anger, or avarice, or fleshly desire violently assail the frail vessel of your soul, look at the star, call upon Mary."

Feast day: September 27.

Soldiers

St. Ignatius Loyola (1491-1556). The son of a noble Basque family, Ignatius Loyola yearned to gain glory on the battlefield. When he was eighteen he entered the service of the Duke of Najera. Three years later, when the French attacked the city of Pamplona, Ignatius saw an opportunity to prove himself. The city had surrendered, but Ignatius, with a handful of troops, retreated to the fortress, where they made a last-ditch effort to drive back the French. During the fight a cannon ball struck Ignatius' legs, shattering the bones in one and wounding the other. During his long recuperation the only books available to him were a life of Christ, with commentary by the Fathers of the Church, and a collection of saints' lives. After reading these books Ignatius resolved to change the course of his life, to strive for the greater glory of God, and to try to always be worthy of the love of the Blessed Virgin Mary.

In 1537 Ignatius and six companions (among them were St. Francis Xavier and Blessed Peter Faber) formed a new religious order: the Society of Jesus, better known as the Jesuits. There was a quasi-military character to the Jesuits. Ignatius was their Father General and the Jesuit priests and brothers were the pope's "foot soldiers," who would use the sacraments, prayer, deep learning, and sound preaching as weapons against the ignorance and heresies of their time to bring souls to God. Because he was once a soldier and because as the founder of the Jesuits he dedicated his life to spiritual warfare, St. Ignatius Loyola is one of the patrons of soldiers.

Feast day: July 31.

The Society of Jesus, or Jesuits

In 1535, during the height of the Reformation, St. Ignatius Loyola founded a new religious community of priests and brothers that became known as the Jesuits. These men dedicated their lives to explaining and defending Catholic doctrine and devotions so that Catholics would have a better grasp of their faith and Protestants would be convinced and return to the Church.

From the beginning the Jesuits have been involved in every facet of Catholic life: parishes; the missions; schools and universities; administrative work at the Vatican; and scientific, historical, and biblical research. Today the Society of Jesus is the largest religious order in the Catholic Church.

ST. JOAN OF ARC (1412–1431). Joan was an illiterate French peasant who at age seventeen heard the voices of St. Michael the Archangel, St. Catherine of Alexandria, and St. Margaret of Antioch reveal that she was commanded by God to lead the French to victory over the English invaders of her homeland. Her sincerity was so absolute that she persuaded a tribunal of theologians that her visions were authentic and convinced the Dauphin, Charles, to give her an army (although he also sent along veteran officers to advise her).

In keeping with the holiness of their mission, Joan banished all prostitutes from the camp and insisted that her troops give up drunkenness, gambling, brawling, and foul language; go to confession; and attend Mass regularly. Joan and her army won victory after victory, culminating in 1429 when she saw Charles crowned king of France in the cathedral of Rheims.

In 1430 Joan was captured, but Charles VII did nothing to try to rescue or ransom her. The English turned her over to an ecclesiastical court on charges of witchcraft and heresy. Her trial was a farce, and the verdict a foregone conclusion: she was found guilty and burned at the stake.

St. Joan of Arc, who led a victorious army, is the patron of soldiers, particularly women in the military.

Feast day: May 30.

What Was a Dauphin?

"Dauphin" was the title for a French prince who would become king of France (just as the Prince of Wales would become king of England). The word "dauphin" is French for "dolphin"; the dolphin was the prince's emblem and appeared on his coat of arms. The title was first given in 1350 to the future King Charles V. The last dauphin was Louis Charles (1785-1795?), the son of Louis XVI and Marie Antoinette, both of whom were guillotined during the French Revolution. Revolutionaries took the dauphin away from his family; the little boy died of abuse and neglect.

St. Foy or Faith (DIED 286). For refusing to sacrifice to the Roman gods this twelve-year-old child was tortured with fire and then beheaded. Her patronage of soldiers is inspired by St. Paul's epistle to the Ephesians: "Stand therefore, having girded your loins with truth, and having put on the breastplate of righteousness, and having shod your feet with the equipment of the gospel of peace; above all taking the shield of faith, with which you can quench all the flaming darts of the evil one" (Eph 6:14-16).

Feast day: October 6.

St. George (DIED c. 303). Always shown in knight's armor and almost always depicted slaying the dragon, St. George has been the patron saint of soldiers for at least fifteen hundred years.

Feast day: April 23.

St. Michael the Archangel. As captain of the heavenly host, St. Michael led the faithful angels to victory over Lucifer and his rebel angels.

Feast day: September 29.

St. Theodore Stratelates (DIED 310). Theodore was a Roman general ("*stratelates*" is Greek for "general") serving in Thrace (now modern-day Bulgaria). In spite of his rank, during a period of persecution he was denounced as a secret Christian, tortured, and crucified. Soldiers in the East took him as one of their patron saints, and he became known to soldiers from the West during the Crusades.

Feast day: February 7.

VICTORY

Our Lady of Victory. In 1571, several Christian princes united to form the Holy League to resist the Ottoman Turks' attempt to seize control of the Mediterranean. The Holy League had 212 ships; the Ottomans had a fleet of 286 ships. In the weeks leading up to the battle, Pope St. Pius V called upon Catholics to invoke the intercession of the Blessed Virgin Mary, particularly by praying the Rosary. On October 7 the two navies met at the Battle of Lepanto, off the Greek coast. After fighting all day, the Ottomans retreated. The Holy League had lost 50 ships, but the Turks lost 210. In addition the Holy League liberated about thirteen thousand Christian galley slaves from the Ottoman fleet. In 1572 Pius V established a new feast, Our Lady of Victory, to be celebrated on the anniversary of the Battle of Lepanto. Today the feast day is known as Our Lady of the Rosary.

Feast day: October 7.

The Month of October

In memory of the role the Blessed Virgin Mary played in the victory at Lepanto, the month of October has been dedicated as the "Month of the Rosary." Many popes have encouraged Catholics to pray the Rosary daily, but especially so during October.

CHAPTER 7

Patron Saints
for Recreation

ACROBATS AND JUGGLERS

ST. JOHN BOSCO (1815-1888). John Bosco was about ten years old when a traveling circus came to his neighborhood, a rural area outside Turin in northern Italy. John was especially attracted to the jugglers and acrobats, who were kind to the boy and taught him a few tricks. Clever and well-coordinated, John learned fast, so his new friends taught him how to walk a tightrope. John's first performance was for his family, and then he invited some of the rough boys in the neighborhood over for a show. John's mini-circus act was the first step in making friends with these boys, and once he had their trust John could talk to them about not using foul language, getting drunk, or pilfering from the farmers and village shopkeepers. It was the beginning of St. John Bosco's lifelong vocation to reclaim at-risk children.

Feast day: January 31.

ARCHERS

ST. SEBASTIAN (DIED C. 300). For Emperor Diocletian, the revelation that one of his bodyguards was a Christian seemed like a betrayal. He ordered Sebastian to be tied to a tree and shot to death with arrows.

Feast day: January 20.

ST. CHRISTOPHER (DIED C. 250). While many Catholics know the story of St. Christopher carrying the Christ Child across a dangerous river, few are aware that Christopher died a martyr. He was arrested by the prefect of Lycia (now in modern-day Turkey), shot with arrows, and then beheaded.

Feast day: July 25.

ST. CHRISTINA OF BOLSENA (DIED C. 250). Christina was a member of Rome's distinguished Anicii family, which for generations had served the empire as senators and consuls. Christina was about fourteen or fifteen when she converted to Christianity. Her outraged father swore to kill her. (Roman fathers had absolute authority over the life and death of their children.) For reasons that the story of St. Christina does not explain, her father took her to Lake Bolsena in Tuscany, where he tied a millstone to her neck and threw her into the water. By a miracle Christina floated. At this point the local magistrate took over the case and put Christina on trial. He condemned her to be shot to death with arrows.

Feast day: July 24.

ARTISTS

ST. LUKE THE EVANGELIST (FIRST CENTURY). We learn more about the Blessed Mother from St. Luke's Gospel than from any of the other Gospels, and there is a long tradition that Mary was one of the evangelist's sources. A legend that has spun off from this tradition of a friendship presents Luke as an artist who painted a portrait of the Virgin and Child on the kitchen table of the Holy Family's house in Nazareth. Several churches in Europe claim to have this painting, including the Shrine of the Black Madonna in Czestochowa, Poland.

Feast day: October 18.

BLESSED FRA ANGELICO (1387-1455). Shortly after Angelico joined the Dominican order, his superiors discovered that this novice was a skillful painter. He was put to work illustrating missals and choir books, and then moved on to small paintings, and ultimately to grand frescoes. He painted a small fresco in the cell, or private room, of every friar in the Dominican Monastery of St. Mark in Florence, as well as larger pieces for the chapter room and the cloister. His reputation spread to Rome, and in 1445 Pope Eugenius IV invited Fra Angelico to fresco the walls of a chapel in the Vatican. Eugenius' successor, Pope Nicholas V, also commissioned Angelico to paint a small Vatican chapel: Eugenius' chapel was destroyed during a renovation of the Vatican Palace, but Nicholas' chapel, with its scenes from the lives of the deacon saints, St. Stephen and St. Lawrence, survives intact. Pope John Paul II beatified Fra Angelico and in 1984 formally named him patron of artists.

Feast day: February 18.

St. CATHERINE OF BOLOGNA (1413-1463). Catherine entered the convent of the Poor Clares in Bologna, Italy. She had a gift for painting, so she worked in the convent library painting illustrations in the manuscripts the nuns copied. Her holiness was rewarded one Christmas when Our Lady and the Christ Child appeared to her.

Feast day: March 9.

ATHLETES

BLESSED PIER GIORGIO FRASSATI (1901-1925). Pier Giorgio Frassati was a natural athlete with a taste for what we call extreme sports. He hung around with a group of energetic young men who called themselves "The Shady Characters." Their two favorite activities were mountain climbing and reckless ski races down the slopes of the Italian Alps.

Even Pier Giorgio's spiritual life was active. He attended Mass and received Communion every morning. He "adopted" needy, desperate people who had no one else to help them. He found doctors who would treat the sick for free; found an apartment for a woman who had lost her home; and persuaded a factory foreman to give a job to an ex-convict.

Tragically, at age twenty-four Pier Giorgio contracted a virulent, deadly form of polio, Just days after he received the diagnosis, he died. To the astonishment of his family, more than one thousand men, women, and children, all of whom had been helped in some way by him, filled the family's parish church for the Requiem Mass.

Feast day: July 4.

St. Sebastian (died c. 300). During the early centuries of the Church preachers often spoke of the martyrs as God's athletes. Just as a boxer, a runner, or a gymnast practiced daily to develop strength and stamina, Christians were expected each day to grow a little closer to God and further from the temptations of the world. Both secular and Christian athletes trained for the ultimate prize: a crown of laurel or oak leaves for the secular athlete, the crown of eternal salvation for the Christian. The martyr St. Sebastian is always depicted as a strong young man, someone who possesses both physical and spiritual strength.

Feast day: January 20.

BICYCLISTS

Our Lady of Ghisallo. The Chapel of Our Lady of Ghisallo marks the spot where, almost nine hundred years ago, the Blessed Mother saved the count of Ghisallo from an attack by robbers. In 1905 the route of the first Tour de Lombardy bicycle race passed the chapel. It became a rest stop for competitors and a destination for other bicyclists. In the 1940s the pastor of the shrine was a cycling fan, Father Ermelindo Vigano. He welcomed bicyclists, and near the chapel he opened a small museum of cycling artifacts. Father Vigano petitioned Pope Pius XII to name Our Lady of Ghisallo the patron of bicyclists, which the Holy Father granted in 1949.

Feast day: October 13.

BOATERS

POPE ST. CLEMENT I (DIED 101). Clement was the fourth pope, and it is believed that he was ordained a priest by St. Peter. One of his letters has survived, the *Epistle to the Corinthians*, in which Pope Clement rebuked the Christians of Corinth who had split into several religious factions. "Why do we wrench and tear apart the members of Christ?" he asked. The letter is interesting in another way as well. It shows that in the first century the bishops of Rome recognized that their authority was not limited to their own diocese, but that they had the responsibility to restore peace and preserve orthodoxy in all Christian churches.

The emperor Trajan had Clement arrested and banished him to the mines in the Crimea. There Clement converted many of his fellow slaves to Christianity, for which he was condemned to death. He was taken by boat two miles out into the Black Sea, an iron anchor was tied to his neck, and he was thrown overboard.

Feast day: November 23.

Popes Who Are Saints or Blesseds

From St. Peter (died c. 67) to St. Pius X (1835-1914), seventy-nine popes have been canonized (that is, declared saints).

From Blessed Victor III (c. 1027-1087) to Blessed John Paul II (1920-2005), eleven popes are now "blessed" (that is, beatified and one step from canonization).

ST. BRENDAN THE NAVIGATOR (C. 486-575). The travel book *The Voyage of St. Brendan* was a best-seller in the Middle Ages. It recounts the adventures of an Irish abbot and fourteen of his monks who sail across the Atlantic Ocean. During their voyage they encounter whales, sea monsters, icebergs, and Judas himself, sitting on a small rock in the middle of the sea. It is an entertaining book, but it should not be taken seriously. Nonetheless, the story of Brendan's voyage has endured over the centuries and led boaters to take him as one of their patron saints.

Feast day: May 16.

COIN COLLECTORS

ST. STEPHEN THE YOUNGER (714-764). In the eighth century a series of Byzantine emperors outlawed the veneration of sacred images and ordered that all icons, mosaics, and paintings that depicted Christ, the Mother of God, and the saints must be destroyed. Stephen, the abbot of a monastery in far-off Bithynia in what is now central Turkey, defied the emperor's order. Stephen was arrested and imprisoned for two years before he was finally brought to trial. The emperor, Constantine V, sat in judgment.

"Is it a crime," Stephen asked, "to trample on the image of the emperor?" To make his point he dropped a coin on the floor and stomped on it.

"It is a great crime to mistreat the emperor's image," Constantine replied.

"If it is a crime to tread on a coin that bears the face of the emperor," Stephen said, "then why is it permissible to burn an image of Christ?"

Stephen's logic infuriated the emperor. Constantine commanded his guards to take Stephen out to the street and beat him to death.

Feast day: November 28.

DANCERS

ST. VITUS (DIED C. 303). According to legend, Vitus was thirteen when his tutor Modestus and his nursemaid Crescentia converted him from paganism to Christianity. To escape the wrath of Vitus' father the three traveled to Rome, where they were caught up in Diocletian's persecution of the Church. All three were beheaded.

In the Middle Ages the medical condition of Sydenham's chorea (which causes involuntary spasms of the body) was known as St. Vitus' Dance because the symptoms resembled dancing, and many sufferers had been healed of this disease after praying at St. Vitus' tomb.

Feast day: June 15.

St. Philemon of Antinoe (died c. 305). Philemon was a professional actor and musician who performed in the Egyptian city of Antinoe. During Emperor Diocletian's persecution of the Church he was arrested and taken to Alexandria, where he was bound hand and foot and thrown into the sea to drown.

Feast day: March 8.

Embroiderers

St. Parasceva (date uncertain). Parasceva was born into a wealthy Christian family in Thrace (now modern-day Bulgaria). She was ten years old when she heard the deacon read the Gospel passage, "If any man would come after me, let him deny himself, take up his cross, and follow me" (Mt 16:24). Parasceva took the words literally and began giving her fine clothes to the poor. When these were gone, she made clothes for the needy. Her parents objected to the expense, so in her early teens Parasceva left home and spent the rest of her life sometimes as a pilgrim, other times as a hermit.

Feast day: October 14.

Fishermen

St. Peter (died c. 67) and St. Andrew (first century). Peter was an impulsive man, the foremost of the apostles whom the Lord appointed the first pope. Andrew was the first apostle to follow Christ. He and Peter were both fishermen, and they had formed a partnership with the two brothers, St. James and St. John. One day when Andrew and Peter were sitting in their fishing boat repairing their nets, Christ approached them. "Follow me," he said, "and I will make you fishers of men" (Mt 4:19).

Feast days: St. Peter, June 29 and February 22 (Chair of St. Peter); St. Andrew, November 30.

St. Anthony of Padua (1195-1231). Many residents of the city of Rimini in Italy belonged to the heretical Cathar sect. Anthony went there to persuade the Cathars to return to the Church, but they would not listen. So Anthony went to the riverbank and cried out, "Listen to the word of God, fishes of the sea and of the river, seeing that the faithless heretics refuse to do so." The water at the saint's feet became turbulent as thousands of fish gathered near the shore and lifted their heads above the surface to hear Anthony preach. The miracle convinced many Cathars to abandon their heresy and return to the Catholic faith.

Feast day: June 13.

St. Nicholas of Myra (died c. 350). A story tells how St. Nicholas was begging for alms for the poor in a certain city, but only three people gave him anything: a woman, a priest, and a fisherman. Each gave him a small fish, which he kept in a bucket of water. At sundown he went to a small house where a poor widow lived with her children. The woman offered Nicholas a bed for the night, but apologized that she had nothing but watery soup and a crust of bread for their supper. "I have three fish," Nicholas said, and when the woman reached inside the bucket she found three large fish, more than enough to feed them all. At the end of the meal only fish bones remained, and Nicholas instructed the woman to place the bones in the bucket. The next morning there were three large fish in the bucket for the family's breakfast. Before he went on his way, Nicholas promised the woman that as long as she returned the fish bones to the bucket, she and her children would always have fresh fish to eat.

Feast day: December 10.

The Corporal Works of Mercy

- *Feed the hungry.*
- *Give drink to the thirsty.*
- *Clothe the naked.*
- *Give shelter to the homeless.*
- *Visit the sick.*

- *Ransom the captive.*
- *Bury the dead.*

ST. BENNO (1010-1106). In the eleventh century the Holy Roman emperor Henry IV tried to make the Catholic Church subservient to the state. He especially wanted the authority to appoint bishops — a power that belongs to the pontiff. Pope St. Gregory VII resisted Henry's attempts to deprive the Church of its independence, and Benno, bishop of Meissen, supported the Holy Father. To punish Benno for his loyalty to the pope, Henry imprisoned him for a year. After he was released, Benno traveled to Rome, but before he left he ordered his clergy to lock the doors of the cathedral so Henry could not seize the church. While Benno was away, Henry broke into the cathedral, took the keys, and threw them in a nearby river. When Benno returned he went down to the river, where he found the keys in the shallows near the shore, guarded by a large fish.

Feast day: June 16.

GARDENERS

ST. FIACRE (DIED 670). Fiacre was an Irish monk whose solitude was constantly disturbed by would-be disciples and people seeking spiritual counsel. To find peace he traveled to Meaux, France, where he asked the bishop, St. Faro, for some land where he could build a hermitage and plant a garden. Bishop Faro said Fiacre was welcome to as much land as he could dig a trench around in a single day. Fiacre found a fine piece of ground and began to walk around it, dragging his spade behind him. Wherever the shovel's blade scored the earth a trench appeared, and if the blade touched a tree or bush, the vegetation was instantly uprooted. In this large garden Fiacre planted vegetables and fruit to feed the hungry and medicinal herbs to heal the sick.

Feast day: August 30.

St. Rose of Lima (1586-1617). Rose wanted to enter a convent, but her parents wanted her to marry. They compromised by permitting Rose to live as a nun in a hermitage in the family garden, which Rose tended. When the family fell on hard times, Rose provided an income by selling her flowers in the Lima marketplace.

Feast day: August 23.

St. Phocas the Gardener (died c. 303). Phocas tended a large garden in Sinope, on the coast of the Black Sea in present-day Turkey. His harvest of vegetables and fruit was always abundant, and he shared his produce with the poor. During Emperor Diocletian's persecution of the Church a detachment of soldiers was sent to execute Phocas. He welcomed them as guests, fed them dinner, gave them a bed for the night, and then dug his grave in his garden. The next day, after Phocas had served the soldiers breakfast, they took him out to his garden and cut off his head.

Feast day: July 23.

Adam. The second and third chapters of Genesis describe God's creation of Adam and Eve and their life in the Garden of Eden. They lived in perfect happiness: they were never sick, they never hurt themselves, they had no worries, all the animals were tame, they would never die, and they saw God face-to-face every evening when he walked through the garden. There is a tradition that Adam and Eve tended the garden, but more as a hobby than labor. After breaking God's command not to eat of the tree of knowledge of good and evil, Adam and Eve were expelled from Eden. God set an angel with a flaming sword at the gate so Adam and Eve could never return to the garden.

Feast day: December 24.

HORSEBACK RIDERS

St. Martin of Tours (c. 336-397). As a Roman officer Martin had a horse, and he is almost always shown in art on horseback, cutting his thick, red woolen cloak in two to give half to a half-naked beggar.

Feast day: November 11.

ST. JAMES THE GREATER (FIRST CENTURY). St. James the Greater, whose tomb is at Compostela in northwestern Spain, is the patron saint of Spain. In the eighth century an army of Moors from North Africa invaded, setting off seven centuries of conflict between Moors and Spaniards. At the Battle of Clavijo (c. 844), Spanish cavalrymen reported that they saw St. James, mounted on a white charger, fighting at their side. After this victory, James received a new title in Spain: Santiago Matamoros, St. James the Moorslayer. Many churches in Spain have a side altar to St. James under this title, with a statue or painting of him on horseback with his sword raised in defense of Catholic Spain.

Feast day: July 25.

HUNTERS

ST. HUBERT (DIED 727). While Hubert was still a pleasure-seeking young man with no regard for the state of his soul, hunting was one of his greatest passions. It was while chasing a magnificent stag on Good Friday that Hubert's conversion began. The animal that would have been his greatest trophy turned to face him, and between the antlers Hubert saw a living Christ on the cross. "Hubert," the crucified Jesus said, "unless you return to the Lord you will fall into hell."

Feast day: November 3.

MARKSMEN

ST. GABRIEL POSSENTI (1838-1862). In his early teens Gabriel Possenti learned to shoot and became a skilled marksman. When he entered the Passionist Fathers' seminary in Isola di Gran Sasso, Italy, he probably assumed his shooting days were over. Then, in 1860, deserters from the army of Giuseppe Garibaldi rode into town. With the permission of his superiors, Gabriel went to the main square to confront the raiders. He found the deserters looting shops and setting houses on fire; one was trying to drag away a young woman. Gabriel intervened, and during the struggle he managed to grab the soldier's pistol from its holster. Pointing the weapon at the man's chest, he ordered him out of town. A moment later the other raiders ran into the piazza with their loot. At the sight of one of their own held at gunpoint by a frail twenty-two-year-old in a cassock, they burst out laughing. They were closing in on Gabriel when a lizard darted across the square. Gabriel took aim and shot the lizard through the head. That made the soldiers stop. Gabriel ordered them to drop their weapons and then, at gunpoint, he escorted them out of town.

Feast day: February 27.

MOTORCYCLISTS

ST. COLUMBANUS (C. 543-615). Columbanus is perhaps the most famous of the hundreds of Irish monks who left their homeland to bring Christianity to the pagan barbarian tribes who had conquered the old Roman imperial provinces that are now Britain, France, Germany, and Switzerland. For thirty years he wandered through those provinces, preaching and founding monasteries and churches until he settled down at last in the town of Bobbio, in Italy. St. Columbanus' desire to travel has led motorcyclists to adopt him as their patron.

Feast day: November 23.

MOUNTAIN AND ROCK CLIMBERS

ST. BERNARD OF MENTHON (C. 1000-C. 1081). Bernard was born to a noble family in the castle of Menthon, at a spot where the French, Italian, and Swiss Alps meet. As a teenager he hiked in these mountains, and as a priest he traveled into them to convert villagers and farmers who had never heard the message of Christ's Gospel. In his travels he often met pilgrims on their way to Rome, or returning from the Eternal City, many of whom told him heart-wrenching stories of companions who died of exposure in the snow or were injured and had no one to help them. In what is now the Great St. Bernard Pass, Bernard founded a monastery where travelers could find shelter. The monks raised giant rescue dogs — St. Bernards — to help find lost or injured pilgrims.

In 1922 Cardinal Achille Ratti was elected pope and took the name Pius XI. Long an enthusiastic mountaineer, as pope he could no longer indulge in his favorite sport, but he promoted the pastime by formally naming St. Bernard of Menthon patron of mountain and rock climbers.

Feast day: May 28.

MUSICIANS AND SINGERS

ST. CECILIA (DIED THIRD CENTURY). Cecilia's parents were Christians who insisted that she give up her desire to consecrate her virginity to Christ and marry instead. They chose a pagan nobleman, Valerian, to be her husband. At the wedding feast, as the hired singers sang bawdy songs, Cecilia sang a song to Christ in her heart.

On her wedding night her guardian angel, armed with a flaming sword, appeared in the bridal chamber. This not only stopped Valerian from consummating the marriage, but led to his baptism. Valerian then brought about the conversion of his brother, Tiburtius. When a period of anti-Christian persecution erupted in Rome, the two brothers collected the bodies of the martyrs and gave them decent burials. This work of mercy led to their own arrest and martyrdom, but not before they had converted one of their prison guards, Maximus.

Later, Cecilia was arrested and sentenced to be suffocated in the steam room of the bathhouse in her palace. Because she was taking a long time to die, an inept soldier tried to kill her quickly with his sword, but she lingered for another three days. She was so well loved by the Christians of Rome that they buried her in a chapel beside the one reserved for the popes in the Catacomb of St. Callixtus. Today Sts. Cecilia, Valerian, Tiburtius, and Maximus lie together in the crypt of Rome's Basilica of St. Cecilia in Trastevere, which was built on the foundations of her house.

Feast day: November 22.

St. Gregory the Great (c. 540-604). After the collapse of the Roman Empire in Western Europe, administration of cities and provinces often fell to bishops. Gregory, who had been praetor, or mayor, of Rome, was later elected pope and worked as diligently as administrator of the city as he did as pastor of the universal Church. Among his many passions as pope was beautifying the Mass; his love for sacred music, particularly chant, led ultimately to the adoption of the Roman style of chant throughout Western Europe. This style became known as Gregorian chant in his honor.

Feast day: September 3.

"The Great"

Of the 263 popes who have led the Catholic Church, only two bear the title "the Great": St. Leo I (reigned 440-461) and St. Gregory I (reigned 590-604). They received this title not only for their tremendous services to the Church, but also for the good they did for the world at large. For example, St. Leo persuaded Attila the Hun not to attack Rome, but to leave the city and its citizens in peace. St. Gregory served as the chief administrator of Rome, maintained good diplomatic relations with kings and barbarian chiefs across Europe, and sent missionaries to convert Anglo-Saxon England. Since his death in 2005, there has been an active movement among Catholics to grant the title "the Great" to Blessed John Paul II.

SKATERS

ST. LYDWINA (1380-1433). One frigid winter day fifteen-year-old Lydwina and several friends went skating on the frozen Schie River in South Holland. Lydwina lost her balance and fell hard, breaking a rib and striking her head on the ice. The fall caused neurological damage that left Lydwina an invalid for the rest of her life. She sank into a profound depression until her parish priest, Father John Pot, suggested that she imitate Our Lord and offer her sufferings for the conversion of sinners. Father Pot helped Lydwina deepen her prayer life and taught her the basics of contemplation. With Father Pot's help she emerged from her depression, learned patience and acceptance, and developed a new compassion for those suffering physical, mental, or spiritual distress.

Feast day: April 14.

SPELUNKERS

ST. BENEDICT (c. 480-550). Benedict was in his late teens when he left his family to live the life of a hermit. In the mountains about forty miles from Rome, at a place called Subiaco, he met a monk named Romanus who directed him to a large cavern that would make a suitable home for a hermit. Benedict spent several years living in solitude in his cave, with virtually no human contact aside from Romanus. In the centuries since Benedict's death, the cave at Subiaco has become a destination for pilgrims, and the interior has been converted to a chapel.

Feast day: July 11.

SWIMMERS

ST. ADJUTOR (DIED 1131). In 1095 Adjutor, a young Norman knight, enlisted in the First Crusade to liberate the Holy Land from the Saracens. Following the defeat of the Saracens, Adjutor stayed on as part of the garrison of Jerusalem. One day when he was on patrol outside the city he was captured by a detachment of Saracens who imprisoned him in a castle on a tiny island off the coast of Palestine. They kept Adjutor in a tower cell with heavy chains locked around his wrists and ankles. With no hope of escape or rescue, Adjutor was on the verge of despair. He prayed to his favorite saint, St. Mary Magdalene, who appeared to him in his cell, broke the chains, and took Adjutor to the castle's battlements. From there he dove into the sea and swam to shore. When he arrived in Crusader territory portions of his chains still hung from hands and feet.

Feast day: April 30.

CHAPTER 8

Patron Saints
for Disasters

BLIZZARDS

OUR LADY OF THE SNOW. On the night of August 4-5 in about the year 352, the Blessed Mother appeared to a Roman senator named John and his wife with instructions to build a church in her honor on Rome's Esquiline Hill. That night Mary also appeared to Pope Liberius with the same message. The next morning the senatorial couple and the pope met on the hill where they saw the outline of a great basilica marked out in snow. The church built on the spot indicated by Our Lady is the Basilica of St. Mary Major, also known as the Basilica of Our Lady of the Snow. Every August 5, at the conclusion of a solemn Mass celebrating the founding of the church, a blizzard of white rose petals are released from the ceiling to recall the miraculous snowfall.

Our Lady of the Snow is invoked against blizzards and its hazards, although generations of Catholic schoolchildren have prayed to her for a snow day.

Feast day: August 5.

DROUGHT

ST. SWITHUN (DIED 862). Swithun was bishop of Winchester in southern England, and especially devoted to the needy. During his pastoral visits around his diocese he held banquets for the poor and hungry rather than the rich lords who expected to dine with the bishop. One market day, while sitting on a bridge that led into Winchester, Swithun saw a heartless man jostle a peasant woman who was carrying a basket of eggs on her head. The basket fell and all the eggs were smashed. After giving the man a piece of his mind, Swithun knelt beside the sobbing woman and made the sign of the cross over the eggs. They were all whole again.

On his deathbed Swithun commanded his monks to bury him in the churchyard with the common people, not in a great tomb inside the cathedral. The monks obeyed him, but more than a century later, in 971, the bishop and monks erected a grand shrine for St. Swithun's relics. When the saint's grave was opened and the procession formed to carry the relics inside the cathedral, a torrential downpour fell — a sign, the people of Winchester agreed, that St. Swithun was displeased. Since then St. Swithun has been invoked to relieve drought, and also to stop too much rain.

Feast day: July 2.

What the Church Teaches Regarding Relics

In the sixteenth century at the Council of Trent, the assembled bishops declared, "The holy bodies of holy martyrs and of others now living with Christ — which bodies were the living members of Christ and 'the temple of the Holy Ghost' (1 Corinthians 6:19) and which are by Him to be raised to eternal life and to be glorified — are to be venerated by the faithful, for through these [relics] many benefits are bestowed by God on men."

This teaching is based not only on tradition (Christians were venerating the relics of the martyrs by 155), but in examples found in the Bible. In the Second Book of Kings we read of a dead man who was being lowered into a grave beside the remains of the prophet Elisha. "As soon as the [dead] man touched the bones of Elisha, he revived, and stood on his feet" (2 Kgs 13:21). Luke 8:43-48 is the account of a woman who suffered a hemorrhage for twelve years, yet she was instantly healed when she touched the fringe of Christ's robe. And Acts 19:11-12 says that "hand-kerchiefs or aprons" that had been touched by St. Paul were carried to the sick and those possessed by evil spirits. As these items were applied to the sick and the possessed, "diseases left them and the evil spirits came out of them."

DROWNING

ST. RADEGUNDE (518-587). Radegunde was born a princess of the Thuringians, a barbarian pagan tribe that lived in eastern Germany. She was twelve when she was carried off by the Franks and eighteen when she was forced to marry their brutal king. During the intervening years Radegunde had become a Christian, and her new faith brought her consolation during the miserable years of her marriage. In 550, the year Radegunde's husband murdered her brother, she left the king and became a nun. She founded a convent dedicated to the Holy Cross in Poitiers, where she found happiness in prayer, study, and the beauty of chanting the Divine Office every day. For her kindness and her wisdom, the local people regarded Radegunde as a saint.

Shortly after her death, one of Radegunde's old servants was fishing when a violent storm came up. A huge wave swamped the boat, and as the man went under he called upon St. Radegunde for help. A moment later he found himself sitting in his boat amid a placid sea.

Feast day: August 13.

ST. ADJUTOR (DIED 1131). There was a turbulent stretch of France's Seine River near the abbey where Adjutor served as a monk. Many boatmen had been caught in the whirlpool and drowned, and Adjutor believed it was time to do something about it. He invited the bishop to the monastery, and together they rowed out to the edge of the whirlpool. While the bishop prayed and sprinkled holy water, Adjutor took a link from the chain that had bound him when he was a prisoner of the

Saracens, and joining his prayers with the bishop's, he tossed it into the dangerous current. Immediately the whirlpool vanished.

Feast day: April 30.

ST. FLORIAN (DIED 304). Florian was a Roman officer serving near what is now the modern-day city of Lorch in Austria. He was arrested during Emperor Diocletian's persecution of the Church, beaten until he could not walk, then dragged to a bridge over the River Emms. There executioners tied a millstone to Florian's neck and shoved him into the water.

Feast day: May 4.

ST. HYACINTH (C. 1185-1257). Hyacinth was a Polish Dominican who founded houses of his order in Russia and modern-day Ukraine in an effort to reunite the Orthodox with the Catholic Church. In 1240 he was in Kiev when the Mongols attacked the city. Racing to the chapel, he took the Blessed Sacrament from the tabernacle. He was hurrying out of the church when he heard Mary's voice say, "My son, will you leave me behind?" Hyacinth hurried over to the alabaster statue of the Blessed Mother and, to his surprise, lifted it easily.

At the banks of the Dnieper River, as the Mongols rampaged through the city, Hyacinth found his brother Dominicans in near panic because they had no boat. "Follow me," Hyacinth said, as he stepped onto the water. He and his community walked over the surface of the river to safety.

Feast day: August 15.

EARTHQUAKE

ST. EMIDIUS (DIED 304). We know very little about St. Emidius except that he was bishop of Ascoli Piceno in eastern Italy. He was a bold bishop who preached the faith in the streets, for which the Roman authorities arrested him and cut off his head. Ascoli Piceno is subject to earthquakes, and over the centuries the people of the region have prayed to their martyred bishop for help. In art St. Emidius is usually shown in bishop's robes, holding up a tottering building.

Feast day: August 5.

St. Agatha (died c. 250). It is said that St. Agatha, after suffering gruesome tortures, was martyred by being rolled over a bed of burning coals. As the executioners began their work an earthquake struck, bringing down a nearby building and crushing two of Agatha's torturers.

Feast day: February 5.

Famine

St. Walburga (c. 710-779). Walburga was an English Benedictine nun, the niece of St. Boniface, the famous missionary to the pagan German tribes. Walburga's brothers, Winnibald and Willibald, had joined their uncle Boniface's mission; they brought so many Germans into the Church that they needed help. The brothers wrote to Walburga, urging her to bring some of her nuns to Germany to teach the faith to the women and children. Outside Wurzburg, Walburga founded a convent where she and her nuns operated a catechism school and a medical clinic.

St. Walburga has two feast days: the day she died (February 25) and the day her relics were moved — the technical term is "translated" — to a shrine (May 1). In Germany, where devotion to St. Walburga has always been especially strong, the beginning of May is the planting season, so farmers prayed to Walburga to make their crops flourish and protect them from famine.

Feast days: February 25 (death) and May 1 (relics moved).

The Translation of Relics

To translate relics may sound odd to modern ears, but the term comes from the Latin word "translatio," which means to transfer or to move. In ancient times, when devotion to a holy man, woman, or child developed, the custom was to

> *exhume the body from its grave and move it into a church or
> chapel, where it would be enshrined and the faithful would
> have access to it. The translation of the relics of a candidate
> for sainthood is still part of the Church's canonization process.*

FIRE

ST. FLORIAN (DIED 304). During a roundup of Christians, Florian, a Roman officer, was arrested by his own men. At his trial, the magistrate, Aquilinus, threatened to burn Florian alive if he did not renounce Christianity. Florian replied, "Then I will rise to heaven in a burst of flames."

Feast day: May 4.

ST. LAWRENCE (DIED 258). The prefect of Rome offered to spare the deacon Lawrence's life if, in three days' time, he surrendered the treasures of the Church. Three days later Lawrence returned to the courthouse with a large crowd of the poor, the lame, and the blind. "These are the treasures of the Church," Lawrence said. The angered prefect condemned Lawrence to be roasted on a grill over a slow fire.

Feast day: August 10.

ST. EUSTACHIUS OR EUSTACE (DIED 118). According to tradition, Emperor Hadrian ordered the arrest of the Roman general, Eustachius, along with his wife, Theopistes, and their two grown sons, Agapitus and Theopistus. The family was exposed to wild lions in the arena, but the animals would not touch them. Then Hadrian had them sealed inside a giant bronze bull; a fire was lit around it, and the martyrs were burned alive.

Feast day: September 20.

FLOOD

ST. GREGORY THAUMATURGUS (C. 213-C. 270). Gregory was converted by the great Christian theologian, Origen (c. 185-254).

After studying theology and philosophy with Origen for seven years, Gregory became bishop of Caesarea in what is now Turkey. Because he performed so many miracles he was called "*Thaumaturgus*," Greek for "the wonder-worker."

The Lycus River ran through Gregory's diocese; during the rainy season it often overflowed its banks, doing a great deal of damage to the region, especially to the crops. One day Gregory walked to the river, planted his staff in the ground, and prayed that floodwaters would never go beyond that point.

Feast day: November 17.

Origen

An African Christian, Origen (c. 185-254) was one of the greatest scholars and theologians of the early Church. He came from a Christian family. His father, Leonides, was very learned and taught his son Latin, Greek, and Hebrew, giving the boy a solid foundation in classical texts as well as Sacred Scripture. Leonides was martyred by the Romans in 202 and is venerated as a saint. Origen, in spite of his many brilliant writings and his own death as a martyr, is not venerated as a saint because some of his ideas, particularly regarding the soul and the fate of the fallen angels in hell, are unorthodox.

ST. CHRISTOPHER (DIED C. 250). Christopher was a tall, immensely strong man. After his conversion to Christianity he built himself a hut beside a dangerous river, where many travelers had drowned. Steadied by a heavy staff, Christopher would wade through the river's strong current, carrying travelers safely on his shoulders.

Feast day: July 25.

ST. JOHN NEPOMUCENE (C. 1340-1393). The queen of Bohemia had gone to confession to John Nepomucene, vicar general of

Prague. The king, Wenceslaus IV, suspected that his wife had been unfaithful to him, and ordered John to reveal what the queen had said in her confession. John replied that the secrecy of the confessional was absolute; he could not divulge what the queen had confessed. Wenceslaus had John tortured, but when he still would not reveal what the queen had confessed, the king had his executioners wrap John in chains and throw him off a bridge into the Moldau River, where he drowned.

Feast day: May 16.

IMPOSSIBLE OR DESPERATE SITUATIONS

St. Jude (FIRST CENTURY). Although one of the twelve apostles (also known as Thaddeus), a cousin of Jesus Christ and the Blessed Virgin Mary, and the likely author of the New Testament Epistle of Jude, for most of the history of the Catholic Church there has been remarkably little devotion to St. Jude. This fact always comes as a surprise to American Catholics, for whom St. Jude is ubiquitous — most churches and chapels have a statue of him, and in the last half of the twentieth century the classified sections of newspapers commonly listed dozens of "Thank you, St. Jude!" notices. Yet devotion to St. Jude as the patron of impossible or desperate situations is an American phenomenon that began in Chicago during the dark days of the Great Depression. According to tradition, St. Jude carried the Christian faith to Persia, where he was martyred by being beaten to death with a club.

Feast day: October 28.

How St. Jude Came to Chicago

The Church of Our Lady of Guadalupe stands amid an industrial neighborhood on the South Side of Chicago. The Claretian Fathers have staffed it for decades. In the late 1920s, the pastor was Father James Tort, who had a special devotion to the forgotten apostle, St. Jude. After the stock market crash of 1929, many of the steel mills in the area closed, and many of Father Tort's parishioners found themselves out of work. In this desperate time he called upon his parishioners to join him in a novena to St. Jude. So many prayers were answered that Father Tort repeated the novena again and again, until it became a regular feature of parish life at Our Lady of Guadalupe. From there, devotion to St. Jude spread to other Chicago parishes and then across the United States. It is a modern religious phenomenon that is still flourishing in the Americas.

St. Rita of Cascia (1381-1457). European Catholics in dire straits invoke the intercession of St. Rita. Her life was filled with sorrow. She longed to enter a convent, but her parents forced her to marry. Her husband was a combative, short-tempered man who was murdered by his enemies. Her sons swore revenge, so she prayed to God to stop them from the sin of murder, and both young men died before they could avenge their father. She joined the Augustinian nuns, and one day received an unusual form of stigmata: an open, bleeding wound in her forehead, such as a thorn would make. The sisters found it repulsive, so Rita often kept out of sight of the community. Because she endured all these troubles without ever losing faith in God, St. Rita is venerated as one of the patrons of impossible situations.

Feast day: May 22.

St. Philomena (date uncertain). After the discovery of her relics in Rome's Catacomb of Priscilla in 1802, devotion to this forgotten martyr flourished. Through her intercession, so many prayers were answered that she became regarded as a great wonder-working saint, who brought relief especially in desperate situations.

Feast day: August 11.

LIGHTNING

ST. THOMAS AQUINAS (1224/25-1274). Thomas Aquinas was the youngest boy of his parents' nine children. The tower room of the family's castle, Roccasecca, was the nursery where five-year-old Thomas slept with his baby sister. One night, during a violent storm, a bolt of lightning flashed into the nursery, killing Thomas' sister. For the rest of his life Thomas was terrified of storms. At the first rumble of thunder he would take refuge in a church until the storm had passed.

Feast day: January 28.

ST. BARBARA (DATE UNCERTAIN). The fire from heaven that struck down Barbara's father immediately after he beheaded her has led Catholics to invoke St. Barbara's protection against lightning.

Feast day: December 4.

SHIPWRECK

ST. PAUL (DIED C. 67). About the year 60 Paul was under arrest and being transported by ship to Rome for trial (the complete story is found in Acts 27 and 28). Near Crete the ship was overtaken by a violent storm that blew it off course, ultimately wrecking it off the island of Malta. St. Paul, some fellow prisoners, their guards and the crew — 276 men in all — survived the wreck. On shore they were discovered by some Maltese, who built a fire for them and sent word of the castaways to the Roman governor, Publius.

St. Paul and his companions remained on the island for three months, during which time he healed Publius' father of dysentery and converted some of the Maltese to Christianity. According to Maltese tradition, Publius was among St. Paul's converts and became the first bishop of the island.

Feast days: June 29, January 25 (conversion), February 10 (shipwreck).

St. Anthony of Padua (1195-1231). In 1221, Anthony, a newly professed member of the Franciscans, sailed to Morocco as a missionary, but he never had an opportunity to preach to the Moors. He fell seriously ill as soon as he arrived in the country. The Franciscans nursed him for several months, but Anthony got no better so they sent him home to Portugal. (Contrary to what most Catholics think, St. Anthony was not Italian, but Portuguese. He was born and raised in Lisbon). A storm in the Mediterranean blew Anthony's ship east, where it ran aground near Messina, Sicily. Anthony found his mission in Italy, and remained there for the rest of his life.

Feast day: June 13.

St. Jodocus (died 668). Jodocus was king of Brittany, one of France's coastal provinces. After a pilgrimage to Rome he abdicated and lived as a hermit. Many Bretons made their living as sailors or fishermen, so Jodocus prayed especially for all seafarers. After his death a town grew up around his tomb, Saint-Josse-sur-Mer, or St. Jodocus-by-the-Sea. It became a tradition among Breton mariners, before setting out on a voyage, to pray at St. Jodocus' tomb, asking him to protect them from shipwreck.

Feast day: December 13.

Storms, Hurricanes, Tornadoes

St. Scholastica (c. 480-547). The twin sister of St. Benedict, Scholastica founded the order of Benedictine nuns shortly after her brother founded the order of Benedictine monks. Scholastica and her nuns were cloistered, but once a year she and some companions met Benedict and a few of his monks at a house halfway between her convent and his monastery. In 547 Scholastica had a premonition that she was about to die. She and Benedict had spent the day together, and as nightfall approached Benedict rose to leave. Scholastica asked him to stay a little longer, but Benedict reminded her of the rule that a monk must be back in his monastery by dark. Scholastica bowed her head, and a moment later a terrible thunderstorm shook the house. "Sister, what have you done?" Benedict exclaimed. "I asked you to grant me a favor and you refused," she replied, "so I asked the same favor from God and he heard my prayer. Go back to your monastery, if you can."

Benedict gave in, and spent the whole night in happy conversation with his sister. The next morning the storm ended, and Scholastica and Benedict went their separate ways. Three days later Benedict saw a white dove being taken up to heaven, which he understood as a sign from God that Scholastica had died. Brother and sister lie buried in the crypt of the great Benedictine Abbey of Monte Cassino.

Feast day: February 10.

Benedictine Nuns

It seems that initially St. Scholastica imagined her community of nuns would live a quiet life of prayer and contemplation behind their convent walls, with very little contact with the outside world. In fact, there have always been cloistered Benedictines, but over the centuries the superiors of the order have also been flexible, permitting the sisters to become more active. In the eighth century, for example, Benedictine nuns from England traveled to Germany to assist St. Boniface in his mission to convert the pagan German tribes. They taught the faith, opened schools for children, and established hospitals. Today, most Benedictine nuns seek a balance between an active apostolate and the contemplative life.

ST. VITUS (DIED C. 303). One version of the martyrdom of St. Vitus tells us that as he, his tutor Modestus, and his nursemaid Crescentia were being martyred, violent winds swept through the area, leveling several pagan temples.

Feast day: June 15.

VOLCANIC ERUPTION

ST. AGATHA (DIED C. 250). A century after Agatha's martyrdom, when Christianity was no longer outlawed in the Roman Empire, the volcano Mount Etna erupted. As a wall of lava rolled down the slope toward the city of Catania, the Christians of the city removed the saint's veil from her shrine and carried it in procession, praying for St. Agatha's intercession. Just outside Catania the lava flow shifted direction, avoided the city altogether, and spilled harmlessly into the sea. In the centuries since the miracle, every time Catania has been threatened by a volcanic eruption, the people of the city have carried St. Agatha's veil through the streets, praying that she will protect them again. Their prayers have been answered many times, most recently during an eruption in the twentieth century.

Feast day: February 5.

ST. JANUARIUS (DIED C. 305). The relics of St. Januarius, also known as San Gennaro, are venerated in Naples. St. Alphonsus Liguori tells us that several times over the centuries Naples has been saved from eruptions of Mount Vesuvius through the intercession of the saint. He wrote: "While the relics of St. Januarius were being brought in procession towards this terrific volcano, the torrents of lava and liquid fire which it emitted have ceased, or turned their course from the city."

Feast day: September 19.

CHAPTER 9

Patron Saints
for Animals

AGAINST MICE, RATS, AND MOLES

ST. MARTIN DE PORRES (1579-1639). Martin de Porres was a lay brother in the Dominican Priory of the Holy Rosary in Lima, Peru. During a severe infestation of mice and rats, the Dominican friars discussed a variety of methods to get rid of the vermin. Martin took a large bowl of leftovers from the kitchen and walked out of the priory. A swarm of rodents followed him. When he was far from the priory he set down the bowl. Every day Martin brought scraps to the same spot, and the priory remained free of mice and rats.

Feast day: November 3.

ST. MAGNUS OF FUESSEN (DIED C. 666). Magnus founded and served as abbot of the Benedictine monastery of Fuessen in Bavaria. For his holiness and charity he was greatly loved by the local people; after his death they told many legends about him. One tells of a dragon that was destroying the crops and villages in the region around Fuessen Abbey. St. Magnus banished the dragon, but kept its baby to hunt mice and rats in the farmers' fields and barns.

Feast day: September 6.

ST. GERTRUDE OF NIVELLES (626-659). Gertrude was in her late teens when she and her mother, Blessed Ida, founded a convent at Nivelles in what is now Belgium. At age twenty, Gertrude became its first abbess. She was a wise administrator, and particularly generous to Irish missionary monks who came to evangelize the Germanic tribes in Belgium, the Netherlands, and northwestern Germany.

For centuries St. Gertrude has been invoked against mice and rats, although the reason is obscure. There has been a suggestion that the mice represent the poor souls in purgatory, for whose deliverance St. Gertrude prayed daily — but that seems to be a stretch.

Feast day: March 17.

St. Ulrich (890-973). For forty-eight years Ulrich labored tirelessly to improve the spiritual and temporal condition of his people. He visited every parish in his diocese; founded new parishes and built new churches; set an example of holiness and selflessness for his priests; opened a hospital; and improved the defenses of Augsburg. When an army of pagan Magyars (from what is now Hungary) besieged Augsburg, Ulrich directed the defense of the city until the emperor arrived with his army to drive out the invaders.

It was the custom in Augsburg to collect dust from St. Ulrich's tomb and sprinkle it in houses and barns to expel mice and rats.

Feast day: July 4.

Against Wild Animals

St. Blaise (died c. 316). Blaise was bishop of Sebaste in what is now Turkey. When anti-Christian persecution erupted in the region, he fled into the mountains, taking refuge in a cave. The wild animals did him no harm, and it is said that when Roman soldiers tracked him to his sanctuary, they found him sitting at the mouth of the cave, surrounded by wolves and bears.

Feast day: February 3.

Bears

St. Columbanus (c. 543-615). Columbanus was an Irish monk who left his homeland to work as a missionary in what is now France, Germany, Switzerland, and Italy. Two bear-related stories are told of St. Columbanus. One planting season the monks at Luxeuil Abbey found themselves shorthanded so Columbanus went into the woods and returned with a bear, which he yoked and used to plough the fields. Toward the end of his life Columbanus left his monastery to live as hermit. He found a cave, but a bear was living in it. At the saint's request, the bear vacated the premises.

Feast day: November 23.

St. Corbinian (670-730). Corbinian was a Frank (the ancestors of the French) who lived as hermit. His wisdom in spiritual matters and his reputation as a miracle-worker attracted visitors and disciples. To escape the attention he made a pilgrimage to Rome, where he was introduced to Pope Gregory II. The pope recognized Corbinian's gifts, consecrated him a bishop, and sent him to evangelize in Bavaria. On his way a bear rushed out of the woods and killed the bishop's mule. Corbinian chided the animal, then unstrapped his luggage from the dead mule and made the bear carry it.

The bear carrying luggage became a symbol of the Diocese of Freising, which St. Corbinian founded. It also appears in the coat of arms of Pope Benedict XVI, who was archbishop of Munich and Freising.

Feast day: September 8.

St. Gall (c. 550-645). Gall was an Irish monk, one of the companions of St. Columbanus who went to the continent to convert the pagan tribes to the Catholic faith. He took Switzerland as his missionary field, and after his death a great monastery was founded there and dedicated to him. Legend tells of a cold night when Gall and his disciples ran out of fuel. Gall saw a bear and commanded it to go into the forest and bring firewood, which the animal did.

Feast day: October 16.

ST. CERBONIUS OF POPULONIA (DIED C. 580). Cerbonius was Catholic bishop of Massa Marittima in North Africa. The Arian Vandals, who ruled North Africa in the sixth century, persecuted their Catholic subjects, particularly targeting Catholic clergy. The Vandal king, Totila, had Cerbonius arrested and condemned him to be mauled to death by a wild bear. But in the arena the bear did not attack the bishop; instead it lay down and licked his feet.

Feast day: October 10.

ST. MAGNUS OF FUESSEN (DIED C. 666). During the Middle Ages Fuessen was renowned for its iron mines, and the first one was uncovered thanks to a friendly bear who led St. Magnus to an exposed vein of ore. Magnus hurried back to his monastery to collect tools and round up a party of workers, but before they set out Magnus rewarded the bear with a cake. Back in the forest, the grateful bear led St. Magnus to several other veins of iron ore.

Feast day: September 6.

BEES

ST. BERNARD OF CLAIRVAUX (1090-1153). Although Bernard could be strict or even irate with persistent, unrepentant sinners, by nature he was warm and affectionate. To read his writings on the mercy of God and the benevolence of the Blessed Mother is to be caught up in the fervor of one who has had a glimpse of the goodness of the Creator and the love of the Mother of God. Bernard is known as the Mellifluous Doctor ("mellifluous" comes from the Latin term for "sweet as honey"). When he wrote and preached about the sweetness of God, he was developing an idea first expressed in the psalms: "O taste and see that the LORD is

good!" (Ps 34:8). And when he spoke of the sweetness of Our
Lady, he presented her as a source of consolation that makes us
forget the troubles of daily life.

Feast day: August 20.

St. Ambrose (c. 340-397). Ambrose began life as a successful
lawyer, whose eloquence persuaded many judges to acquit his
clients. Once he became bishop of Milan, Ambrose used his
persuasive gifts to convert non-Christians (most famously, St.
Augustine), to defend the faith against the Arian heretics, and
to encourage practicing Catholics to live holier lives. His sister
was a nun, and Ambrose thought highly of consecrated virginity, so much so that it was one of his favorite sermon topics. On
this subject he was so convincing that Catholic mothers with
daughters of marriageable age would not go to Mass at Ambrose' cathedral if he was preaching. St. Ambrose is known as
"the Honey-Tongued Doctor," and to reinforce the point he is
often shown with a beehive, which has led to his patronage of
bees and beekeepers.

Feast day: December 7.

St. Modomnoc (died c. 550). Modomnoc was a prince of the
royal O'Neill clan that ruled Ulster in northern Ireland. As a
young man he traveled to Wales to become a monk at St. David's
monastery, where he was appointed beekeeper. When Modomnoc completed his studies and returned to Ireland, his bees left
their hives and followed his ship to Ireland.

Feast day: February 13.

BIRDS

St. Francis of Assisi (1181-1226). Francis and his disciples
were walking through the Spoleto Valley when he saw a vast
congregation of birds of all types. As he went over to investigate,
Francis was surprised that the birds did not take fright and fly
away; instead, they remained where they were, as if they were

waiting for him. And so Francis preached a brief sermon to the birds. "My brother and sister birds," he said, "you should praise your Creator and always love him." This story has become so popular over the centuries that many gardens contain statues of Francis with a few birds; often such a statue is perched on the edge of a birdbath. There is a joke among Catholics that St. Francis is not only the patron of birds, but also of birdbaths.

Feast days: October 4 and September 15 (stigmata).

St. Kevin (c. 498-618). Shortly after his ordination to the priesthood, Kevin traveled into the Wicklow Mountains south of Dublin and settled in the beautiful valley of Glendalough. He intended to live as a hermit, but as more and more disciples joined him he built a monastery and became its first abbot. As is often the case with Irish saints, many of the miracle stories told about Kevin are associated with animals. One day he was praying with his arms stretched out like Christ on the cross. A blackbird perched herself in one of Kevin's hands and laid an egg. To safeguard the egg, Kevin remained in this position for weeks until the egg hatched and the hatchling could fly off. St. Kevin is the patron of birds, especially blackbirds.

Feast day: June 3.

St. Milburga (died 727). Milburga was an English princess who became a nun at the Abbey of Much Wenlock in Shropshire. Among the local people she had a reputation as a saint. One year at harvest time thousands of birds descended on the fields, and nothing the farmers tried — not loud noises and not even fire — drove the birds away. A ruined harvest meant famine. Hearing of the farmers' plight Milburga began to pray, and as she prayed the birds flew off and the fields were saved. During the Middle Ages farmers invoked St. Milburga to preserve their crops from the ravages of wild birds. In recent times she has become the patron of pet birds, too.

Feast day: February 23.

CATS

ST. GERTRUDE OF NIVELLES (626-659). St. Gertrude, a Benedictine abbess from southern Belgium, is invoked against mice and rats, which has led cat lovers to assume that Gertrude was a cat person, and so the ideal patron of their favorite pet.

Feast day: March 17.

CATTLE

STS. PERPETUA AND FELICITY (DIED 203). Incredibly, a handful of eyewitness accounts of the trials and deaths of some of the early martyrs have survived. By far the most moving is the prison diary of Perpetua, a Roman noblewoman of Carthage in North Africa, who was arrested with her slave Felicity, or Felicitas. Perpetua had an infant son whom she was still nursing, so she took him with her to prison; Felicity was eight months pregnant and gave birth to a daughter in prison. Perpetua's son was cared for by her family, while Felicity's daughter was adopted by a Christian family. Perpetua and Felicity were martyred by being exposed to a wild heifer, which gored and threw them; they were then killed by a gladiator.

Feast day: March 7.

ST. BRIGID OF KILDARE (C. 450-525). Many of the miracle stories the Irish tell of St. Brigid speak of abundance: a pan of fried bacon that is never diminished, a cask of ale that never runs dry. It is also said that at her convent in Kildare, Brigid's herd of dairy cows gave a lake of milk every day. To this day it is customary on Irish farms to weave straw into a cross — St. Brigid's cross — and hang it over the door of the dairy barn.

Feast day: February 1.

DOGS

ST. ROCH (DIED 1378). Roch was a young French nobleman who left his home for a prolonged pilgrimage to Rome and the other holy places in Italy. In 1372 he was returning home and had gotten to the city of Piacenza during an outbreak of the Black Death. Rather than run away, Roch stayed at Piacenza to nurse the sick.

One morning he awoke to find black swellings on his body — the first symptom of the plague. So as not to infect anyone else, he left the city and walked deep into the woods to die alone. Suddenly a dog trotted up to him with its tail wagging, carrying a loaf of fresh bread in its mouth. The dog returned every day until Roch recovered.

In art, St. Roch is usually depicted with a plague sore on one leg and a dog at his side.

Feast day: August 16.

ST. HUBERT (DIED 727). Hubert's conversion from a life of thoughtless pleasure occurred on Good Friday when he was hunting in the Ardennes Forest (in what is now modern-day Belgium). Spotting a magnificent stag, he spurred his horse and gave chase. Hubert pursued the stag for miles, when suddenly it stopped and turned to face the hunter. Between the antlers Hubert saw a living Christ on the cross. "Hubert," the crucified Jesus said, "unless you return to the Lord you will fall into hell."

Leaping off his horse, Hubert knelt on the ground. "What should I do, Lord?" he asked.

"Go find Lambert the bishop," Jesus replied. "He will guide you."

Typically, when artists depict this dramatic scene, they include a pack of hunting hounds, which has led to St. Hubert's patronage of all dogs.

Feast day: November 3.

DONKEYS AND ASSES

ST. ANTHONY OF PADUA (1195-1231). Anthony was preaching a mission in the town of Rimini where a Cathar lived. The Cathars were a heretical sect that among other things denied the Real Presence of Christ in the Blessed Sacrament. Anthony visited the man and tried to persuade him, but the Cathar was adamant in his disbelief.

A few days later, as Anthony was carrying a monstrance bearing the Blessed Sacrament in procession, he saw the Cathar with his donkey. As the procession passed them the donkey knelt in the street. The Cathar tugged at the animal's bridle to make it rise, and even offered it a bundle of fresh hay, but as long as it was in the presence of the Eucharist the donkey remained on its knees. Convinced by this miracle, the Cathar professed his faith in the Real Presence and returned to the Catholic faith.

Feast day: June 13.

DOVES

ST. SCHOLASTICA (C. 480-547). Scholastica and her twin brother St. Benedict were very close. Together they founded the Benedictine order of monks and nuns. As a cloistered nun Scholastica was forbidden to leave her convent to make social calls, but one day a year she was dispensed from this rule so she and Benedict could visit with each other. Three days after their last visit, Benedict saw his sister's soul in the form of a dove ascending to heaven. Today at the Abbey of Monte Casino — where Scholastica and Benedict lie buried in the crypt — the monks keep doves in memory of St. Scholastica.

Feast day: February 10.

ST. DAVID OF WALES (DIED C. 600). David was a Welsh monk and later a bishop who founded monasteries and churches throughout his native land. He was an inspired preacher, frequently attracting crowds so large that no church could hold them, so he often preached outdoors. While he was speaking at a place known today as Llanddewi Brefi, people at the back of the crowd complained that they could not see or hear him.

The ground beneath David's feet rose up, creating a rise so all could see him, and his voice became so strong that all could hear him. The congregation noticed that a dove was perched on his shoulder, seeming to whisper in his ear — a manifestation of the inspiration of the Holy Spirit, who is often depicted as a dove.

Feast day: March 1.

HORSES

ST. HIPPOLYTUS OF ROME (DIED C. 236). The name "Hippolytus" is Greek for "unleasher of horses." St. Hippolytus was a priest in Rome who was martyred by being torn apart by wild horses.

Feast day: August 13.

ST. GUY OF ANDERLECHT (C. 950-1012). Guy was a poor field hand who spent all his non-working hours in prayer at his parish church. Impressed by Guy's devotion, the priest hired him as sacristan. After Guy's death his grave was lost, until it was exposed by a horse.

Feast day: September 12.

LAMBS

ST. JOHN THE BAPTIST (FIRST CENTURY). A cousin of Jesus and Mary, and the last of the biblical prophets, John the Baptist was the man chosen by God to prepare the people of Israel for the coming of the Messiah. He was preaching repentance to a crowd when he saw Jesus approaching. "Behold, the Lamb of God," John cried, "who takes away the sin of the world!" (Jn 1:29). To recall this dramatic moment, St. John the Baptist is often depicted with a lamb. At every Mass, the priest repeats St. John's declaration as he elevates the Host before distributing Communion.

Feast days: June 24 (nativity) and August 29 (beheading).

ST. AGNES (DIED C. 304). The name "Agnes" comes from a Greek word for "pure" or "holy." The twelve-year-old Roman martyr was both pure and holy, and in art she is usually shown with a lamb, a traditional emblem of purity and innocence. As it happens, the lamb is also a pun, since the Latin word for lamb is "*agnus.*"

On St. Agnes' feast day two lambs are carried into Rome's Basilica of St. Agnes Outside the Walls and blessed. The wool from these lambs will be woven into the palliums the pope presents to new archbishops.

Feast day: January 21.

The Pallium

The pallium is a liturgical vestment worn only by the pope and archbishops. It is a circular band of white wool adorned with six black crosses. The pallium is worn over the chasuble as a symbol of the spiritual authority of the pope and his archbishops.

LIONS

ST. MARK THE EVANGELIST (DIED 68). The four evangelists are represented by four winged creatures the Hebrew prophet Ezekiel saw in a vision supporting the throne of God: one had the face of a man, the second of a lion, the third of an ox, and the fourth of an eagle. St. Matthew is represented by a winged man because his Gospel begins with a list of the ancestors of Jesus Christ. St. Luke's symbol is the winged ox because his Gospel begins in the Jerusalem Temple where oxen were offered in sacrifice. The eagle is St. John's emblem because the beginning of his Gospel is so theologically sophisticated that it seems to soar up to heaven. And because St. Mark's Gospel begins in the wilderness, his emblem is the winged lion.

It is possible, even likely, that Mark the Evangelist is the John Mark mentioned in the Acts of the Apostles, as the cousin of St. Barnabas. St. Paul found John Mark so immature, unreliable, and irritating that the apostle's friendship with Barnabas ended because of the young man. John Mark's character must have improved because years later St. Peter, in his first epistle, referred to him as "my son."

According to tradition, St. Mark was the first bishop of Alexandria. On Easter Sunday, 68, he was arrested, a noose was tightened around his neck, and he was dragged through the streets until he was dead.

Feast day: April 25.

LOST ANIMALS

ST. FELIX OF NOLA (DIED 260). Felix was a priest in Nola, a town near Naples in southern Italy. During a time of persecution, he helped his elderly bishop, Maximus, escape to a place of safety but then was arrested and beaten almost to death. An angel delivered him from prison, and Felix went directly to Maximus' hiding place to look after the old man. After Maximus' death and the end of the persecution, Felix lived quietly as a priest and farmer outside Nola. After St. Felix's death, devotion to him was very strong (as it remains to this day in southern Italy). In the fifth century St. Paulinus of Nola appointed himself caretaker of St. Felix's shrine and left a record of the miracles attributed to the saint's intercession. Paulinus tells us that one day a farmer came to the tomb to pray for the return of his stolen oxen. "Restore these same animals," the farmer prayed. "I shall not accept any others." When the man returned to his farm he found his missing oxen in their stalls. Today St. Felix is more likely to be invoked for missing pets than missing livestock.

Feast day: January 14.

RABBITS

ST. MELANGELL (DIED C. 590). Melangell was an Irish princess who traveled to Wales to live as a hermit nun. She built herself a hut and planted a garden in the neighborhood of what is now

Pennant. One day she was reading in her garden when she heard the blare of hunting horns and the barking of hunting dogs. Suddenly a frightened rabbit ran into her garden, jumped into her lap, and climbed up her sleeve, just as the hunters and their dogs crashed through Melangell's hedge. The leader of the hunting party was a Welsh prince named Brochwel. Surprised to see a nun in the forest, he asked Melangell who she was. Impressed by her calm and dignity, Brochwell declared Melangell was "a true handmaiden of the true God" and gave her vast tracks of forestland where hunting was outlawed and all animals would live in safety. St. Melangell is the patron of rabbits, but in medieval Wales she was venerated as another St. Francis, the patron of all animals.

Feast day: May 27.

SALMON

ST. KENTIGERN (C. 520-603). One day the queen of the Picts came to see Kentigern, the bishop of Glasgow. She was in great distress because she had begun an affair with a knight at court and given her lover a ring that the king had given to her. The king had noticed the item missing from the queen's finger and asked her to produce it, but she could not because the knight had lost it. Seeing how penitent and distraught she was, Kentigern promised to help and sent her home. Then he called one of his monks and instructed him to go fishing in the Clyde River. As soon as he cast his line the monk caught a beautiful salmon, which he carried back to Kentigern. The bishop took a knife, cut open the fish, and there lay the queen's ring. He sent the ring to the queen and the salmon to the kitchen.

Feast day: January 13.

A Patron Saint for Salmon?

When the world was mostly rural and virtually everyone was involved in some form of farming, the health of livestock, poultry, horses, and hunting dogs, as well as the extermination of vermin, were all vital concerns. Naturally, Christians in the West and the East turned to the saints for help. Based on episodes in the saints' lives, farmers identified patrons for virtually every animal in the barnyard.

Until the modern era the forests of Europe were filled with wolves, bears, and other animals that were dangerous to livestock, and so patron saints were found to protect farm animals from these predators.

There are also cases when patronage is a bit whimsical: swans are lovely but not especially useful (although they were a delicacy served at medieval banquets); there were no lions in Europe, but because of St. Mark the king of beasts got a patron saint; and in the case of St. Kentigern and the salmon, we have a kind of sacred folk tale that teaches us about the boundless mercy of God.

Like the popularity of certain saints, saintly patronage is cyclical: it changes to keep up with the times. An example of this phenomenon is St. Brendan's patronage of whales — a recent development that has grown out of the movement to save the whales.

SHEEP

ST. DROGO (1105-c. 1186). Drogo's parents were Flemish nobility. His mother died giving birth to him, and all his life Drogo felt that he was somehow responsible. At age eighteen he renounced his title, wealth, and lands, and went on pilgrimage to Rome. He did not return to Flanders (now part of present-day Belgium), but went to France, where at Sebourg he was hired as a shepherd. The villagers said he could bilocate; some saw him in the fields with the sheep at the exact time that others saw him in the church attending Mass.

Feast day: April 16.

ST. GEORGE (DIED 303). According to one version of the St. George legend, the dragon left the people in peace as long as they supplied him with sheep. But when the sheep were all gone, they had to surrender a maiden to it. George arrived just in time — after the maiden had been delivered to the dragon's lair, but before it had had a chance to devour her.

Feast day: April 23.

SPIDERS

ST. FELIX OF NOLA (DIED 260). After Felix escaped from prison the Roman authorities sent troops to hunt down the fugitive priest. In his hiding place in the woods Felix heard the soldiers coming. Filled with dread, he ran deeper into the forest until he came to a ruined house. Fallen timbers blocked the door, so Felix climbed in through the building's only window and hid in the rubble. The soldiers were getting closer, yet as frightened as Felix was he found himself watching intently a spider that was spinning a web over the window. Within minutes Felix's pursuers arrived at the ruined house, but they did not search it. The door was blocked, and over the only window was an unbroken spider web.

Feast day: January 14.

SWANS

ST. HUGH OF LINCOLN (1140-1200). In 1181, as part of his penance for the murder of St. Thomas Becket, Henry II founded England's first Carthusian monastery. Hugh, a French Carthusian monk, was sent by his superiors to England as prior of the new foundation. In England everyone — the king, the bishops, the common people — was taken with Hugh's goodness, wisdom, and warmth. Henry and the English bishops petitioned Hugh's superiors to permit them to appoint him bishop of Lincoln. At the bishop's residence there was a swan that became attached to Hugh, following him about the grounds, eating from his hand, and even sleeping in his room. In art, St. Hugh is usually shown with his pet swan.

Feast day: November 17.

WHALES

ST. BRENDAN THE NAVIGATOR (C. 486-575). St. Brendan was abbot of a monastery in western Ireland. According to a medieval book titled *The Voyage of Brendan*, he and several monks sailed west across the Atlantic Ocean in search of the Promised Land of the Saints. One morning Brendan and his companions anchored their boat off a barren island and went ashore to make breakfast. They had just lit a fire when the "island" heaved up. It was the back of a giant whale.

Feast day: May 16.

WOLVES

ST. EDMUND THE KING (841-869). In November 869, King Edmund led his army against a Viking horde that had invaded his realm. The Vikings scattered the English troops and took the king prisoner. Ingvar, the Viking chief, promised to spare Edmund's life if he renounced his Christian faith and swore to serve the Vikings. Edmund refused. Ingvar had Edmund tied to a tree and shot through with arrows. When he was dead, one of the Vikings cut off the king's head and threw it deep into the woods. Later, Englishmen returned to collect Edmund's body. They found the corpse easily enough, but they could not find the head. Then they heard a voice calling, "Here! Here!" They followed the sound and discovered a wolf lying on the ground with Edmund's head between its paws. The wolf let the Englishmen take the head and then followed them to a nearby town, where Edmund would be buried. Once the saint's relics were safe, the wolf returned to the forest.

Feast day: November 20.

CHAPTER 10

Patron Saints
for Unexpected Causes

CRIMINALS

ST. DISMAS (DIED C. 30). St. Luke's Gospel tells us that as Christ was dying on the cross, one of the two thieves crucified with him mocked him saying, "Are you not the Christ? Save yourself and us!" But the other thief said to his fellow criminal, "Do you not fear God, since you are under the same sentence of condemnation? And we indeed justly, for we are receiving the due reward of our deeds; but this man has done nothing wrong." Then the thief said to Our Lord, "Jesus, remember me when you come in your kingly power." Christ replied, "Truly, I say to you, today you will be with me in Paradise" (Lk 23:39-43).

About the year 600 Christians gave the good thief a name: Dismas. Since then he has become the patron of all criminals and convicts, especially thieves. In recent times various prison ministries have adopted St. Dismas as their patron.

Feast day: March 25.

ST. VLADIMIR (C. 956-1015). Vladimir was one of the least likely individuals to become a saint. The illegitimate son of the prince of Kiev, in what is now Ukraine, he came to power by murdering his half-brother. He was an enthusiastic pagan who erected an immense temple to every god in that part of the world and consecrated it with human sacrifice. His victims were two

Christians, a father and his son. Vladimir had seven wives and kept a harem of eight hundred concubines, among whom was his widowed sister-in-law.

About the year 987 Vladimir came to the aid of the Byzantine emperor Basil II, defeating his enemies the Bulgars. As his reward Vladimir demanded the hand of Basil's sister, Anna. Anna refused to be the eighth wife of a blood-thirsty heathen, but Basil was in an awkward position. He wrung from Vladimir a promise to be baptized and dismiss his other wives and all his concubines. To everyone's surprise, after his baptism and marriage Vladimir sent away his women. He brought back to Kiev bishops, priests, and deacons, along with carts filled with icons, liturgical vessels, and sacred books. He erected churches, instituted a program that fed the poor every day, and even abolished the death penalty. His dramatic conversion from a violent life led to St. Vladimir being venerated as one of the patrons of penitent criminals.

Feast day: July 15.

ECOLOGY AND ENVIRONMENT

ST. FRANCIS OF ASSISI (1182-1226). It has been said that no saint imitated Jesus Christ more closely than Francis of Assisi, even to the point of bearing on his body the stigmata, the wounds of the crucifixion. (St. Francis was the first saint to be granted this grace.) Just as he saw Christ in all men and women, Francis saw the glory of God in all creation. This is beautifully expressed in his hymn, "Canticle of the Sun." Like the troubadour poets he had admired and imitated when he was a young man, Francis wrote his hymn in Italian rather than Latin. "All praise be yours, my Lord," Francis sang, "through all that you have made, and first my lord Brother Sun, who brings the day; and light you give to us through him." In the verses that follow, Francis gives thanks to God for the magnificent universe which he, out of love, created for us. At the end of his life Francis added the final verses in praise of "Sister Death . . . from whom no man alive will escape."

In 1980, Blessed John Paul II formally proclaimed St. Francis of Assisi patron of ecology and the environmental movement. *Feast days:* October 4 and September 15 (stigmata).

IMMIGRANTS

ST. FRANCES XAVIER CABRINI (1850-1917). Mother Cabrini, an Italian nun, founded the Missionaries of the Sacred Heart to serve as missionaries in China. But Pope Leo XIII informed her that her mission lay "not in the East, but to the West." Hundreds of thousands of poor Italians were emigrating to the United States. They needed schools, hospitals, orphanages, and homes for the elderly, so Mother Cabrini and six sisters traveled to New York in 1889 to serve their fellow Italians. For the next twenty-nine years Mother Cabrini and her nuns opened countless schools and charitable institutions for Italians all across the United States, including sixty-seven hospitals. In 1946, when Pope Pius XII canonized Mother Cabrini, he also formally proclaimed her the patron of immigrants.

Feast day: November 13.

INTERNET

ST. ISIDORE OF SEVILLE (560-636). Isidore, bishop of Seville, was descended from a family that for generations had served as administrators of Rome's province of Hispania (now modern-day Spain and Portugal). By the time Isidore was born, the Roman Empire in Western Europe was only a memory. Various barbarian nations had conquered and carved up the provinces. Everywhere he looked Isidore saw the achievements of the empire collapsing: the paved roads were overgrown, the libraries and schools had been looted and burned, the aqueducts were broken. Fearing that the world he loved would be completely forgotten, Isidore began writing an encyclopedia of Roman society, ranging from education to engineering, from architecture to cuisine. It was the labor of a lifetime, and when he completed the work, it ran to twenty volumes.

In the 1990s, when the Internet was new, Catholics working in the online industry wanted a patron saint. They chose St. Isidore because they interpreted his multivolume encyclopedia of all existing knowledge as the world's first database.

Feast day: April 4.

TELEVISION

ST. CLARE OF ASSISI (1193-1253). One Christmas Eve, Clare of Assisi was so ill that she could not leave her bed to attend midnight Mass. While all the other nuns went off to the convent chapel, Clare sat up by herself in her cell. "See, Lord," she said, "I have been left here all alone with you." Suddenly she experienced a remarkable vision: Clare saw and heard the Mass as it was being celebrated, as if she were in her choir stall near the altar. In 1958, recalling this miracle, Pope Pius XII declared St. Clare the patron of television.

Feast day: August 11.

The Patience of a Saint

Late at night on Palm Sunday, 1212, Clare Scifi, the daughter of the count and countess of Sasso-Rosso, crept out of her family's palace in Assisi and walked quickly to a chapel, where St. Francis and his followers were waiting for her. There, Francis cut off her hair and covered her with a nun's veil: with that act, Clare became the first female disciple of St. Francis. Together they founded a new community of women, originally known as the Poor Ladies of San Damiano, later known as the Poor Clares.

Clare, like Francis, vowed herself to absolute poverty. Her sisters would have no source of income and would depend entirely on whatever people were moved to give them. At the time it was unheard of for cloistered nuns to live a hand-to-mouth existence; all other convents owned farmland and livestock or perhaps rental properties in a city or town, which guaranteed them an income. Each time a pope died and a new one was elected, Clare submitted her Rule to him, but each declined to approve such a severe way of life. Nonetheless, Clare and her nuns persisted in their commitment to radical, Christ-like poverty.

In the summer of 1253 word came to Pope Innocent IV that Clare was dying. With his entourage the pontiff traveled to Assisi, entered Clare's sickroom, and placed in her hand a document he had signed approving her Rule. She had waited forty-two years for that moment. She died only a short time later.

Travelers

St. Christopher (died c. 250). After his conversion to Christianity, Christopher built a hut beside a dangerous river and lived as a kind of human ferry. He lifted onto his shoulders every traveler who came to the river and carried the person safely to the opposite shore.

One day Christopher heard a child's voice calling him. He stepped outside his hut and saw a little boy who asked him to be taken across. Christopher lifted the boy, grabbed his staff, and waded into the river. With each step the current grew stronger, and the little boy grew heavier. By the time he reached the riverbank Christopher was exhausted. "Boy," he said, "who are you?" The little boy replied, "Christopher, today you carried on your shoulder the Creator of the world." Then the Christ Child disappeared.

Feast day: July 25.

St. Nicholas of Myra (died c. 350). The miraculous intervention of St. Nicholas on behalf of endangered pilgrims has led to him being venerated as one of the patrons of travelers.

Feast day: December 6.

Sᴛ. Rᴀᴘʜᴀᴇʟ ᴛʜᴇ Aʀᴄʜᴀɴɢᴇʟ. The Book of Tobit, or Tobias, in the Old Testament tells the story of Raphael accompanying a young man named Tobias on a dangerous journey and keeping him safe the entire way.

Feast day: September 29.

Tʜᴇ Tʜʀᴇᴇ Kɪɴɢs (ꜰɪʀsᴛ ᴄᴇɴᴛᴜʀʏ). The Gospel of St. Matthew tells us how the Magi, also known as the Three Kings or Wise Men, traveled from countries far to the east of Israel to find the newborn King of the Jews. They traveled at night, following a wondrous star, which led them to Bethlehem and the house where the Holy Family was staying.

Feast day: January 6.

He's Still the Patron Saint of Travelers

Poor St. Christopher. For more than forty years, many Catholics have come to believe either that the pope expelled St. Christopher from the calendar of saints because he never existed or that the pope demoted St. Christopher and he is no longer a saint (in which case maybe we should call him "Mr. Christopher"). Both notions are way off the mark. St. Christopher is still a saint in good standing. In fact, there is no doubt among hagiographers — the scholars who study saints' lives — that there was an early martyr named Christopher.

The misinformation about St. Christopher began in 1969, when Pope Paul VI authorized a complete revision of the Church's liturgical calendar. Some popular saints, such as St. Barbara, were removed from the calendar because Vatican hagiographers believed they were mythical characters. Other saints had their feast days lowered in rank to an optional memorial, which lets local churches decide if they will commemorate the saint or not.

Media reports at the time of the shake-up often got the facts wrong, only adding to the confusion. Many bishops and parish priests failed to explain to the people in the pews what was happening. St. Christopher was one of the victims of this mess.

With approximately forty thousand saints on the books but only 365 days in a year, every day is the feast of dozens of saints. July 25 is the feast day of the apostle St. James the Greater, St. Christopher, and other less-well-known saints. Since any of the apostles outranks a martyr, even a martyr as famous as St. Christopher, the 1969 calendar instructed priests throughout the world to offer Mass on July 25 in honor of St. James. This is the general rule. Parishes and chapels dedicated to St. Christopher, however, or regions where St. Christopher is especially honored, have the option of celebrating his Mass on July 25.

There was a real St. Christopher. The Roman Martyrology, the ancient compendium of Christians who were martyred during the first centuries of the Church, records Christopher's death in Lycia, now in present-day Turkey, during the persecution by Emperor Decius (reigned 249-251).

So put your doubts to rest, and put St. Christopher's statue back on the dashboard, hang his medal from your keychain, and pray to him with confidence before you set out on any journey.

VEGETARIANS

ST. NICHOLAS OF TOLENTINO (1245-1305). Nicholas of Tolentino was a priest of the Augustinian order. Although the Augustinians did not forbid their members to eat meat, Nicholas gave it up completely as a personal penance. Once, when Nicholas was served roasted chicken, he made the sign of the cross over the dish, and the meat was changed to roasted vegetables.

Feast day: September 10.

CHAPTER 11

Patron Saints
for the Nations of the World

Note: Not all countries have a patron saint. In a few cases we were able to identify the patron saint of a particular country, but could not find the reason behind the patronage. In such cases, we did not include an entry for that country.

ALBANIA

OUR LADY OF GOOD COUNSEL. According to an Albanian legend, this image of the Virgin and Child was originally venerated in Shkodra. In or about the year 1467, an unseen power removed the icon from Shkodra and transported it to a church in Genazzano, Italy, a town about thirty miles south of Rome, where it has been a pilgrimage destination ever since.

Feast day: April 26.

ALGERIA

OUR LADY OF AFRICA. No one knows when a wayside statue of the Blessed Virgin was first erected outside Algiers. In 1872 it was moved into a grand seaside basilica and became known as Our Lady of Africa. Both Algerian Catholics and Algerian Muslims pray before this image of Mary.

Feast day: April 30.

ST. CYPRIAN OF CARTHAGE (C. 200-258). A North African lawyer who converted to Christianity, Cyprian went on to become a priest, then bishop of the North African city of Carthage. He was arrested and beheaded during Emperor Valerian's persecution of the Church.

Feast day: September 16.

ANDORRA

OUR LADY OF MERITXELL. On the feast of the Epiphany, January 6, sometime in the late twelfth century, villagers in this small, landlocked country in southwestern Europe discovered a wooden statue of the Virgin and Child standing beneath a wild rose bush. They enshrined the statue in the parish church in Canillo, but three times it vanished and reappeared under the wild rose. The villagers of Meritxell took this as a sign and erected a chapel for the statue on the spot where they had found it. In 1873 the General Council of Andorra named Our Lady of Meritxell the national patroness.

Feast day: September 8.

ANGOLA

IMMACULATE HEART OF MARY. It is likely that Catholic Angolans adopted Mary under this title as their patron through the influence of the Scheut Fathers, a Belgian missionary order whose official name is the Congregation of the Immaculate Heart of Mary. Since the mid-nineteenth century the Scheut Fathers have been active missionaries in Africa.

Feast day: Saturday before the Solemnity of the Sacred Heart of Jesus.

The Immaculate Heart of Mary

Devotion to Mary's Immaculate Heart is rooted in the Gospel of St. Luke. In his account of the night Christ was born, after describing the wonders of the event, Luke says, "Mary kept all these things, pondering them in her heart" (Lk 2:19).

> *Like her soul, which God kept free from all stain of original sin, Mary's heart is immaculate because it never harbored any sinful thoughts or impulses. Instead, it was filled with love for God and all humankind. St. Bernardine of Siena (1380-1444), who actively promoted devotion to Mary's Immaculate Heart, wrote that "from her heart, as from a furnace of Divine Love, the Blessed Virgin spoke the words of the most ardent love."*
>
> *In 1917 at Fátima in Portugal, the Blessed Mother told the three children, Jacinta and Francisco Marto and their cousin Lúcia dos Santos, "to save poor sinners, God wishes to establish in the world devotion to my Immaculate Heart." In 1942, Pope Pius XII consecrated the world to the Immaculate Heart of Mary.*

ARGENTINA

ST. FRANCIS SOLANO (1549-1610). A Spanish Franciscan, Francis Solano carried the faith to Indian tribes in western and central South America, including northern Argentina.

Feast day: July 14.

BLESSED LAURA VICUNA (1891-1904). Although born in Chile, Laura Vicuna passed her early childhood years with her mother in Argentina. From a young age she fought off the sexual advances of her mother's lover, who ultimately beat her to death for refusing him.

Feast day: January 22.

OUR LADY OF THE IMMACULATE CONCEPTION OF LUJAN. This statue, carved in Brazil, was sent to Argentina, where it was venerated in a private chapel near Lujan. As the devotion spread, the statue was moved to ever more grand churches. Since 1763 it has been housed in a Gothic-style basilica; that same year Argentinians adopted Our Lady of Lujan as one of their patron saints.

Feast day: December 8.

ARMENIA

ST. BARTHOLOMEW (FIRST CENTURY). According to tradition, the apostle Bartholomew preached the Gospel in Armenia. He was martyred there by being flayed alive.

Feast day: August 24.

ST. GREGORY THE ILLUMINATOR (C. 240-332). Gregory was born in Armenia and was educated in Caesarea (now in modern-day Israel). When he reached adulthood Gregory became a priest and then traveled as a missionary to his homeland. He converted tens of thousands of Armenians to Christianity, including the king. About the year 300 Armenia became the world's first Christian nation.

Feast day: September 30.

AUSTRALIA

ST. FRANCIS XAVIER (1506-1552) AND ST. THÉRÈSE OF LISIEUX (1873-1897). For most of Australia's history the Catholic Church considered it mission territory and so the country was placed under the patronage of the patron saints of missionaries, St. Francis Xavier and St. Thérèse of Lisieux. In 1976, the Congregation for the Propagation of the Faith in Rome formally declared that the Church in Australia was firmly established, at which point Australian bishops confirmed that the continent was under the patronage of Our Lady Help of Christians but not of St. Francis and St. Thérèse.

Feast days: St. Francis Xavier, December 3; St. Thérèse of Lisieux, October 1.

OUR LADY, HELP OF CHRISTIANS. In 1844 the Catholic bishops of Australia declared the Blessed Mother, under this title, one of the patrons of the country.

Feast day: May 24.

St. Mary MacKillop (1842-1909). Mary MacKillop was born in Melbourne, Australia, at a time when the population of Australia was booming. Catholic schools, hospitals, orphanages, and other institutions operated by the Church were overwhelmed. To meet these pressing needs MacKillop, in conjunction with Father Julian Tennison Woods, founded a new community of nuns, the Sisters of St. Joseph of the Sacred Heart. By the end of her life, there were seven hundred fifty Sisters of St. Joseph in Australia and New Zealand, operating dozens of charitable institutions, and teaching twelve thousand children. Since St. Mary MacKillop's canonization in 2010, she has been venerated as a patron saint of Australia.

Feast day: August 8.

AUSTRIA

St. Colman of Stockerau (died 1012). Colman was a pilgrim, from either Ireland or Scotland, who passed through the Austrian village of Stockerau on his way to Jerusalem. He was falsely accused of being a spy and hanged. His body was left dangling from the gallows, but it never showed any sign of decomposition, which led the villagers to believe that they had executed not just an innocent man but a saint.

Feast day: October 13.

St. Florian (died 304). Florian, an officer in the Roman legions, was martyred in the Austrian city of Linz. His tomb has been a popular goal for Austrian pilgrims for seventeen centuries.

Feast day: May 4.

St. Leopold the Good (1073-1136). As ruler of Austria, Leopold kept his country out of war, opened new lands to peasant farmers, and founded monasteries, including Heligenkreuz Abbey outside Vienna.

Feast day: November 15.

St. Maurice (died c. 287). The head from the lance of St. Maurice (the chief officer of the Theban Legion, which was martyred just across the border in Switzerland) was one of the prized relics of Austria's imperial family. It is still displayed in Vienna.

Feast day: September 22.

St. Severinus of Noricum (died 482). Severinus was a monk who was among the first to preach the Christian faith in Austria. He founded several monasteries near present-day Vienna, and cared for Austrians who had fallen victim to the Huns.

Feast day: January 8.

Our Lady of Mariazell. A Benedictine monk named Magnus built a chapel and placed a limewood statue of the Blessed Virgin in it. After miracles were reported at the chapel, Mariazell became the most frequented Marian pilgrimage destination in Austria. The statue bears the title "*Magna Mater Austriae*" ("Great Mother of Austria").

Feast day: September 13.

BELGIUM

St. Columbanus of Ghent (died 959). Columbanus was a wandering Irishman who settled at last in the town of Ghent as a hermit. The city's Cathedral of St. Bavo was built on the site of his hut.

Feast day: February 2.

Our Lady of Banneux. In 1933 an eleven-year-old Belgian girl, Mariette Beco, received a series of visions of the Blessed Mother. She instructed the child to pray often and, in return, promised to relieve suffering on earth. In 1949 the Vatican declared the apparitions were "worthy of belief."

Feast day: January 15.

OUR LADY OF BEAURAING. Over a period of five weeks in 1932 and 1933, the Blessed Virgin appeared to four young girls and one boy, bearing the message, "Pray always." In 1943, the local bishop authorized public devotion at the site of the apparitions.

Feast day: November 29.

Apparitions

Since the third century, when St. Gregory Thaumaturgus became the first Christian to receive a vision of the Blessed Virgin, countless apparitions of Mary have been reported. Among the most famous are the apparitions at Guadalupe, Mexico, in 1531; Lourdes, France, in 1858; and Fátima, Portugal, in 1917.

It is the duty of the local bishop to investigate a reported apparition. In judging the phenomenon he uses four criteria:

1. *Is the event inexplicable, in the sense of miraculous?*
2. *Is the visionary or seer of sound mind, of good moral character, and obedient to the pastors of the Church?*
3. *Is the vision's message consistent with Catholic doctrine and moral teachings?*
4. *Has the vision brought about positive spiritual benefits to people who have visited the site of the apparition, such as the conversion of sinners, increase of religious devotion, or more generous acts of charity?*

If the apparition meets all four criteria the bishop may declare it "worthy of belief." The bishop is also free to refer the case for a final assessment to the Congregation for the Doctrine of the Faith in Rome.

BOLIVIA

ST. FRANCIS SOLANO (1549-1610). Bolivia is one of the regions in South America where this Franciscan missionary strengthened the faith of Spanish colonists and converted the Indians.

Feast day: July 14.

Our Lady of La Candelaria of Copacabana. An Indian artisan carved a statue of the Blessed Virgin as an act of personal devotion. After the statue was enshrined in a chapel in the town of Copacabana, miracles were reported. During Bolivia's struggle for independence from Spain, the Bolivian people called upon the intercession of Our Lady of La Candelaria of Copacabana. When the country achieved its independence in 1825, Bolivians attributed it to Mary's prayers.

Feast days: February 2 and August 5.

BORNEO

St. Francis Xavier (1506-1552). The Catholics of Borneo adopted Francis Xavier as their patron because during the decade he served as a missionary in Asia (1542-1552), he traveled through their part of the world.

Feast day: December 3.

BRAZIL

St. Anthony of Padua (1195-1231). As the most popular saint among the Portuguese, it was natural that Portuguese colonists in Brazil would make St. Anthony one of the patrons of their country.

Feast day: June 13.

St. Peter of Alcantara (1499-1562). Peter of Alcantara founded a reformed branch of the Franciscans that became known as the Alcantarines. He sent many of these friars to the Spanish and Portuguese colonies in the New World, including Brazil. In 1926, St. Peter of Alcantara was named one of the patrons of Brazil.

Feast day: October 19.

Our Lady of Nazareth. In 1182 a Portuguese knight, in danger of tumbling off a cliff, called upon Our Lady of Nazareth and was saved. Portuguese colonists carried this devotion to Brazil, erecting a shrine to Mary in the city of Belem do Para.

Feast day: March 6.

OUR LADY OF THE IMMACULATE CONCEPTION OF APARACIDA. In 1717 three fishermen pulled a clay statue of the Immaculate Conception out of the Paraiba River. A chapel was built for the image, which became known as Our Lady of the Immaculate Conception Who Appeared from the Waters, or in Portuguese, "*Aparecida.*" In 1904 Pope St. Pius X proclaimed Our Lady of Aparacida patron of Brazil.

Feast day: October 12.

The Immaculate Conception

From the moment Mary was conceived in the womb of her mother, St. Anne, God kept her soul free from all stain of original sin. This unique privilege was granted to Mary alone because God had chosen her to be the mother of the Savior, Jesus Christ. On December 8, 1854, Blessed Pius IX declared that the Immaculate Conception of the Blessed Virgin Mary was dogma, which all the Catholic faithful must believe.

BULGARIA

STS. CYRIL (DIED 869) AND METHODIUS (DIED 885). These Greek brothers carried Christianity to the Slavic lands of Eastern Europe. Although they did not preach in Bulgaria, the Bulgarians have taken them as their patron saints.

Feast day: February 14.

CANADA

ST. ANNE (FIRST CENTURY B.C.). In 1658 French colonists placed a little wooden statue of St. Anne, the mother of the Blessed Virgin Mary and the grandmother of Jesus Christ, inside a small chapel at Beaupré on the St. Lawrence River in the province of Quebec. That year two miracles occurred: a crippled man praying to St. Anne was healed, and a boatful of sailors in danger of drowning in a storm invoked St. Anne and were saved. The shrine became a major destination for pilgrims, and St. Anne was named patron of Canada.

Feast day: July 26.

ST. JOSEPH (FIRST CENTURY). French Jesuit missionaries established devotion to St. Joseph among the Indian tribes of Canada and fostered it among the French colonists. The grandest expression of Canada's devotion to the husband of Mary and the foster father of Jesus is the magnificent Oratory of St. Joseph, built by St. André Bessette on Mount Royal, overlooking Montreal.

Feast days: March 19 (St. Joseph, Husband of the Blessed Virgin Mary) and May 1 (St. Joseph the Worker).

ST. GEORGE (DIED C. 303). In 1763 the French and Indian War came to an end, and France's possessions in the New World, including Canada, passed to the English. St. George, who was already the patron of England, also became patron of British Canada.

Feast day: April 23.

NORTH AMERICAN MARTYRS (DIED BETWEEN 1642 AND 1649). Between 1642 and 1649, six French Jesuit priests (St. John de Brébeuf, St. Gabriel Lalemant, St. Isaac Jogues, St. Anthony Daniel, St. Charles Garnier, and St. Noël Chabanel) and two French lay assistants (St. René Goupil and St. John de La Lande) who labored as missionaries in Canada were tortured and killed by the Iroquois. Canonized in 1930, they were the first saints of Canada.

Feast day: October 19 (September 26 in Canada).

ST. MARY OF THE HURONS. In 1639 the Jesuits established a mission, Sainte-Marie among the Hurons on the Wye River, about 750 miles from the little settlement of Quebec. It became the queen of their missions in Indian territory, but it survived only ten years. In 1649, under pressure from repeated attacks by the

Iroquois, the French and the Hurons burned the mission and fled to the safety of Quebec.

Feast day: None.

OUR LADY OF THE CAPE. In 1854 a parishioner donated a statue of the Blessed Mother to the Church of Our Lady of the Cape. In the years that followed, a series of miracles occurred at the church. In 1904 St. Pius X proclaimed Our Lady of the Cape "Queen of Canada." In 1909, the bishops of Canada named the church the National Shrine of the Blessed Mother.

Feast day: First Sunday in October.

CENTRAL AFRICAN REPUBLIC

IMMACULATE HEART OF MARY. A Belgian missionary order, the Congregation of the Immaculate Heart of Mary, has been active in Africa since the mid-nineteenth century. As a tribute to these priests, popularly known as the Scheut Fathers, Catholics of the Central African Republic took the Immaculate Heart of Mary as their patron.

Feast day: Saturday after the Solemnity of the Sacred Heart of Jesus.

CHILE

ST. FRANCIS SOLANO (1549-1610). This Spanish Franciscan was active in establishing the Church in South America, working among Spanish colonists as well as converting the Indian tribes in Chile.

Feast day: July 14.

ST. JAMES THE GREATER (FIRST CENTURY). In 1541 Spanish conquistador Pedro de Valdivia founded a town in Chile and named it Santiago in honor of the apostle who is the patron saint of Spain (Santiago is Spanish for St. James).

Feast day: July 25.

OUR LADY OF MOUNT CARMEL OF THE MAIPU. In the early nineteenth century, during Chile's war for independence from Spain, the commanders General José Miguel Carrera, General

Bernardo O'Higgins, and General José de San Martín invoked the aid of Our Lady of Mount Carmel of the Maipu. After a victory in 1817, General San Martín donated his baton, his emblem of office, to the statue. In 1923, at the request of the bishops of Chile, Pope Pius XI proclaimed Our Lady of Mount Carmel of the Maipu the patron of Chile.

Feast day: July 16.

CHINA

OUR LADY OF SHESHAN. Catholics of Shanghai, China, erected a basilica on a mountain called Sheshan in thanksgiving to Our Lady for saving them from anti-Christian rioters. The church held a painting of the Virgin and Child dressed in Chinese imperial robes. Our Lady of Sheshan was proclaimed patron of the Diocese of Shanghai, and then of all China.

Feast day: May 24.

ST. JOSEPH (FIRST CENTURY). Missionaries in many countries, including China, have adopted St. Joseph as their patron because he is one of the most popular and beloved saints of the Church, and is venerated as one of the most powerful intercessors in heaven. The custom began in the sixteenth century, when European missionaries placed Mexico under the patronage of St. Joseph to help them bring souls to the Catholic faith.

Feast days: March 19 (St. Joseph, Husband of the Blessed Virgin Mary) and May 1 (St. Joseph the Worker).

ST. FRANCIS XAVIER (1506-1552). The great Jesuit missionary Francis Xavier was en route to China when he fell ill and died on an island off the China coast.

Feast day: December 3.

COLOMBIA

ST. PETER CLAVER (1581-1654). A Spanish Jesuit missionary, Peter Claver spent forty-four years serving and caring for the hundreds of thousands of African slaves who passed through the port of Cartagena, Colombia.

Feast day: September 9.

St. Louis Bertran (1526-1581). Louis Bertran's Dominican superiors sent him as a missionary to Panama and Colombia.

Feast day: October 9.

Our Lady of the Rosary of Chiquinquirá. Over the years this painting of the Virgin and Child with St. Andrew the Apostle and St. Anthony of Padua faded, but in 1586, as the pious woman who cared for the painting watched, the painting was miraculously restored to its original beauty. The image is enshrined in the Basilica of Our Lady of the Rosary in Chiquinquirá, Colombia. In 1829 Pope Pius VII proclaimed Our Lady of the Rosary of Chiquinquirá the patron of Colombia.

Feast day: July 9.

Costa Rica

Our Lady of the Angels. In 1635 a woman of mixed race found a three-inch-high stone figurine of the Virgin and Child. The local people built a chapel on the site, which became a popular pilgrimage destination for Indians, the poor, and other outcasts of Costa Rican society. The statuette became known as Our Lady of the Angels, and Mary under this title became patron of Costa Rica.

Feast day: August 2.

Cuba

Our Lady of Charity of El Cobre. Two Indians and an African slave boy found a statue of the Virgin and Child floating off the Cuban coast. After the statue was enshrined in a chapel on a hill above the mining town of El Cobre, people reported countless miracles. In 1916 Pope Benedict XV named Our Lady of Charity of El Cobre Cuba's patron saint.

Feast day: September 8.

OUR LADY OF REGLA. The town of Chipiona in Spain safeguards a statue of the Virgin Child that, according to legend, once belonged to St. Augustine of Hippo. The Spanish carried devotion to this Madonna to the New World, but it especially flourished in Cuba, where Our Lady of Regla became one of the patrons of the island.

Feast day: September 8.

CYPRUS

ST. BARNABAS (FIRST CENTURY). One of the first Christians and one of the most respected members of the Church, Barnabas introduced the newly converted Paul to the apostles. He traveled on missionary journeys with St. Paul before traveling on his own to Cyprus, where he became the island's first bishop and was martyred there.

Feast day: June 11.

CZECH REPUBLIC

ST. ADALBERT (C. 957-997). Although a Czech and archbishop of Prague, Adalbert encountered so much resistance from pagan Bohemians that he gave up trying to convert them and carried the faith to Poland, Prussia, Hungary, and Russia, where he had much greater success.

Feast day: June 20.

STS. CYRIL (DIED 869) AND METHODIUS (DIED 885). As is customary in every Slavic nation of Europe, these Greek brothers who brought to Christianity to the Slavs are venerated as patrons of the Czech Republic.

Feast day: February 14.

ST. LUDMILA (DIED 921). The first Christian duchess of Bohemia (now part of the Czech Republic), Ludmila was assassinated by her daughter-in-law, a leader of Bohemia's anti-Christian faction.

Feast day: September 16.

ST. WENCESLAUS (907-929). Raised a devout Catholic by his grandmother, St. Ludmila, Wenceslaus tried to expand Christianity in Bohemia. He was murdered by his brother, who had aligned himself with their mother against increasing Catholic influence in the country.
Feast day: September 28.

ST. PROCOPIUS OF SAZAVA (C. 970-1053). After a brief period as a hermit, Procopius founded the monastery of Sazava outside Prague and served as its first abbot.
Feast day: July 14.

ST. VITUS (DIED C. 303). St. Vitus became a patron of Bohemia after some of his relics were brought from Rome to Prague and enshrined in the cathedral that bears his name.
Feast day: June 15.

ST. JOHN NEPOMUCENE (1340-1393). For his refusal to compromise the Church or reveal what he had heard in confession, John Nepomucene, vicar general of the Archdiocese of Prague, was tortured and killed by the king of Bohemia.
Feast day: May 16.

The Seal of the Confessional

Everything a penitent tells a priest in confession is kept in strictest secrecy, known as the seal of the confessional. Priests are absolutely forbidden to divulge, in any way, anything they hear in confession. A priest who breaks the seal of the confessional is automatically excommunicated and can only be absolved of this terrible sin by the pope.

ST. SIGISMUND OF BURGUNDY (DIED 524). St. Sigismund became one of the patrons of Bohemia after his relics were transferred from their tomb in France to a new shrine in Prague.
Feast day: May 6.

DENMARK

ST. ANSGAR (801-865). This French Benedictine monk was invited by King Harold to bring Christianity to his people, the Danes.
Feast day: February 3.

ST. CANUTE (DIED 1086). King of Denmark, Canute was tireless in strengthening the Church in his country. One day a group of his opponents followed him into a church and murdered him.
Feast day: January 19.

DOMINICAN REPUBLIC

ST. DOMINIC (1170-1221). The first city in the Americas, Santo Domingo, was founded by Bartholomew Columbus (Christopher's brother) in 1498 and named in honor of St. Dominic, the founder of the order of preaching friars who became known as Dominicans.
Feast day: August 5.

Naming the New World

It was routine for Catholic explorers in the New World to give religious names to islands, mountains, bodies of water, and other prominent landmarks. For example, the Caribbean island of St. Kitts was named for St. Christopher, San Francisco Bay in California was named for St. Francis of Assisi, and what is now Lake George in New York was originally named the Lake of the Blessed Sacrament.

OUR LADY OF MERCY OF ALTAGRACIA. A painting of the Virgin Mary and the newborn Infant Jesus was painted in Spain around 1500 and brought to Santo Domingo in 1502 by two brothers, Alfonso and Antonio Trejo. They donated the painting to a church, where it became an object of great devotion among the settlers. The people of the island named the image Our Lady of Altagracia, or High Grace, and venerated her as the patron of their country.
Feast day: January 21.

ECUADOR

OUR LADY OF QUINCHE. A Spanish sculptor working in the city of Quito, Ecuador, carved this statue of the Virgin and Child, then traded it to Indians for a load of cedar wood. In time many of the Indians of Ecuador developed a profound devotion for Our Lady of Quinche, as they named her. She became one of the national patrons.

Feast day: November 21.

EGYPT

ST. MARK THE EVANGELIST (DIED 68). It is likely that Mark is John Mark, the young cousin of St. Barnabas. He traveled for a time with Barnabas and St. Paul on one of their missionary journeys; Paul found him unreliable and irritating (see Acts of the Apostles). This falling out over John Mark broke the friendship of Paul and Barnabas. According to tradition, Mark was the first bishop of Alexandria, Egypt. On Easter Day 68, Roman soldiers seized Mark, tightened a noose around his neck, and dragged him through the streets until he was dead.

Feast day: April 25.

EL SALVADOR

OUR LADY OF PEACE. The statue was found by chance on the shore of the Mar del Sur and placed in a church in the city of San Miguel. In 1833, when El Salvador was on the brink of civil war, the antagonists met before the statue and swore to make peace.

Feast day: November 21.

ENGLAND

ST. GEORGE (DIED C. 303). King Edward III (reigned 1327-1377) adopted the dragon-slayer, St. George, as patron of England. In the early fifteenth century, the English bishops declared St. George's feast day a national holiday, on par with Christmas.

Feast day: April 23.

OUR LADY OF WALSINGHAM. Following a vision of the Blessed Virgin Mary, Richeldis de Faverches erected a shrine in the village of Walsingham. It became the premier Marian shrine in England until its destruction under Henry VIII in 1538. The shrine was restored in 1897.

Feast day: September 24.

ST. AUGUSTINE OF CANTERBURY (DIED 604). With forty Benedictine monks, Augustine, a Roman abbot, sailed to England to bring the Catholic faith to the Anglo-Saxons. He succeeded in converting Ethelbert, king of Kent. Augustine established his diocese in Canterbury, which became the primatial see, or most important diocese, of England.

Feast day: May 27.

What Is a "See"?

"See" can be a noun as well as a verb. As a verb, it means to perceive something with your eyes. As a noun, a see is a diocese or archdiocese. The root of the noun is the Latin word "sedes," which means seat. In every cathedral of the Catholic Church there is a chair reserved for the bishop or archbishop; it is one of the symbols of his spiritual authority. To refer to the See of Philadelphia or the See of Boston is just an elegant way to refer to these archdioceses. The Holy See refers to the pope, the bishop of Rome, who has spiritual authority over the Catholic Church throughout the world.

ST. GREGORY THE GREAT (C. 540-604). In 597 Pope Gregory sent the abbot Augustine to plant the faith in England.

Feast day: September 3.

ST. CUTHBERT (DIED 687). Cuthbert was a shepherd boy who became bishop and abbot of Lindisfarne Abbey, one of the holiest places in northern England. He was beloved in his day as a peacemaker and a wonder-worker. After his death he ranked among the popular saints in England. Even Henry VIII's commissioners could not bring themselves to destroy his relics. Instead, they buried them in Durham Cathedral.

Feast day: September 4.

EQUATORIAL GUINEA

IMMACULATE CONCEPTION. In 1986 the Catholic bishops of Equatorial Guinea proclaimed Our Lady, under her title of the Immaculate Conception, to be the national patron.

Feast day: December 8.

ESTONIA

BLESSED VIRGIN MARY (FIRST CENTURY). The first Catholic church erected in Estonia around 1219 was dedicated to the Blessed Mother. Over time her patronage extended from that original church to the entire nation.

Feast day: September 8.

ETHIOPIA

ST. FRUMENTIUS (DIED C. 380). Frumentius was a Lebanese Christian who was shipwrecked on the coast of Ethiopia. He was taken to the court of the king, where in time he achieved high office as a royal servant. Frumentius used his influence to plant Christianity among the Ethiopians.

Feast day: October 27.

ST. GEORGE (DIED C. 303). By the time Frumentius arrived in Ethiopia, veneration of St. George was already widespread in the Middle East. It is likely that he brought devotion to the saint to Ethiopia.

Feast day: April 23.

FINLAND

ST. HENRY OF UPPSALA (DIED C. 1156). Henry was an English

monk who traveled to Scandinavia on Church business and decided to stay. After being named archbishop of Uppsala in Sweden, he traveled to Finland to establish the faith there. He was murdered by a Finn whom he had excommunicated. The Finns venerate him as a martyr and national saint.

Feast day: June 9.

What Is a Martyr?

"Martyr" comes from the Greek word "martyria," which means a witness. A Christian martyr is someone who bears witness to the faith by his or her willingness to die rather than renounce it. The first Christian martyr was the deacon St. Stephen, who was stoned to death about the year 35. His story can be found in the Acts of the Apostles (chapters 6 and 7).

FRANCE

St. Anne (FIRST CENTURY B.C.). The mother of Mary and the grandmother of Jesus became one of the patrons of France after her relics were discovered in Brittany in 1625.

Feast day: July 26.

St. Denis (DIED C. 250). The first bishop of Paris, Denis was martyred on the hill that would become known as Montmartre. The church of St. Denis, built over his tomb, became the preferred burial spot for the kings and queens of France.

Feast day: October 9.

St. Joan of Arc (1412-1431). Inspired by heavenly voices, Joan, an illiterate French peasant, convinced the king of France to give her an army to drive the English invaders from their country.

Feast day: May 30.

St. Martin of Tours (c. 316-397). A tireless bishop, Martin founded new churches and monasteries for the Christians of Gaul and carried the faith into parts of the country that were still pagan.

Feast day: November 11.

St. Remigius (died c. 533). Remigius, archbishop of Rheims, instructed and baptized Clovis, the first Christian king of France.

Feast day: October 1.

St. Thérèse of Lisieux (1873-1897). In 1944 the bishops of France named St. Thérèse one of the patrons of the country.

Feast day: October 1.

Our Lady of Chartres. The great Gothic Cathedral of Chartres stands about fifty miles from Paris on a site where Mary has been venerated since the first centuries of the Church. The cathedral also preserves one of France's holiest relics: Our Lady's veil.

Feast day: July 13.

Our Lady's Veil

According to tradition, Charlemagne, the first Holy Roman emperor, received the Blessed Mother's veil from the emperor and empress of the Byzantine Empire. In 876 Charlemagne's grandson, Charles the Bald, donated the veil to the bishop of Chartres. It has been venerated in the Cathedral of Chartres ever since.

Our Lady of La Salette. In 1846 the Blessed Mother appeared to a boy and girl in La Salette and called upon all Catholics to do penance for their sins.

Feast day: September 19.

OUR LADY OF LOURDES. In 1858 the Blessed Virgin appeared to St. Bernadette Soubirous and revealed to her the location of a healing spring. The shrine at Lourdes has become one of the most popular pilgrimage destinations in the Catholic world.

Feast day: February 11.

OUR LADY OF THE MIRACULOUS MEDAL. In 1830, Mary appeared to St. Catherine Labouré in the chapel of the Daughters of Charity on the Rue du Bac in Paris. She gave Catherine the design for a new Marian medal and promised abundant graces to all who wore it.

Feast day: November 27.

What Are Sacramentals?

As the glossary to the Catechism of the Catholic Church *explains: "[Sacramentals] … are sacred signs which bear a resemblance to the sacraments. They signify effects, particularly of a spiritual nature, which are obtained through the intercession of the Church" (CCC 1667). They can be objects, such as medals, scapulars, and rosaries, or actions such as blessings.*

GEORGIA

ST. GEORGE (DIED C. 303). In the fourth century, when this country in Caucasus Mountains adopted Christianity, the king took St. George as the national patron and renamed his nation in the saint's honor.

Feast day: April 23.

ST. NINO (DIED C. 320). A Christian slave from Cappadocia (now in modern-day Turkey), Nino was the first to introduce Christianity to Georgia.

Feast day: December 15.

GERMANY

ST. BONIFACE (680-754). This English Benedictine monk began the evangelization of Germany in 718. In 723 Pope Gregory II consecrated Boniface a bishop. He established his cathedral at Mainz and founded many monasteries and convents for the newly converted Germans. In 544 Boniface traveled to Dokkum in what is now the Netherlands to confirm a group of German converts. Before the ceremony began, a group of German pagans attacked the crowd, slaying St. Boniface and fifty-two other Christians.

Feast day: June 5.

ST. GEORGE (DIED C. 303). As is true of so many countries in Europe, Germany adopted the ever-popular St. George as one of its patrons.

Feast day: April 23.

ST. MICHAEL THE ARCHANGEL. After Germany became Christian in the eighth century, mountaintop sanctuaries that had been dedicated to the god Wotan were reconsecrated in honor of St. Michael. Consequently, St. Michael became one of the patrons of Germany.

Feast day: September 29.

ST. PETER CANISIUS (1521-1597). This Dutch Jesuit dedicated his life to bringing German-speaking Protestants back to the Catholic Church. Canisius wrote a German catechism that explained and defended Catholic doctrine and religious practices. He traveled throughout Germany, Austria, Bohemia, and even into Poland, preaching and reconciling thousands to the Catholic faith. After Boniface, he is considered the "Second Apostle" of Germany.

Feast day: December 21.

OUR LADY OF ALTÖTTING. Arguably the oldest surviving Christian house of worship in Germany, the chapel enshrines a small wooden statue of the Virgin and Child. In 1489 the body of a drowned child was brought to the chapel. As family and friends prayed to Our Lady for help, the child came back to life. From that day throngs of the sick have traveled to Altötting, and many have reported that they were cured. The shrine is known as "the Lourdes of Germany."

Feast days: Ash Wednesday and Holy Saturday.

OUR LADY OF KEVELAER. In 1641 the Blessed Mother commanded a peddler and his wife to build a chapel in her honor at Kevelaer on the German/Holland border. When the chapel was completed, a small picture of the Virgin and Child was placed on the altar. Soon there were reports of miraculous healings. To this day the shrine of Our Lady of Kevelaer is one of the most popular Marian pilgrimage destinations in Germany.

Feast day: June 1.

GREECE

ST. ANDREW (FIRST CENTURY). According to tradition, Andrew the Apostle, brother of St. Peter, was martyred at Patras, Greece, tied to an X-shaped cross.

Feast day: November 30.

St. Andrew

St. John's Gospel tells us that Andrew was the first apostle called by Jesus (see Jn 1:35-42). St. Andrew and his brother St. Peter were born in Bethsaida, a village on the shore of the Sea of Galilee; they were fishermen. Before he joined Jesus, Andrew had been a disciple of St. John the Baptist.

According to tradition, Andrew preached the Gospel in Eastern Europe, as far as present-day Ukraine and Russia.

ST. GEORGE (DIED C. 303). Greek Christians gave St. George the title *"Megalomartyr"* — "the Great Martyr" — and considered his feast day second in importance only to Easter and Christmas.

Feast day: April 23.

St. Nicholas of Myra (died c. 350). St. Nicholas is another saint so popular in Greece that he became one of the country's patrons.

Feast day: December 6.

Our Lady of Mount Athos. There is a legend that the Virgin Mary and St. John were shipwrecked on Mount Athos. Mary was enchanted by the beauty of the place and asked her Son to give it to her. She heard his voice from heaven say, "Let this place be your lot, your garden, and your paradise, as well as a haven for those who seek salvation." From that day Athos was known as "the Holy Mountain" and "the Garden of the Virgin Mary."

Feast day: February 12.

Guatemala

St. James the Greater (first century). The first capital of the Spanish colony of Guatemala was founded on July 25, 1524 — an auspicious day for the conquistadors, as St. James is the patron of Spain. They named the new settlement City of St. James of the Knights of Guatemala, and so the apostle became the patron of the nation.

Feast day: July 25.

Our Lady of the Rosary. The statue of Our Lady of the Rosary is made of silver. In 1821, leaders of Guatemala's independence movement proclaimed Our Lady of the Rosary its national patron. In 1833 the bishops of the country gave Mary a new title: Queen of Guatemala.

Feast day: October 6.

Haiti

Our Lady of Perpetual Help. In 1882, as an epidemic swept across Haiti, the bishops gathered at the Chapel of Our Lady of Perpetual Help in Bel Air and invoked her aid. That day, everyone sick with the disease was healed. In 1942, the bishops of

Haiti formally proclaimed Our Lady of Perpetual Help patron of the nation.

Feast day: June 27.

Our Lady of Perpetual Help

About the year 1450 an unknown Greek artist on the island of Crete painted this icon of the Virgin and Child, flanked by the archangels St. Michael and St. Gabriel. In 1495 an Italian merchant traveling through Crete stole the icon and carried it back to his house in Rome. It can be found today over the altar of Rome's Church of St. Alphonsus, just a few steps from the Basilica of St. Mary Major.

The title of this icon, "Perpetual Help," pays tribute to Mary as our constant and most powerful intercessor in heaven.

HONDURAS

OUR LADY OF SUYAPA. Two peasants, a teenager and a young boy, discovered a statuette of the Virgin Mary outside the village of Suyapa. The image was mounted in a silver frame and exposed for veneration. The little Madonna became very dear to the Honduran people, and in 1925 Pope Pius XI declared Our Lady of Suyapa patron of Honduras.

Feast day: February 3.

HUNGARY

ST. ASTRICUS (DIED. C. 1035). Abbot of Pannonhalma Abbey, the first Benedictine monastery in Hungary, Astricus traveled to Rome to win Pope Gregory II's recognition of the new Christian kingdom of Hungary. He returned home with the pope's blessing and the Holy Crown of Hungary, Gregory's personal gift to King Stephen and all future Hungarian kings.

Feast day: November 12.

ST. GERARD SEGRADO (DIED 1046). A Benedictine monk from Venice, Gerard was persuaded by King Stephen to tutor his son and heir, St. Emeric, and to preach the Gospel to the pagan Magyar tribes. St. Gerard won many souls for Christ, but after Stephen's death he was murdered by anti-Christian Hungarians.

Feast day: September 24.

ST. STEPHEN OF HUNGARY (C. 935-1038). The first Christian king of Hungary, Stephen united the Magyar tribes into a single nation and brought in bishops and monks from Christian Europe to convert his people.

Feast day: August 16.

ICELAND

ST. THORLAC THORHALLSSON (1133-1193). A native of Iceland, Thorlac Thorhallsson studied at the University of Paris. He was ordained a priest and appointed bishop of Skalholt in Iceland, where he labored to eradicate corruption among the clergy. After his death the Althing, the Icelandic assembly, declared Thorlac a saint.

Feast day: December 23.

INDIA

ST. THOMAS THE APOSTLE (FIRST CENTURY). An ancient tradition tells us that Thomas the Apostle carried the Gospel to India and was martyred there.

Feast day: July 3.

St. Thomas in the Gospels

Although all the lists of the apostles in the four Gospels include Thomas, he is not a prominent player. He is recorded as speaking only three times, all of them in St. John's Gospel. When Jesus is about to go to Bethany to see Lazarus,

Martha, and Mary, some of the apostles fear that the Lord's enemies will try to kill him. Thomas says to his fellow apostles, "Let us also go, that we may die with him" (Jn 11:16).

During the Last Supper, when Christ says that he is going away and will prepare a place for his apostles, Thomas asks, "Lord, we do not know where you are going; how can we know the way?" This leads to Christ's great answer, "I am the way, and the truth, and the life" (Jn 14:5-6).

The most famous episode comes after Christ's resurrection: Thomas refuses to believe the apostles when they tell him the Lord is risen from the dead (Jn 20:24-29).

ST. FRANCIS XAVIER (1506-1552). In 1542 Francis Xavier arrived at Goa, India, as the first Jesuit missionary. He taught the catechism to children, nursed lepers, cared for prisoners, and attempted to restrain Portuguese colonists from abusing and exploiting the Indians.

Feast day: December 3.

ST. ROSE OF LIMA (1586-1617). Although she was born in Lima, Peru, of mixed Spanish and Incan descent, at Rose's canonization in 1671 Pope Clement X pronounced her patron saint of "the Indies," including India.

Feast day: August 23.

OUR LADY OF BANDEL. The original church was built in 1599 at Bandel, about sixty miles from Calcutta. The statue of the Blessed Mother enshrined in the church is known as Our Lady of Good Voyage, in memory of a Portuguese ship whose captain and crew were saved from drowning in the Bay of Bengal through Mary's intercession.

Feast day: Second Sunday of November.

Our Lady of Bandra. Also known as Our Lady of the Mount, the church preserves a statue of Mary brought to India by the Jesuits in the sixteenth century. Both Catholics and non-Christians visit this shrine.

Feast day: September 8.

Our Lady of the Assumption. According to legend, as Mary lay dying, all the apostles returned to Jerusalem to see her one last time, but St. Thomas, because he had to travel from India, arrived late. He found the apostles standing around Our Lady's tomb. It was filled with lilies and roses, but her body was gone. When the apostles told Thomas that Mary had been taken up to heaven, body and soul, he refused to believe, just as he had refused to believe them when they told him Christ had risen from the dead. To prove what the apostles said was true, Our Lady dropped her sash from heaven. It fluttered down to Thomas, who at once put aside his doubts and believed.

Feast day: August 15.

IRAN

St. Maruthas (died c. 415). A Syrian bishop, Maruthas rebuilt the Church in Persia (now modern-day Iran) after the persecution under King Shapur II. He also collected the stories of the Persian martyrs.

Feast day: December 4.

IRELAND

St. Patrick (c. 390-c. 461). The Apostle of Ireland was born near the Scottish border. At age sixteen Irish raiders captured Patrick and sold him into slavery in Ireland. After six years as a slave he escaped and returned home to his family. He joined the priesthood, and shortly after his ordination he dreamed that he heard the voices of the Irish crying out to him, "Come back, young man, and walk among us once again." Patrick believed that God had chosen him to carry the faith to the Irish, a belief that was confirmed when Pope Celestine named Patrick bishop of Ireland. He made a great many converts, particularly in the eastern and northern parts of the island. The conversion of the Irish was completed by St. Patrick's disciples.

Feast day: March 17.

ST. BRIGID OF KILDARE (c. 450-525). Brigid's father was a pagan Irish chieftain, and her mother was a Christian slave. It is said that when Brigid was a little girl she met St. Patrick. As an adult she founded a convent at Kildare and opened a school — the first Christian school in Ireland — where the Catholic faith and Irish culture were taught to the students. Countless miracle stories are told of St. Brigid, and in the Middle Ages the Irish venerated her almost as highly as they did the Blessed Mother.

Feast day: February 1.

ST. COLUMBA (c. 521-597). As a young monk Columba prized books above all things. Secretly he made an illicit copy of an exquisite book of psalms that belonged to Abbot Finnian of Clonnard Abbey. Finnian discovered what Columba had done and took him to court, where the judge ruled that Columba must surrender the bootleg copy. Enraged, Columba asked his kinsmen for help. Finnian called up the men of his own clan, and the battle that followed took the lives of three thousand troops. As punishment, the bishops and abbots of Ireland exiled Columba to Scotland, with orders to convert three thousand Scots to atone for the three thousand dead. In exile Columba learned patience and charity, and he proved to be a remarkable missionary. His own sincere conversion made him beloved among the Irish.

Feast day: June 9.

ST. KEVIN (c. 498-618). Kevin founded a monastery at Glendalough, a lovely valley in the Wicklow Mountains south of Dublin.

He governed his monks like a kindly father, and had such a sweet disposition that even wild animals were drawn to him.

Feast day: June 3.

St. Malachy O'More (1094-1148). As archbishop of Armagh, Malachy rooted out corruption in the Church in Ireland and introduced the Cistercian monks to a new standard for holiness among the Irish clergy. Prophecies concerning the popes and the end of the world have been attributed to him, but they are forgeries that were written in his name more than four centuries after his death.

Feast day: November 3.

Our Lady of Knock. On August 21, 1879, fifteen residents of the village of Knock saw Our Lady, St. Joseph, and St. John the Evangelist outside the village church. Knock became the Lourdes of Ireland, where many pilgrims have reported miraculous healings from a host of ailments.

Feast day: August 21.

ISRAEL

St. George (died c. 303). George was born in Palestine (present-day Israel) and was martyred in the city of Lod, which lies south of the capital of modern Israel, Tel Aviv.

Feast day: April 23.

ITALY

St. Francis of Assisi (1181-1226). The saint considered most Christ-like, St. Francis of Assisi is beloved around the world. In 1939 Pope Pius XII named St. Francis one of the patrons of Italy.

Feast days: October 4 and September 17 (stigmata).

St. Catherine of Siena (1347-1380). A member of the Dominican order, Catherine of Siena — by unremitting, patient persistence — convinced Pope Gregory XI to leave Avignon, France (where the popes had lived under the French king's thumb for seventy years), and return to Rome, where he belonged. In 1939 Pope Pius XII named St. Catherine one of the patrons of Italy.

Feast day: April 29.

St. Bernardine of Siena (1380-1444). Considered the Apostle of Italy, Bernardine traveled throughout the country bringing peace to warring cities and aristocratic families, reviving religious devotion, and reforming the Franciscan order.

Feast day: May 20.

Our Lady of the Snow. In August 352 the Blessed Virgin appeared to a Roman senator and his wife, then to Pope Liberius, requesting that a church be built in her honor on the Esquiline Hill. The next day the three visionaries met on the hilltop and found the outline of a basilica laid out on the ground in snow.

Feast day: August 5.

Our Lady of Perpetual Help. Sometime in the fifteenth century an Italian merchant traveling through Crete saw this icon of the Virgin and Child, stole it, and carried it to his house in Rome. After his death the icon passed to another Roman merchant. The Blessed Mother appeared to the merchant's daughter and instructed her to place the icon in a church between the basilicas of St. Mary Major and St. John Lateran. That was done, and today the icon of Our Lady of Perpetual Help is venerated in a small church near the Basilica of St. Mary Major.

Feast day: June 27.

Our Lady of Loreto. According to tradition, after the Turks drove the last of the Crusaders from the Holy Land in 1291, angels carried the house of the Holy Family from Nazareth to the town of Loreto, Italy, where it became the country's premier Marian shrine.

Feast day: December 10.

OUR LADY OF POMPEII. In the late nineteenth century Bartolo Longo, a sometime Satanist who repented and returned to the Catholic faith, acquired a painting of Our Lady of the Rosary. To promote frequent recitation of the Rosary, he built a shrine church outside the ruined Roman city of Pompeii. The shrine is a destination for pilgrims throughout Italy and across the globe.

Feast day: May 8.

OUR LADY OF TEARS. In 1953 Antonina and Angelo Jannuso of Syracuse, Sicily, were poor newlyweds expecting their first child. Antonina was having a difficult pregnancy and prayed to Our Lady for help. On August 29 she saw tears running down the cheeks of a plaster plaque of the Immaculate Heart of Mary. The Jannusos collected some of the tears and gave them to their parish priest, who submitted them for scientific evaluation. They were found to be human. Antonina gave birth to a healthy son, and the plaque of the weeping Madonna was transferred to a shrine.

Feast day: April 1.

JAPAN

ST. FRANCIS XAVIER (1506-1552). In 1549 Francis Xavier became the first Christian missionary to reach Japan. The converts he made were the beginning of a Catholic community that in a few decades would number more than four hundred thousand souls.

Feast day: December 3.

ST. PETER BAPTIST (1545-1597). A Spanish Franciscan who became superior of the Franciscan missionaries in Japan, Peter Baptist was among the twenty-six European and Japanese Catholics arrested and crucified on a hill overlooking Nagasaki in 1597. These were the first martyrs of Japan.

Feast day: February 6.

JORDAN

ST. JOHN THE BAPTIST (FIRST CENTURY). John the Baptist, the

precursor of the Savior and the last of the biblical prophets, preached that the Messiah was coming, and he baptized penitent sinners in the Jordan River. St. John exercised his ministry in a region now part of present-day Israel and Jordan.

Feast days: June 24 (nativity) and August 29 (beheading).

KOREA

BLESSED VIRGIN MARY AND ST. JOSEPH (FIRST CENTURY). European missionaries introduced Catholicism to Korea beginning in the seventeenth century. It was customary to place their work under the protection of Mary and Joseph. As the faith spread, Korean Catholics adopted Our Lady and St. Joseph as their national patrons.

Feast days: Blessed Virgin Mary, January 1 (Mary, Mother of God), March 25 (Annunciation), August 15 (Assumption), September 8 (Nativity), December 8 (Immaculate Conception); St. Joseph, March 19 (St. Joseph, Husband of the Blessed Virgin Mary) and May 1 (St. Joseph the Worker).

LATVIA

BLESSED VIRGIN MARY (FIRST CENTURY). The Teutonic Knights, an order of warrior monks from Germany, colonized the region known today as Latvia. In honor of Our Lady they named it Terra Mariana, or the Land of Mary.

Feast days: January 1 (Mary, Mother of God), March 25 (Annunciation), August 15 (Assumption), September 8 (Nativity), December 8 (Immaculate Conception).

LEBANON

ST. GEORGE (DIED C. 303). St. George was born, lived, and was martyred just across the border from Lebanon in what is now Israel.

Feast day: April 23.

Popular St. George

Over the centuries, many cities, provinces, and countries have chosen St. George as their patron. At least a dozen countries are under his protection, including England, Ethiopia, and Canada.

OUR LADY OF LEBANON. In 1907 Lebanese Catholics erected a sixty-foot-tall bronze sculpture of Mary on a hill overlooking the Bay of Jounieh. In 1908 the Maronite patriarch of Antioch proclaimed this image of Our Lady as "Queen of Lebanon."

Feast day: May 2.

LIECHTENSTEIN

ST. FLORIN (DIED 856). Florin was an English pilgrim-turned-priest who ministered in what is now the Liechtenstein Diocese of Vaduz. Some of his relics are enshrined in Vaduz's Cathedral of St. Florin.

Feast day: November 17.

ST. LUCIUS (SIXTH CENTURY). Lucius came from Switzerland as a missionary to what is now Liechtenstein in the year 500. We know nothing else about him.

Feast day: December 3.

LITHUANIA

ST. CASIMIR (1460-1483). In the fifteenth century the kings of Poland ruled Lithuania. At age eleven Prince Casimir's father, the king, named him Grand Duke of Lithuania.

Feast day: March 4.

ST. CUNEGUNDES (DIED 1040). A German empress who passed her widowhood as a nun, St. Cunegundes was very popular in

Poland and Lithuania as well as Germany. Lithuanians took her as one of their national patrons.

Feast day: March 3.

St. George (died c. 303). As is the case with so many countries, Lithuania placed itself under the protection of the dragon-slayer St. George.

Feast day: April 23.

St. Hyacinth (1185-1257). A Dominican missionary, Hyacinth carried the faith from Poland to Scandinavia, across Lithuania, and into Russia.

Feast day: August 17.

St. John of Dukla (1414-1484). John was a Polish Franciscan who made it his mission to preach in Poland, Lithuania, and the Ukraine, in an effort to bring union between the Catholic and Orthodox Churches.

Feast day: October 1.

St. John Kanty (c. 1390-1473). A much-loved theology professor at the University of Cracow, John of Kanty was regarded as a living saint by the townspeople as well as his students. In 1737 Pope Clement XII proclaimed St. John one of the patrons of Lithuania.

Feast day: December 23.

St. Ladislaus of Gielniow (1440-1505). As the superior of the Polish province of Franciscans, Ladislaus sent friars to Lithuania to bring back to the Catholic faith those who had gone into schism.

Feast day: September 25.

Luxembourg

St. Willibrord (c. 658-739). With eleven fellow Benedictine monks, St. Willibrord traveled from his home in England to the

Low Countries (the Netherlands, Belgium, and Luxemburg) to preach the Gospel. The missionary monks met with great success, and in 696 Pope Sergius recognized their achievement by naming Willibrord bishop of Utrecht. Willibrord was buried in Luxemburg's Abbey of Echternacht, which he founded in 698.

Feast day: November 7.

St. Cunegundes (died 1040). Cunegundes was a member of the Luxemburg aristocracy. After her marriage to St. Henry II, duke of Bavaria, she spent the rest of her life in Germany.

Feast day: March 3.

St. Philip (first century). One of the twelve apostles, it is a mystery why St. Philip is one of the patrons of Luxemburg. Nonetheless, devotion to St. Philip was strong in the Low Countries in the Middle Ages and Renaissance, when many members of the nobility were baptized "Philip."

Feast day: May 3.

Our Lady of Consolation. During the seventeenth century an epidemic swept across Luxemburg. The people prayed to Our Lady of Consolation, and the plague abated. In thanksgiving, Mary under this title was proclaimed patron of the Grand Duchy of Luxemburg. The statue of Our Lady of Consolation is enshrined in the cathedral in Luxemburg City. A replica is enshrined in the Basilica and National Shrine of Our Lady of Consolation in Carey, Ohio.

Feast day: Sixth Sunday of Easter.

MACEDONIA

St. Clement of Ohrid (c. 840-916). At the time Clement was born, his homeland, Macedonia, was part of the Bulgarian Empire. He became a priest, and as a disciple of Sts. Cyril and Methodius brought Christianity to the Macedonians and the Bulgarians.

Feast day: July 17.

MADAGASCAR

ST. VINCENT DE PAUL (1581-1660). Beginning in 1648, St. Vincent de Paul, founder of the Congregation of the Mission, sent priests of his order to plant Christianity in Madagascar. Today, approximately twenty-five percent of the population of Madagascar is Catholic.

Feast day: September 27.

MALTA

ST. PAUL (DIED C. 67). About the year 60, Paul was being transported to Rome as a prisoner for trial. En route his ship was overtaken by a storm and Paul, his guards, and the crew — more than two hundred men — were shipwrecked on the island of Malta. During his three-month stay, Paul made many converts (see Acts of the Apostles, chapters 27 and 28).

Feast days: June 29, January 25 (conversion), February 10 (shipwreck).

ST. PUBLIUS (DIED C. 112). The governor of Malta, Publius befriended St. Paul and was converted by him. He became the first bishop of Malta.

Feast day: January 21.

ST. GEORGE (DIED C. 303). In yet another sign of St. George's popularity, the inhabitants of the island of Malta took him as one of their patrons.

Feast day: April 23.

ST. AGATHA (DIED C. 250). St. Agatha was martyred in Sicily, her homeland, but there is a longstanding tradition among the Maltese that to escape persecution she and several fellow Christians fled to Malta, hiding in a crypt at Rabat. The crypt survives, part of a complex that includes an early Christian catacomb and a church — all dedicated to St. Agatha.

Feast day: February 5.

OUR LADY OF THE ASSUMPTION. On August 15, 1942, a convoy of fifteen British merchant ships, filled with food, medical supplies, and ammunition, evaded Nazi bombers and delivered their cargo safely to the besieged island of Malta. The Maltese referred to the successful mission as the "Santa Marija Convoy," and since it arrived on the feast of the Assumption, Our Lady of the Assumption became one of the island's patrons.

Feast day: August 15.

MEXICO

OUR LADY OF GUADALUPE. In December 1531 the Blessed Virgin appeared to a fifty-five-year-old Indian named Juan Diego Cuautlatoatzin. Speaking to him in Nahuatl, his native language, Mary instructed Juan Diego to go to the bishop of Mexico City and tell him that Our Lady wanted a chapel built in her honor on Tepeyac Hill. The bishop resisted, until Mary sent Juan Diego with a cloak full of Castilian roses that he found growing on the hill, months out of season. When he spilled the roses at the bishop's feet, an image of the Virgin Mary was revealed on Juan Diego's tilma: she was dark-skinned like an Indian, wearing both European and Aztec dress. Within a decade, eight million Indians in Mexico, inspired by the miraculous image, were converted to the Catholic faith. Pope Benedict XIV named Our Lady of Guadalupe patron of Mexico.

Feast day: December 12.

ST. JOSEPH (FIRST CENTURY). In the sixteenth century Spanish missionaries chose St. Joseph as the first patron of Mexico.

Feast days: March 19 (St. Joseph, Husband of the Blessed Virgin Mary) and May 1 (St. Joseph the Worker).

BLESSED ELIAS NIEVES (1882-1928). Since his beatification in 1997, Elias Nieves has been venerated as one of the patrons of Mexico. He was an Augustinian priest who, during the persecution of the Catholic Church in the 1920s, went underground to serve his parishioners. He was arrested and executed by firing squad. Father Nieves' last words were, "Long live Christ the King!"

Feast day: March 10.

MONACO

ST. DEVOTA (DIED 303). Devota was a Christian who was tortured to death for her faith on the island of Corsica. Her relics were transferred to Monaco, where she is venerated as patron of the tiny principality.

Feast day: January 27.

NETHERLANDS

ST. BAVO (C. 589-654). A sinner who repented and became a hermit, Bavo is one of the most popular saints in the Low Countries (the Netherlands, Belgium, and Luxemburg). He founded a Benedictine monastery in Ghent, Belgium, which he dedicated to St. Peter. After his death, the monastery was renamed "St. Bavo."

Feast day: October 1.

ST. WILLIBRORD (C. 658-739). An English Benedictine monk who evangelized the Low Countries, Willibrord was the first bishop of Utrecht, which became the most important diocese in the Netherlands.

Feast day: November 7.

ST. PLECHELM (DIED C. 730). One of the Benedictine missionary monks who came from England to the Low Countries with St. Willibrord, Plechelm was second bishop of Utrecht in the Netherlands and founded the Abbey of Sint Odilienberg, one of the first monasteries in the country.

Feast day: July 15.

NEW ZEALAND

ST. FRANCIS XAVIER (1506-1552). As the patron saint of the missions, Francis Xavier was patron of New Zealand until

1976, when the Society for the Propagation of the Faith, which oversees and supports the Church's missions, declared that the Church in the country was self-sufficient and that New Zealand was no longer mission territory.

Feast day: December 3.

Our Lady, Help of Christians. To replace St. Francis Xavier, the bishops of New Zealand named Mary, Help of Christians as the national patron saint.

Feast day: May 24.

Nicaragua

St. James the Greater (first century). Managua, the current capital of Nicaragua, was founded in 1811 and given the name Leal Villa de Santiago de Managua, or the Loyal City of St. James of Managua. Nicaraguans venerate St. James as the patron of their capital and their country.

Feast day: July 25.

Our Lady of the Immaculate Conception of El Viejo. According to tradition, this statue of the Blessed Virgin was brought to Nicaragua in the sixteenth century by a relative of St. Teresa of Ávila. The statue was enshrined in the Franciscan mission of El Viejo, on the Pacific coast. Over time it became the most revered image of Our Lady in the country.

Feast day: December 8.

Nigeria

St. Patrick (c. 390-c. 461). Irish members of the Society of Missionaries of Africa (better known as the White Fathers, from their white habits) were active in Nigeria, which led to Nigerian Catholics taking St. Patrick as one of their patrons.

Feast day: March 17.

OUR LADY, QUEEN OF NIGERIA. In 1960 the Catholic bishops of Nigeria entrusted their country to Mary under the title "Our Lady, Queen of Nigeria."

Feast day: October 1.

NORWAY

ST. OLAF II (995-1030). The first Christian king of Norway, Olaf was zealous in establishing Christianity in his kingdom. He was killed at the Battle of Stiklestadt, where he fought to recover his kingdom from rebels. St. Olaf was Norway's first saint.

Feast day: July 29.

PAKISTAN

ST. THOMAS THE APOSTLE (FIRST CENTURY). Until 1947, Pakistan was considered part of India, and so would have as its patron St. Thomas, who is said to have brought Christianity to this region.

Feast day: July 3.

PANAMA

OUR LADY OF LA ANTIGUA. The national patron of Panama traces its roots to a late seventeenth-century painting of the Virgin and Child, which is displayed in a church in the town of Tunja.

Feast day: Third Sunday of January.

PAPUA NEW GUINEA

ST. MICHAEL THE ARCHANGEL. Catholics of Papua New Guinea chose St. Michael as their national patron in honor of the Michaelite missionaries, who have served the faithful for nearly a century.

Feast day: September 29.

PARAGUAY

ST. FRANCIS SOLANO (1549-1610). Paraguay was part of the mission territory assigned to Francis Solano by his Franciscan superiors.

Feast day: July 14.

Our Lady of the Miracles of Caacupé. In the sixteenth century a Christian Guarani Indian was hiding in the forest from an enemy tribe. He promised Our Lady he would carve a statue of her if she saved his life; the man's enemies passed by without seeing him, and he fulfilled his vow. The sculpture of Mary was enshrined in Caacupé. So many prayers were answered through Mary's intercession that the image became known as "Our Lady of the Miracles of Caacupé." Since the statue is usually dressed in a blue cloak, she is also known as "the Blue Virgin of Paraguay."

Feast day: December 8.

PERU

St. Francis Solano (1549-1610). Francis Solano traveled extensively through South America, but his main base of operation was Peru, especially Lima and the surrounding region. Toward the end of his life, when he was too old to travel through jungles and across mountain ranges, he was called home to Lima and elected guardian, or superior, of the Franciscan residence in Lima.

Feast day: July 14.

St. Rose of Lima (1586-1617). The beautiful daughter of a well-to-do colonial family, Rose could expect to marry well, but she wanted to enter a convent. Her parents refused their permission, but offered a compromise: she could join the Dominican Third Order, which granted her the privilege of wearing the habit while living at home. Rose's brothers built her a hermitage in the garden, and she lived there. She persuaded her parents to give her one room of the house as a hospital for the poor; Rose's patients reported that at her touch they were miraculously healed. The people of Lima also believed that it was through Rose's prayers that the city had been saved from a pirate fleet.

Feast day: August 23.

What Is a Third Order?

Some religious orders, including the Dominicans, the Franciscans, and the Carmelites have a Third Order. Priests

> *belong to the First Order, nuns to the Second Order, and the Third Order is open to the laity. Lay men and women become associated with the order, promising to strive to live the spirit or mission of the religious community while working at their job and raising their family. Typically, members of the Third Order are obligated to recite certain prayers that are also part of the daily spiritual life of the First and Second Orders.*

St. Martin de Porres (1579-1639). Martin represents the interracial character of Spanish America: his mother was a freed African slave, his father was a Spanish nobleman, and Martin spent his adult life as the only lay brother of mixed race in Lima's Dominican Monastery of the Rosary. During his lifetime he was regarded as a living saint, and many miracles were attributed to him. At his funeral, two bishops, the king of Spain's viceroy, and the justice of the royal court served as Martin's pallbearers.

Feast day: November 3.

St. Turibius de Mongrovejo (1538-1606). In 1579 Pope Gregory XIII appointed Turibius de Mongrovejo archbishop of Lima, Peru. The archdiocese covered 180,000 square miles, and the archbishop covered it three times on foot. He baptized and confirmed half a million souls, including St. Rose of Lima and St. Martin de Porres. He studied the Indians' languages so he could preach to them and hear their confessions; to the outrage of the Spanish colonists he was a champion of the rights of the Indians. Turibius opened schools and hospitals, founded new churches and monasteries and convents, and established the first seminary in the New World.

Feast day: March 23.

St. Joseph (first century). In the sixteenth century the Jesuits, the Carmelites, and the Franciscans were all devoted to spreading devotion to St. Joseph. It is likely that missionaries from one (or perhaps all) of these religious orders adopted St. Joseph as the patron of Peru.

Feast days: March 19 (St. Joseph, Husband of the Blessed Virgin Mary) and May 1 (St. Joseph the Worker).

OUR LADY OF MERCY. Spanish Mercedarian friars built a chapel in Lima, Peru, about 1535 and introduced devotion to their patron, Our Lady of Mercy. Their statue became an object of intense devotion: in 1730 Our Lady of Mercy was formally proclaimed patron of Peru; in 1921 Mary was given the military rank of Grand Marshall of Peru; in 1971 she received the Great Peruvian Cross of Naval Merit.

Feast day: September 24.

The Mercedarians

In 1223 a Spaniard, St. Peter Nolasco, founded the Order of the Blessed Virgin Mary of Mercy, or the Mercedarians, to ransom Christian prisoners and slaves from the Muslims. It is said that Our Lady herself encouraged the order by appearing to St. Peter, King Peter of Aragon, and St. Raymond of Peñafort and telling them that all Mercedarians would be under her protection.

In addition to promising to observe poverty, chastity, and obedience, the Mercedarians also swore to give their own lives in exchange for Christian captives. Surviving records tell us that for some four centuries the Mercedarians were very active in buying back thousands of Christian prisoners and slaves. Some collections of saints' lives claim that between the Mercedarians and the Trinitarians, 1.5 million captives were liberated. That number is probably a pious exaggeration, but the number of Christians ransomed certainly ran to many thousands.

Today Mercedarian priests work as prison and hospital chaplains, as parish priests, and as missionaries.

PHILIPPINES

ST. ROSE OF LIMA (1586-1617). Although Rose is a saint of the Americas — the first saint of the New World — at her canonization in 1671 Pope Clement X declared her the patron of all the Indies, a loose term at the time that included all lands from India to the Philippines.

Feast day: August 23.

OUR LADY OF PEACE AND OF GOOD VOYAGE. This statue of the Blessed Mother is enshrined in Antipolo City, the Philippines. On at least eight occasions, the Virgin Mary, under this title, kept Spanish galleons safe from British and Dutch privateers, bringing the ships safely across the Pacific. In 1926 the archbishop of Manila declared Our Lady of Peace and of Good Voyage one of the patrons of the Philippines.

Feast day: Entire month of May.

POLAND

OUR LADY OF CZESTOCHOWA. According to legend, St. Luke the Evangelist painted this portrait of the Virgin and Child upon the surface of the kitchen table of the Holy Family's house in Nazareth. It is said that St. Helena discovered the painting in Jerusalem in 326 and sent it to Constantinople; one thousand years later it came into the possession of the monks of Jasna Gora Monastery, outside the town of Czestochowa (the first documentation of this was in 1382). In 1655 the king of Sweden invaded Poland. Jasna Gora was besieged, but the monks defended their monastery and after forty days drove off the invaders. In the wake of the victory, Poland's King Jan Casimirus crowned the image and declared Our Lady of Czestochowa "Queen and Patron of Poland."

Feast day: August 26.

ST. ADALBERT (c. 957-997). One of the first missionaries to Poland, Adalbert was martyred by pagan tribesmen on the site of the modern-day Polish city of Gdansk.

Feast day: April 23.

ST. ANDREW BOBOLA (1592-1657). A Polish Jesuit, Andrew Bobola dedicated his life to reconciling Orthodox Christians with the Catholic Church. His success enraged the Cossacks, who captured "the soul-stealer," as they called him, and tortured him to death.

Feast days: May 16, May 23 (among the Jesuits), February 21 (in Poland).

ST. CASIMIR (1460-1483). A prince of Poland, Casimir lived a semi-monastic life within his family's palace. At one point Hungarian nobles offered to make him their king if he would lead a Polish army into their country to secure the crown. Casimir refused to spill Polish or Hungarian blood in an unjust war.

Feast day: March 4.

ST. CUNEGUNDES (DIED 1040). A Luxemburg noblewoman who became empress of Germany, Cunegundes had a reputation for innocence and piety. After her death devotion to the saint was strong in Central Europe, including Poland.

Feast day: March 3.

ST. FLORIAN (DIED 304). A Roman officer who was martyred in Austria, the Poles took St. Florian as one of their national patrons after a portion of his relics were given to the archbishop of Cracow.

Feast day: May 4.

ST. HYACINTH (1185-1257). One of the first Dominican priests in Poland (he received the habit from St. Dominic), Hyacinth traveled across his homeland reviving among the clergy zeal for living a life of service to the Church and the faithful, and fostering religious devotion among the Polish laity. He is regarded as a "Second Apostle" of Poland (St. Adalbert being the first).

Feast day: August 17.

ST. JOHN OF DUKLA (1414-1484). In the fifteenth century many Poles belonged to the Orthodox Church. John, a Polish

Franciscan, devoted himself to reconciling the Orthodox to the Catholic Church so that all Poles would be united under the Holy Father.

Feast day: October 1.

St. John Kanty (c. 1390-1473). A respected professor of theology and biblical studies at the University of Cracow, John was also a compassionate man who shared his university stipend with the poor.

Feast day: December 23.

St. Ladislaus of Gielniow (1440-1505). Superior of the Franciscan province in Warsaw, Ladislaus ministered to the Poles and sent Franciscan missionaries to Lithuania.

Feast day: September 25.

St. Stanislaus Szczepanowsky (1030-1079). Stanislaus was forty-two years old when the pope named him bishop of Cracow, his birthplace. Almost immediately he clashed with Boleslaus the Cruel, over the king's vicious way of life. Unable to bring the king to repentance, Stanislaus excommunicated him. The king retaliated by attacking the bishop as he said Mass, hacking him to death at the altar.

Feast day: April 11.

PORTUGAL

St. Anthony of Padua (1195-1231). It is a common misconception among Catholics that St. Anthony was Italian. Although he spent most of his ministry in Italy, he was born in Lisbon, in a house just a few steps from the city's cathedral. St. Anthony's house still stands, and has been made into a church.

Feast day: June 13.

St. George (died c. 303). The hilltop fortress built in the Middle Ages to defend the city of Lisbon is dedicated to St.

George. As a warrior saint, he became especially popular as the Portuguese Christians fought to drive the Moorish invaders from their country.

Feast day: April 23.

ST. VINCENT (DIED 304). Vincent, a Spanish deacon, was cruelly tortured to death. His body was left exposed to the elements, but a group of Christians recovered it and took it to what is now Cape St. Vincent in Portugal, where they buried it.

Feast day: January 22.

ST. JOHN DE BRITO (1643-1693). A Portuguese Jesuit, John de Brito carried the Catholic faith to India. To make himself more acceptable to potential converts he became a vegetarian and dressed in the yellow cotton robes of a member of the Hindu elite. He enjoyed remarkable success, which won John the enmity of the king of Marava. The king ordered John to leave the country; John refused. For his refusal he was beheaded.

Feast day: February 4.

ST. FRANCIS BORGIA (1510-1572). Francis Borgia, a Spanish duke, became connected to Portugal by marriage: his wife Eleanor was a member of the Portuguese aristocracy. The couple had eight children, but after Eleanor's death Borgia entered the Jesuits in 1550. In 1565 he was elected general of the Society of Jesus and is considered the greatest the Jesuits have ever known, after their founder, St. Ignatius Loyola. Popes and kings sought his advice, he founded the Roman College for the training of Jesuit priests, and he sent waves of Jesuit missionaries to Asia, Africa, and the New World.

Feast day: October 10.

OUR LADY OF FÁTIMA. For six consecutive months in 1917, the Blessed Virgin appeared to three children, all cousins, at Fátima,

Portugal. Our Lady's messages at Fátima — including telling people to pray the Rosary and her warnings regarding the spread of Communism from Russia and the coming of the Second World War — became one of the religious phenomena of the twentieth century.

Feast day: May 13.

The Fátima Prayer

Many Catholics, when reciting the Rosary, add a prayer at the end of each decade: "O my Jesus, forgive us our sins, save us from the fires of hell, lead all souls to heaven, especially those who have most need of your mercy." At Fátima, the Blessed Mother taught the three children this prayer and asked that it be recited when saying the Rosary.

IMMACULATE CONCEPTION. In 1166 Gilberto, the first bishop of Lisbon, encouraged devotion to Mary under her title of the Immaculate Conception. This devotion spread rapidly throughout Portugal, and Mary, under this title, became one of the national patrons. The Portuguese celebrate the feast of the Immaculate Conception as a public holiday.

Feast day: December 8.

ROMANIA

ST. NICETAS (DIED C. 414). Probably a Greek, Nicetas carried the Gospel to what is now Romania, as well as the Balkan nations. St. Jerome knew him and praised his zeal in establishing Christianity in such a far-off place.

Feast day: June 22.

RUSSIA

ST. ANDREW (FIRST CENTURY). According to an ancient legend, St. Andrew the Apostle, the brother of St. Peter, preached the

Gospel along the shores of the Black Sea, on Russia's southern border. Then he traveled up the Dnieper River and preached at the site of present-day Kiev, Ukraine.

Feast day: November 30.

St. Basil the Great (c. 330-379). Basil's parents, grandparents, two brothers, and one sister are all venerated as saints. After inspecting monasteries throughout the Middle East he developed a monastic rule that is still followed by monks and nuns of the Eastern-rite Catholic and Orthodox Churches. He is one of the great theologians of the early Church, hailed as one of the Three Holy Hierarchs in the East and a Doctor of the Church in the West. Devotion to him came early to Russia, probably with the first group of clergy to evangelize the country in the tenth century.

Feast day: January 2.

Three Holy Hierarchs

The Orthodox Church and Eastern-rite Catholics venerated three bishops as the Three Holy Hierarchs ("hierarch" is another term for bishop). They are St. Basil the Great (c. 330-379), St. Gregory of Nazianzus (329-389), and St. John Chrysostom (349-407). They are considered the three greatest theologians of the Church in the East. The Orthodox Church and the Eastern-rite Catholics celebrate the feast of Three Holy Hierarchs on January 30.

Sts. Boris and Gleb (died c. 1019). These were the prince sons of St. Vladimir. After their father's death an anti-Christian faction sprang up in Kiev, and Boris and Gleb became targets of this movement. Boris was stabbed to death in his sleep by one of his servants; Gleb was attacked and killed by his cook.

Feast day: July 24.

St. Nicholas of Myra (died c. 350). St. Vladimir introduced devotion to St. Nicholas to the Russian people. After the Blessed Virgin Mary, Nicholas became the most beloved saint in Russia.

Feast day: December 6.

St. Thérèse of Lisieux (1873-1897). So much money had been contributed to the Carmelites to defray the expenses of promoting her cause for sainthood that after Thérèse was canonized a great deal was left over. The Carmelite prior general asked Pope Pius XI what should be done with the funds. The Holy Father requested it be used to found a seminary for the training of Byzantine-rite Catholic priests for Russia. The seminary was dedicated as the College of St. Thérèse (although it is commonly known in Rome as the Russicum, or the Russian College).

Feast day: October 1.

St. Vladimir (c. 956-1015). Fratricide, rapist, bigamist, and practitioner of human sacrifice, Vladimir, prince of Kiev, was an unlikely saint. In order to marry a Byzantine princess he accepted baptism, and the grace of the sacrament brought about an extraordinary change in him. He sent away his other wives and his concubines; he brought bishops, priests, and deacons to his realm to instruct his people in the Christian faith; he built churches; and every day he sent out wagons full of food to feed the poor. St. Vladimir is revered as the Apostle of Russia.

Feast day: July 15.

Saint Kitts

St. Christopher (died c. 250). In 1493 Christopher Columbus sailed past a Caribbean island and named it after his patron, St. Christopher. "St. Kitts" is the informal nickname for the island, which is formally known as the Island of St. Christopher.

Feast day: July 25.

SAINT LUCIA

ST. LUCY (DIED 304). On December 13, 1502, French sailors discovered a Caribbean island unknown to Europeans. They named it after St. Lucy, because December 13 is her feast day.

Feast day: December 13.

SAINT VINCENT AND THE GRENADINES

ST. VINCENT (DIED 304). On January 22, 1498, Christopher Columbus discovered a string of islands that he named in honor of the Spanish martyr, St. Vincent, whose feast was celebrated that day.

Feast day: January 22.

SAN MARINO

ST. MARINUS (FOURTH CENTURY). A stonemason from the island of Rab (off the coast of what is now Croatia), Marinus found work at Rimini in Italy. Later he traveled to Monte Titano, where he lived as a hermit. The Republic of San Marino, the longest-surviving sovereign state in Europe, grew up around his hermitage.

Feast day: September 3.

ST. AGATHA (DIED C. 250). The great virgin martyr of Catania, Sicily, Agatha is venerated as the patron of San Marino because on her feast day in 1739 the people of San Marino successfully liberated their republic from occupation troops sent from the Papal States.

Feast day: February 5.

SÃO TOMÉ AND PRÍNCIPE

ST. THOMAS THE APOSTLE (FIRST CENTURY). In or about the year 1470, Portuguese explorers sailing along the coast of Africa discovered these islands. Since it was the feast day of St. Thomas the Apostle, they named the main island after him.

Feast day: July 3.

SCOTLAND

ST. ANDREW (FIRST CENTURY). According to legend, in the fourth century a Greek monk named Regulus, or Rule, took some of the bones of St. Andrew from his tomb in Patras, Greece, and carried them to Scotland. He built a church in which he enshrined the bones, and the city of St. Andrews grew around it. Scottish Christians took the apostle as their national patron.

Feast day: November 30.

ST. COLUMBA (C. 521-597). In his native Ireland, Columba, in a fit of jealousy, started a war that took the lives of three thousand men. The bishops and abbots of Ireland exiled Columba to Scotland, and assigned him the penance of converting at least three thousand Scots — one for each of the men killed. Columba's mission was more fruitful than that, and Scots venerate him as one of the apostles of their nation.

Feast day: June 9.

ST. MARGARET OF SCOTLAND (C. 1045-1093). Beautiful, intelligent, and devout, Margaret exercised her influence as queen to introduce Catholic culture from the Continent to rough-hewn Scotland. She promoted schools and libraries, and she increased charity for the poor.

Feast day: November 16.

SERBIA

ST. SAVA OR SABAS (1176-1235). A Serbian prince, Sava left his father's castle to become a monk on Mount Athos in Greece. Later he returned home, where he was named archbishop of Serbia. Sava became renowned as a church-builder and an advocate of education in Serbia.

Feast day: January 14.

SLOVAKIA

OUR LADY OF SORROWS. In 1564 Angelika Bakicova, a Slovak

gentlewomen, was experiencing great difficulties in her life when Our Lady of Sorrows appeared and consoled her. To commemorate the vision, Angelika commissioned a sculptor to create a pietà, an image of Mary holding in her arms the dead Christ, which she placed in a small chapel. Pilgrims who prayed before the holy image reported miraculous cures. In 1927 Pope Pius XI proclaimed Our Lady of Sorrows patron of Slovakia.

Feast day: September 15.

SLOVENIA

ST. VIRGILIUS (DIED 784). Virgilius was an Irishman who went on a pilgrimage to the Holy Land. On his return home he passed through the German-speaking lands of Central Europe, where he met St. Rupert. Under the saint's influence, Virgilius became a Benedictine monk and a missionary in what is now Austria and Slovenia.

Feast day: November 27.

SOUTH AFRICA

OUR LADY OF SHONGWENI. At the outbreak of World War II, a French missionary priest, Father Wagner, was called home from South Africa to serve in the military. During an especially fierce battle he hid himself amid the corpses of dead soldiers and made a vow to the Blessed Mother: if she permitted him to survive the war, he would celebrate an annual feast day in her honor at his mission in South Africa. Father Wagner did survive, and he was returned to his mission at Shongweni. In the church he placed a statue of the Virgin and Child, and every year on the feast of the Annunciation he led his parishioners in prayers of thanksgiving to Our Lady.

Feast day: March 25.

OUR LADY OF THE ASSUMPTION. In 1952 a Marian congress was held in South Africa. On that occasion the pope's representative in the country, Archbishop Martin H. Lucas, S.V.D., placed South Africa under the patronage of Our Lady of the Assumption.

Feast day: August 15.

SPAIN

ST. JAMES THE GREATER (FIRST CENTURY). A longstanding tradition tells us that St. James carried the Gospel to Spain. After his martyrdom in Jerusalem, his body was miraculously transported and buried in northern Spain at the site of present-day Compostela. His relics were discovered in the ninth century and were enshrined in a church. The Christians of Spain took the apostle as their patron. Several times during their seven-centuries-long war against the Moorish forces of occupation, Spanish soldiers reported that St. James rode into battle with them and granted them victory.

Feast day: July 25.

OUR LADY OF THE PILLAR. Initially St. James made few converts to Christianity in Spain. Then Our Lady appeared to him, standing upon a pillar, and promised her assistance. From that moment James' mission was a success. The Basilica of Our Lady of the Pillar in Saragosa claims to possess that actual pillar upon which Mary stood.

Feast day: February 4.

OUR LADY OF GUADALUPE. Legend tells us that St. Luke carved this statue of Our Lady. It was passed down to St. Gregory the Great, who gave it to St. Leander, archbishop of Seville. Since the fourteenth century it has been venerated in the Monastery of Our Lady of Guadalupe in Spain (not to be confused with the Guadalupe shrine in Mexico).

Feast day: September 6.

OUR LADY OF MONTSERRAT. By tradition this statue of the enthroned Virgin and Child was created during the early years of the Church; it is more likely that the statue was carved about the twelfth century. Pilgrims have visited Our Lady of Montser-rat's shrine for centuries. Most famously among them was St. Ignatius Loyola, who began the vocation that would lead to his founding of the Society of Jesus by spending a night in prayer before the image and leaving his sword on Mary's altar.

Feast day: January 14.

OUR LADY OF RANSOM. In 1218 the Blessed Mother appeared to St. Peter Nolasco, St. Raymond Peñafort, and King James of Aragon, instructing them to establish a new religious order dedicated to ransoming Christians who had been taken captive by the Moors. The vision resulted in the foundation of the Mercedarians, who placed themselves under the protection of Our Lady of Ransom (also known as Our Lady of Mercy). Over the next 550 years, the Mercedarians would buy back thousands of Christian prisoners.

Feast day: September 24.

ST. TERESA OF ÁVILA (1515-1582). By 1533, the time Teresa entered the Carmelite convent, the order had lost its original rigor. A nun could have a comfortable suite of rooms, and many nuns brought their servants to care for them. They could receive visitors, including men, inside the cloister, and the routine of prayer had dwindled to almost nothing. Teresa set out to reform the Carmelites, reviving her order's original austerity and devotion to a life of poverty and prayer. She met with resistance from Carmelite nuns who did not want to be reformed, but she won the support of the king of Spain and the superior of the Carmelites. Her writings on the interior life became not only spiritual classics, but also classics of Spanish literature.

Feast day: October 15.

SRI LANKA

ST. THOMAS THE APOSTLE (FIRST CENTURY). Tradition claims that St. Thomas carried the faith to Sri Lanka, establishing Christian communities on the northern and western coast of the island.

Feast day: July 3.

St. Lawrence (died 258). The first Portuguese colonists to arrive in Sri Lanka were commanded by Lawrence de Almeida. On the site of present-day Colombo the settlers erected a chapel and dedicated it to St. Lawrence, the patron of their leader. St. Lawrence became the patron of Colombo, and then of Sri Lanka.

Feast day: August 10.

Our Lady of Madhu. In 1670 the Dutch invaded Sri Lanka and began to persecute Catholics. About twenty Catholic families of the town of Mantai took a century-old statue of Our Lady and fled to Madhu, where they were safe from the Dutch. Another seven hundred Catholic families arrived, and together they built a church and a town. After the British seized Sri Lanka from the Dutch, anti-Catholic persecution ceased. Madhu became the foremost Marian shrine on the island, and Our Lady of Madhu patron of Sri Lanka.

Feast days: July 2 and August 15.

Sudan

St. Josephine Bakhita (1868-1947). Bakhita, the child of a well-to-do Sudanese family, was kidnapped at age nine by slave traders. She was sold several times before she was purchased by Italy's consul to Khartoum, who bought her in order to free her. She became a member of the consul's household, and when they returned to Italy she accompanied them. There she became acquainted with Canossian Daughters of Charity; she took instruction, was baptized Josephine, and then applied to join the order. Sister Josephine proved to be a compelling speaker. Her superiors sent her on missions throughout Italy to collect funds for the African missions.

Feast day: February 8.

Sweden

St. Ansgar (801-865). A French Benedictine monk, Ansgar was the first to carry the Catholic faith to the Swedes. He made many converts, but after his death the fledgling Church in Sweden was destroyed by anti-Christian forces.

Feast day: February 3.

St. Bridget of Sweden (1303-1373). Bridget was related to the Swedish royal family. She enjoyed a happy life with her husband and their eight children. After her husband's death, she became more profoundly religious. She founded the Order of the Holy Savior, which spread across northern Europe. She then traveled to Rome, where she spent the rest of her life caring for the sick and the poor, visiting the tombs of the saints, and experiencing especially vivid visions of episodes from the life of Jesus and Mary.

Feast day: July 23.

Apparitions and Visions

During the two-thousand-year history of the Catholic Church many thousands of individuals have claimed to have received visions or revelations. Some of these visionaries were saints, many others were deluded, and some were frauds.

Church authorities are very cautious when dealing with such claims. If the visions and the message delivered during the visions are not contrary to Catholic doctrine and moral teachings, if the visionary is of good moral character and faithful to the Church, if the visions have had a positive effect on the spiritual life of people who have visited the site, then the local bishop, after a thorough investigation, may pronounce the apparition "worthy of belief."

Even so, no Catholic is obligated to believe in a vision or its message. The way to salvation is through the message Christ gave us in the Gospel, not through any revelation made to a private individual.

St. Eric of Sweden (D. 1160). As king of Sweden, Eric did his utmost to convert his entire nation to Christianity. He also formulated a new law code based on Christian principles. Political rivals murdered him as he was leaving church after Mass.

Feast day: May 18.

St. Sigfrid (died c. 1045). Sigfrid was a monk at the English Benedictine Abbey of Glastonbury when he, along with other Benedictines, was invited by the king of Norway to bring the Gospel to Scandinavia. The English missionaries made many converts; Sigfrid personally converted and baptized the king of Sweden.

Feast day: February 15.

Switzerland

St. Gall (c. 550-645). An Irish monk, Gall traveled with St. Columbanus to bring Christianity to the pagan tribes of Continental Europe. He worked extensively in Switzerland, and is considered the apostle of that country. There he founded a monastery that became the great Abbey of St. Gall, renowned in later centuries for its splendid library.

Feast day: October 16.

St. Nicholas of Flüe (1417-1487). A prosperous Swiss farmer and the father of ten children, Nicholas was respected among his neighbors as a peacemaker. Toward the end of his life, when civil war threatened to tear Switzerland apart, representatives of the various cantons called upon Nicholas to arbitrate. He brokered a peace and then returned home.

Feast day: March 21.

Our Lady of the Hermits. The little statue of Our Lady of the Hermits once belonged to the ninth-century hermit St. Meinrad. After his death it was enshrined at Einsiedeln Abbey, which became the most important Marian pilgrimage destination in Switzerland.

Feast day: September 14.

SYRIA

ST. BARBARA (DATE UNKNOWN). Syria claims to be the place where the virgin martyr St. Barbara lived in a tower and was martyred by her own father.

Feast day: December 4.

ST. SERGIUS (DIED 303). Sergius was a Roman officer serving in Syria. For refusing to participate in a sacrifice to pagan gods he was arrested, savagely beaten, and then beheaded. He was buried in Resafa, where a basilica was erected over his tomb; Christians renamed the city Sergiopolis.

Feast day: October 7.

UGANDA

OUR LADY, QUEEN OF AFRICA. Veneration of the Blessed Mother under this title was introduced by members of the Society of Missionaries of Africa, better known as the White Fathers because of their white habits. The first group of White Fathers arrived in Uganda in 1878.

Feast day: April 30.

UKRAINE

ST. JOSAPHAT (1584-1623). Josaphat was born in what is now Ukraine and raised in the Russian Orthodox Church. As a young man he was reconciled to the Catholic Church and became a monk of the Church's Byzantine rite. He devoted himself to bringing Orthodox Christians back to union with Rome. In 1617 he was named archbishop of Polotsk in what is now Belarus. He was attacked by an anti-Catholic mob and beaten to death in the archbishop's residence.

Feast day: November 12.

UNITED STATES

IMMACULATE CONCEPTION. On February 7, 1847, the bishops of the United States, meeting in Baltimore, Maryland, chose the

Blessed Virgin Mary, under her title of the Immaculate Conception, as the patron of the United States.

Feast day: December 8.

URUGUAY

STS. PHILIP AND JAMES (FIRST CENTURY). On May 1, 1726, the city of Montevideo was founded in Uruguay. At this time the feast day of the two apostles was celebrated on May 1, so they became first the patrons of the capital city and then of the nation.

Feast day: May 3.

OUR LADY OF THE THIRTY-THREE. In 1825, thirty-three Uruguayan patriots made a pilgrimage to the town of Florida to pray before a wooden sculpture of the Immaculate Conception and beg her to grant Uruguay political independence. When the independence movement was successful, the patriots returned to give thanks to Our Lady. In 1857 her statue was crowned and she was declared "Liberator of Uruguay." In 1961 Blessed Pope John XXIII officially declared Our Lady of the Thirty-Three patron of Uruguay.

Feast day: Second Sunday of November.

VENEZUELA

OUR LADY OF COROMOTO. In 1652 the Virgin Mary appeared to the chief of the Coromoto tribe and instructed him, his wife, and all their people to become Christians. Then she presented the chief with a holy card bearing her image and disappeared. The Coromotos traveled to a Spanish settlement, where all were baptized. The holy card is enshrined in the National Sanctuary of the Virgin of Coromoto. In 1944 Pope Pius XII declared Our Lady of Coromoto patron of Venezuela.

Feast day: September 8.

VIETNAM

ST. JOSEPH (FIRST CENTURY). European missionaries active in Vietnam placed the country under the patronage of St. Joseph.

Feast days: March 19 (St. Joseph, Husband of the Blessed Virgin Mary) and May 1 (St. Joseph the Worker).

OUR LADY OF LA VANG. Around the year 1800, a group of Vietnamese Christians hid in the jungle of La Vang to escape arrest and execution. They were hungry, frightened, and falling ill with all manner of diseases. Then the Blessed Mother appeared to them and promised to hear the prayers of all who called upon her for aid. After the period of persecution ended, the Christians built a chapel on the site of the apparition. During a second wave of persecution (1820-1885), when one hundred thousand Vietnamese Catholics were martyred, the chapel was destroyed. After that persecution came to an end, the Christians built a new church for Our Lady of La Vang. In 1959 Our Lady of La Vang was declared the national patron.

Feast day: November 22.

WALES

ST. DAVID OF WALES (DIED C. 600). The son of Welsh Christians, David was born in southern Wales. He founded a monastery at what is now St. Davids, and subsequently became the place's first bishop. He founded monasteries across Wales, and dozens of his pupils and monks became saints.

Feast day: March 1.

Index